Me, But Better

Also by Olga Khazan

Weird: The Power of Being an Outsider in an Insider World

Me, But Better

The Science and Promise of Personality Change

Olga Khazan

Simon Element

New York   Amsterdam/Antwerp   London   Toronto   Sydney   New Delhi

Portions of this book first appeared in the magazine article "I Gave Myself Three Months to Change My Personality" (*Atlantic*, February 10, 2022). Reprinted with permission of the *Atlantic*.

Grateful acknowledgment is made for the use of the following:

"To be of use" from *Circles on the Water* by Marge Piercy, copyright © 1982 by Middlemarsh, Inc. Used by permission of Alfred A. Knopf, an imprint of the Knopf Doubleday Publishing Group, a division of Penguin Random House LLC. All rights reserved.

"This Be the Verse" from *Collected Poems* by Philip Larkin, copyright © 1983, 2003 by the Estate of Philip Larkin. Originally published in 2003 by The Marvell Press, Australia, and Faber and Faber Limited, Great Britain. Published in the United States by Farrar, Straus and Giroux. Used by permission of Farrar, Straus and Giroux and Faber and Faber Ltd. All rights reserved.

"A Point of Age" from *Collected Poems of Berryman* by John Berryman, copyright © 1989 by Kate Donahue Berryman. Used by permission of Farrar, Straus and Giroux. All rights reserved.

For Rich, my favorite personality

Contents

Me, But Better

Introduction

Only those who have personality and emotions
know what it means to want to escape from these things.

—T. S. Eliot

In December of 2021, I was waiting for my lunch at a vegan restaurant in Miami when I got a call from the art director of the magazine where I work. She wanted a photographer to take photos of me to accompany an article of mine that was going into print production.

At first, my heart leapt. I glowed with flattery: *Photos! Of me!* Every woman for whom *Sex and the City* is canon has dreamed of having her headshot appear alongside her words. Briefly, the words "photo shoot" conjured a gleaming version of me—one who would look out, gorgeously yet somehow still intelligently, from the glossy pages. Outside, the sun beamed and South Beach hopped with promise. "Tofu BLT!" the counter guy cried.

None of this, I admit, evokes struggle. And if this were a different world—and if I were a different person—this is where the story would end. I would have sauntered home smiling, toting my sandwich and the smug knowledge that I had triumphed over my haters. I'd uneventfully drive to my first (and probably only) professional photography session, enjoy myself, and spend the next few days feeling nothing but cheer, gratitude, and most of all, serenity that my life was turning out well.

But I was not that person. At least not yet. Instead, I possessed a unique ability to find suffering in even the best of circumstances. I'd long wished I had a slightly different personality, and this tendency was one of the main reasons why.

Over the phone, the art director explained that she had planned everything: She found a local photographer. She arranged the COVID safety protocols. She came up with ideas for the poses. I just needed to buy a black shirt, which I could expense. Perhaps sensing that she would need to reassure me the way one would a skittish horse, the art director said this would all be fun and easy.

I thanked her and hung up. Then came my old friend, anxiety, gliding in to poison my day, dragging behind it endless, dire *what ifs*. I went home to fret. Though I understood that this was an amazing opportunity, the reality is that I hate having my photo taken—and this was a photo that hundreds of thousands of people would see. If I have enough time, makeup, and liquor, I can usually arrange my face into an image I can tolerate, but the process is more psychodynamic than cosmetic.

I was in Miami for a work-cation of sorts, staying in an old art deco building with tile floors and cologned hallways. *I'll just do a lot of primping beforehand, and it should be okay,* I told myself as I examined my pores in the Airbnb's cocaine-den mirror-walls.

My hair had grown long and splintered, and the only time I had for a haircut was right before the photo session. *No problem.* I carefully researched salons and booked an appointment at a well-reviewed spot for the morning of the shoot.

I walked into the salon feeling optimistic, but when my hairstylist introduced herself to me, I noted with some alarm that she was, herself, completely bald. (I did not work up the nerve to ask why.) I asked for my usual—a trim with discreet, blended layers. She said something like "You want some texture and some face shaping mid-length," and I, a policy blogger with terrible taste, let out a quick and confused "Yes."

About twenty-five minutes later, she was blow-drying my hair into a choppy, avant-garde mushroom. When she asked if I thought it looked good, I mustered an "mm-hmm" and avoided eye contact. Then I ran across the street to a Chipotle, chugged a Dos Equis, and wondered whether haircuts are legally actionable.

I drove to the photo studio, where I met the photographer, a thin, fashionable man with a bouncy energy. He asked me right away if I wanted to "fix my hair." Then he said he was going to take some photos of me in profile.

"I'll give you any amount of money right now to not do that," I said.

I hate having my photo taken, but I *especially* hate having my photo taken from the side. Is this internalized antisemitism from growing up the only Jewish girl in the most goyish town in Texas? Probably. Is it nevertheless a very real and strong phobia? Absolutely. I tried to tamp down the panic climbing my throat. *Just be cool!* I yelled at myself silently. *It's not a big deal! Antisemites don't read the* Atlantic *anyway!*

The photographer said, "Sure, whatever you want," and proceeded to *click-click-click* a bunch of photos of me in profile. The nature of the photos dictated that I not be smiling. Instead, I was to stare into the middle distance, my face fixed into my usual look of vague displeasure, the broad lights accentuating all my worst angles. When he was done, the photographer asked me to examine what looked, to me, like a plastic surgeon's "before" picture.

"Looks great," I lied briskly.

The shoot ended just as rush hour picked up. My mom was flying in that evening, but before she landed I needed to get to the grocery store to buy special food for the diet she was on for her gastritis. As I fought traffic, my boss messaged me about a different story that was going through edits. Pecking with one finger, I responded—and missed my exit. The highway whisked me away through a tunnel that led to a little island that cruise ships launch from, the circumnavigation of which added thirty minutes to my journey.

In my head, two dueling narratives duked it out: One reminded me that this was all fine, since my mom wasn't arriving for hours and my boss knew I was doing the photos that day. The other, shriller, one insisted I was about to be fired and also about to strand my mom at Miami International Airport.

Eventually, I made it to the Publix. I bought the salmon and sweet potatoes and other stuff recommended by a site called something like "Heal Gastritis Naturally." I wheeled the cart full of food back to my car—or tried to. I was parked on an upper level of the garage, and in the distance I could just see the gray roof of my Prius when the wheels on the cart locked abruptly. I was still about a dozen yards away.

I looked at the car. I looked at the food. There was too much to carry by hand. I began lugging the locked shopping cart, scraping it across the concrete floor of the sweltering garage in my photo clothes. A man watching me yelled, "Is it stuck?!"

Back inside the car, I checked my phone. The editor had messaged me more questions. He wondered if I could open the document and just fix the paragraph he was asking about. Sweat rolled down my face as I slid my seat back, opened my laptop, and turned my phone into a hotspot. I made the edits and sent the editor back the document while, in the trunk, the ice cream melted into soup.

I inched through more traffic, back to the Airbnb. I gathered up all the groceries and stumbled inside, arms loaded with lukewarm, gastritis-friendly foods. My boyfriend, Rich, put everything away. Then some membrane inside me ruptured. Without quite being able to describe why, I melted down.

"My life is nothing but nonstop stress and torture!" I screamed. "I hate everyone and everything! I can't take this anymore!" Then, apropos of nothing, I added, "And we are *not* having a fucking kid!"

I poured wine to the brim of a glass and gulped hard between sobs. I felt awful to be crying, but I couldn't stop. Why did it feel like everything good in my life always turned rotten? Why did seemingly every vacation feature a hundred-year storm, every glimmering prospect a dark caveat, and every new friendship a secret expiration date?

Or was that even true? Was I stitching together a few unfortunate events into a misleading pattern of misery? *And ugh, why can't I stop doing that!?*

Rich looked on, mystified. Whether it's because he's an American, a man, a gentile, or some combination of the three, he doesn't experience anxiety. This, along with his bald head and perfectly round, blue eyes, makes him look like a cartoon baby, perpetually tranquil and innocent.

He tried to comfort me: My hair didn't look that bad! He would go pick up my mom! I didn't have to get pregnant if I didn't want! This worked about as well as blowing gently on a kitchen fire.

Of course, nothing I was saying was true; I knew my words were hyperbolic even as I spat them out. I was looking at a series of low-level aggravations in the worst way possible. Even as I stood there sobbing, I knew I was less a victim of circumstance than a victim of myself. Behind the terrifying projection, it was my small, scared personality talking.

Specifically, that day I was undermined by my extreme neuroticism, one of the "Big Five" traits that scientists say make up personality. Neuroticism, or a person's penchant for feeling anxious and negative, not only fueled my wine rant, it also clouded my decision-making in the moment. Neuroticism turns the mundane into an emergency, and if I were less neurotic, I might have found ways to release the pressure building up inside me. Had my brain not clanged with worry, I might have thought to order the groceries to be delivered. I could have told my editor I wasn't available to talk just then. And, as my dumbfounded boyfriend intoned multiple times that night, I could have remembered that *everything worked out, anyway.* I saw everyone—the hairstylist, the photographer, the Publix—as the enemy that day. But really, the enemy was inside me all along.

Seeing through the Mirage

That wasn't an isolated incident. I often had moments like these, in which I snatched dissatisfaction from the jaws of happiness.

My life, after all, is and was objectively excellent: I have a solid relationship, an interesting job, and a stable place to live. But neuroticism kept me from enjoying this bounty, and it meant that when some calamity—unemployment, a health scare—did inevitably strike, I crumbled more quickly than most. My personality blinded me to the ways I could expand my life and make it even better, or even just appreciate my good fortune.

In addition to neuroticism, personality consists of four other "factors," or traits: extroversion (which is basically sociability); agreeableness (or niceness); openness to experience (vaguely, creativity); and conscientiousness (or orderliness). Together, your levels of these five traits predict how you'll respond to various situations—like, say, if you'll relish your special photo shoot in a tropical paradise or have a cosmic breakdown.

I had always felt unusually neurotic, introverted, and disagreeable. Over time, I stuck those labels to myself proudly, and I mostly lived by them, even when doing so made me miserable. I avoided anything that didn't suit my personality perfectly.

For instance, for years I almost reflexively declined to socialize. Rich had to invite me to his happy-hour group a dozen times before I agreed to make an appearance. *You're an introvert, remember!* I'd tell myself as I watched TV alone again. Even as I wallowed in the comfort of yet another *Great British Bake Off* season, I wondered why I often had virtually no one to talk to, and why I relied so heavily on Twitter for social interaction.

I also knew I churned with anxiety, but I saw that as a good thing. I took any quiver of instability at my job as a sign that I should work even longer hours. The resulting back pain and physical-therapy appointments served as perverse signs of success. *You're right to be anxious*, I'd tell myself. *Anxiety is keeping you safe.*

It was through my job, though, that I came across some scientific research that showed that you can change your personality traits by behaving in ways that align with the kind of person you'd *like* to be. If you don't want to be quite so anxious or isolated anymore, you can live differently. A new and slightly improved personality, I learned, can make you happier, more successful, and more fulfilled. It can help you enjoy your life, rather than just endure it.

I took a scientific personality test whose results showed that my particular combination of traits correlated with unhappiness and dysfunction. Personality traits are supposed to help you achieve your goals, but my traits were thwarting me. I started to wonder if I could peel off those personality labels and throw them in the trash. Who would I act like if I could act like anyone? Though I had tried therapy and various medications, I decided to attempt something more radical, and possibly more lasting: to change my personality.

For an *Atlantic* magazine article on which this book is based—the one I was getting photographed for in Miami—I spent a few months performing a series of personality-changing activities. Over the course of a summer, I tried to make new friends. I reluctantly meditated, and I journaled like an unpopular teen on prom night. After three months, the personality-test website revealed that my experiment had worked, sort of: I had become slightly more extroverted and less neurotic. (Yes, that means the Airbnb tirade reflected the marginally *better* version of my personality.) For the article, I had gone through the motions of sociability, tranquility, and niceness, and my personality had shifted modestly. In science writing, we would consider this a small pilot study—a proof of concept that might hold up, but also might not.

After the story was published, I shelved my gratitude journal and meditation pillow and went back to being a high-strung misanthrope for a while. *Who needs meditation when you have alcohol?* I asked myself. Inevitably, as the day in Miami that winter showed, I backtracked.

However, some upcoming transitions prompted me to give personality change another, more serious attempt. Despite what I had said during my post-photo diatribe, Rich and I did want to try to start a family. But the daily travails of child rearing, I knew, would be far worse than a combination of bad lighting, a broken shopping cart, and competing work pressures. Parenting requires an ability not to form every molehill into a mountain, and to keep things firmly in perspective—not strengths I possessed.

What's more, my score on agreeableness, the trait associated with niceness and benevolence, was low, and agreeable people make better parents. I wanted to be more like the very agreeable Rich, who has a calm, loving presence that children gravitate toward.

Rich and I met when I was in grad school in LA, as I was moving into his former room in a group house. Even then, it was clear to me that he brimmed with kindness. Because of a paperwork snafu, after he relinquished his room he had nowhere to stay for a few months, so, while I slept in his former bed, he slept on the couch in the living room.

During one of my first nights in the house, the smoke alarm in my/his room started beeping, jolting me awake the night before a big test. I had no idea what to do; my attempts to get any kind of assistance in LA at that point had generally resulted in my getting ripped off or yelled at. Of the seven people who lived in the house, Rich seemed like the one who would be the most willing to help me. I crept to the couch and stood over him while he snored.

"Rich, the smoke detector is beeping," I whispered.

Without a word, he shot up, walked into the room, and, with a hyperextension of his six-three frame, jabbed the alarm into silence. Then he left me, a total stranger, to go back to sleep in his bed, while he returned to the couch. Even then, his presence felt load-bearing, a beam holding up my rickety structure.

Both because of his selflessness and his tolerance of middle-of-the-night noise, I knew Rich would make a great father. But for the sake of this Hypothetical Future Child, as we had taken to calling it, I felt *I* needed to become less sharp and critical and more cuddly and easygoing. I hoped to adopt the "bless this mess" attitude of cheerful Instagram moms. I figured I would like parenting more if I learned to see my child as an especially uncoordinated friend rather than an irrational enemy.

I was also tired of viewing my life through the dingy pane of neuroticism, the trait that signifies depression and anxiety. Over time, I started to notice that rather than protecting me, neuroticism restrains me. It cordons off choices that would have made me happy, robs me of the joy of an accomplishment, and keeps me so preoccupied with survival that the future becomes unfathomable. Another reason I hadn't tried to have a baby yet was the neurotic tendency toward fear: I was terrified I'd be a bad mom.

On top of all this, we were hoping to relocate permanently to Florida—we liked it there, despite the long day of minor stressors. For years, my extreme introversion had kept me trapped in DC, a city in which I had never really wanted to live. I had always assumed the meager number of friends I had made in DC were all I would ever have as an adult, and that there was no way to meet new people after college, so I should never move. But while writing the article, my short experiment with extroversion suggested that a social life can be cultivated at any age. It had sparked a belief in second chances.

I saw my personality project as a midlife tune-up. I hoped to learn to socialize without dread—and maybe even without alcohol. I wanted to be described—literally just once!—as a "good friend." I thought back to that glorious summer between high school and college, when everyone reinvents themselves and reenters the world projecting how they'd *like* to be seen. Who says you can't do that when you're thirty-six?

I wondered, what if I had spent more time on my personality-change experiment? Would I have been able to better handle mildly stressful days like the one in Miami? What if I found activities I liked enough to stick with them? What if I pushed past mild inconvenience to all-out, fidgety discomfort—like the discomfort of leading a Meetup group, of entering the forty-fifth minute of a meditation session, of making myself see new ways of living? What if, rather than trying to make everything in the world go my way, I changed the way I responded to the world?

I decided to spend at least a year trying to change my personality. I had completed my earlier, brief pilot study, but now, to extend the science metaphor, I wanted the large experiment that makes the lab technician rip off his bifocals in amazement. I decided to behave like the healthiest, happiest, and most successful people—the people with the scientifically "best" personalities. This book is for people who have ever thought about doing something similar. The circumstances of our lives will differ, and so will the personality traits we're grappling with. But stress, loneliness, anger, distraction, impulse, and fear are universal—and they can change.

For the next year, whenever I hovered my cursor over a sign-up sheet for an activity that seemed truly daunting, I would force myself to click "submit." I would act like the kind of person who wanted to do it. I embraced the words of Jorge Luis Borges, who wrote, "Personality is a mirage maintained by conceit and custom, without metaphysical foundation or visceral reality." For those who yearn to see through the mirage of their own personalities, I hope to be an example.

But Why Personality Change?

Personality change is not the most intuitive concept. When I told one acquaintance that I was working on a book about personality change, she said, "You mean like from brain damage?" Another friend said that, rather than changing myself, I should focus on fighting the patriarchy, the real source of all our problems.

When I first heard about some of these personality-change studies, I, too, was a little skeptical. For one thing, there were parts of my personality that I found helpful. I always saw anxiety as my secret weapon, the edge that an immigrant kid like me had on my rich, pedigreed peers. Sure, *they* went to Yale, but *I* could have a huge panic attack about my career and work straight through the weekend like it was nothing. I knew I wasn't perfect, but I worried that by changing my personality I would lose my drive, my intuition, and my determination.

But I would later learn that there are ways to hold on to beneficial traits—or even the beneficial *aspects* of certain traits—while adjusting the ones that aren't serving you. Introversion, for instance, isn't necessarily a negative quality—many introverts are thoughtful, witty, and sensitive. But in my case, introversion was too often becoming an excuse to withdraw from life. Not just sometimes, to recharge, but all the time. I hoped that becoming slightly more extroverted would make me happier—*even if* I still called myself "an introvert" in the end.

Whenever I'm feeling anxious, my therapist likes to say that I have a "true self" and an "anxious self" inside me. That is, my anxiety (aka neuroticism) isn't really my true self; the True Olga is the one who knows her own capability. You can think of your less-desired personality traits this way, too: as false selves whose voices deceive you. I wanted to listen to the best of my personality and learn to ignore the worst of it.

When I started this project, Rich sometimes reminded me that I didn't have to change my personality, because he liked me the way I was. Unlike with every other man I'd ever been with, with him I never had to do my "boiled frog" approach to dating, in which I'd create a fake, relaxed personality that I gradually faded into my real one, hoping the guy wouldn't notice when months later he found himself arm in arm with just another sad girl who wanted commitment. Even early on, Rich seemed okay with my crying jags and my earnest passion for watchdog journalism. Being loved within my relationship, in fact, was how I started to love myself. At times I saw my own flaws soften under his infatuated gaze.

In part through that relationship, I came to see that I do have some strengths: I work extremely hard, I can be loyal, and my analytical side is indispensable when it comes time to pick a health-care plan or file taxes. Far from implying you don't like yourself, learning new ways of being can be an act of self-love, just like learning to cook can be a way to nourish yourself. Personality traits are a spectrum, so wanting an increase in, say, agreeableness doesn't mean you're a self-loathing grinch. It just means there's something about that trait that could improve your life, and you want to try it on.

If you don't feel you need to do even one thing in your life differently, I congratulate you and humbly ask which SSRI you're on. But studies suggest most people—around 90 percent—do want to change at least one of their personality traits. Even in global surveys across many different cultures, about 60 percent of people say they are currently trying to change their personalities. Personality change appears to be something many people want to undertake, even if they don't always realize it. (I'm also not talking here about dissociative identity disorder, formerly called multiple personality disorder—a mental illness in which people develop distinct internal identities. Though a worthy topic, it belongs in a different book entirely.)

Personality change *can* feel like an overwhelming proposition, and I was privileged to spend hundreds of hours on this project—in part because I was on book leave and didn't have children. Almost no one can go all out like this, and they don't have to. Some of the activities I describe are short: brief bouts of meditating, quick conversations with acquaintances, an afternoon spent throwing away unnecessary belongings. In the studies that I cite, most interventions take just a few minutes a day, yet they're enough to create meaningful personality change.

You don't have to put your life on hold to change your personality; you can introduce small habits that add up to a big difference.

The most important reason to change your personality, though, is that it might make you happier. Finding happiness, or at least contentment, often requires changing your daily thoughts and behaviors, and those happen to be the two elements of personality. Psychological research suggests that agency—the sense that you can create a positive difference in the world, or at least in your life—is linked to reduced levels of depression and helplessness. "Agency causes progress," the positive-psychology pioneer Martin Seligman has said, while "lack of agency causes stagnation." Agency imbues you with the sense that you can do something about your problems.

What I like about the idea of personality change is precisely this— that it allows you to seize the reins of your own destiny. In the brilliantly simple words of my (newfound) meditation teacher, "Sometimes things happen that we don't like." But you can still live in a way that you *do* like. You can use science, effort, and an unfortunate number of iPhone apps to behave differently—and eventually, to think differently. You can change your life, even if nothing in your life changes.

1

The OCEAN Within:

What Is Personality?

I confess that before I became a science writer, I wasn't sure what, exactly, personality was. In high school, I had taken a form of the Myers-Briggs test, which suggested I was judgy and should therefore become a judge. Wasn't "INTJ" my personality? Or what about some of the Freudian theories we learned about in Psych 101—with all my gum-chewing and nail-biting, I was pretty sure I had an oral fixation. Was that part of my personality?

The layman's definition of personality seems akin to "what you're naturally like on the inside," but I've also heard the term used as shorthand for a person's likes and dislikes, their general mood, or even whether they have interesting things to say. (It turns out these all describe parts of personality, but not its entirety.)

I knew personality was partly genetic—a fact that was unideal for my change efforts. My father, for example, is so anxious that he once declined to buy a car manufactured near Hiroshima, Japan, because he worried that a particle of the residual radiation from the atomic bomb dropped there in 1945 might somehow have nestled into the glove compartment, and, upon the car's arrival at Pat Lobb Toyota in Texas, would jump out and give him instantaneous, fatal cancer. Given this tremendous level of neuroticism running through my veins, could I even do anything about my personality? How can you change something that's inherited?

Gradually, I figured out that to understand personality, you have to understand the stories of two prominent, early psychologists: Gordon Allport and Sigmund Freud. Our modern, scientific concept of personality arose from a day these two men met—and clashed—in 1920.

Allport was then a midwestern twenty-two-year-old with a budding interest in personality. He took psychology courses as an undergraduate and found he liked to "help people with their problems," he wrote. From early in his career, Allport was obsessed with one question: "How shall a psychological life history be written?" He seemed to be rummaging through the pottery shards of early psychology, wondering, What *is* personality?

Allport had just left Constantinople, where he had spent a year teaching English during the twilight of the Ottoman Sultanate, and he was headed to Boston, where a PhD program at Harvard awaited him. Along the way, he made a pit stop in Vienna, and, with the characteristic moxie of a twentysomething, wrote Freud to ask for a meeting.

Freud, meanwhile, was a white-bearded man in his sixties who had already significantly influenced the science of the mind. Freud believed our behaviors resulted from subconscious conflicts between the pleasure-seeking id, the moralistic superego, and the realistic ego. To Freud, these battles were rooted in childhood and were often sexual in nature. His famed "talking cure," or psychoanalysis, had already swept continental Europe, and it would eventually colonize wealthy American neighborhoods, too. Freud was, in short, a very big deal. Allport was just some kid.

Still, Freud agreed to the meeting, and on the appointed day, Allport entered Freud's "red burlap room with pictures of dreams on the wall," as he later described it. To Allport, it was an encounter of "pungent significance."

At first, Freud stared at Allport in total silence.

In an attempt to make conversation, Allport told Freud a story he thought would appeal to him: On the tram on the way over, Allport had seen a four-year-old boy who refused to sit on the soiled seats. The boy kept saying everything was *"schmutzig"*—dirty. The boy appeared to have dirt phobia, Allport noted.

When he finished his story, Freud "fixed his kindly therapeutic eyes" on Allport.

"And was that little boy you?" Freud asked.

Allport was surprised that Freud had misunderstood the situation so dramatically. *Of course it wasn't him.* To Freud, everything seemed to be about repressed neuroses. Allport thought that was too simplistic an explanation for human behavior. The experience, Allport wrote, "taught me . . . that psychologists would do well to give full recognition to manifest motives before probing the unconscious." Not everything has a hidden meaning, in other words. Sometimes people know what they're like.

What made people have different personalities, Allport would later determine, was not whether they harbored secret urges to marry their mothers or kill their fathers, as Freud would have it. It's that we all have different traits that determine how we pursue goals, think about the world, and react to adversity. Eventually, this view—trait theory—would come to define personality psychology and would give rise to the five-trait model of personality that most psychologists use today. (These are the same five that appeared on that online personality test I took—the one that prompted me to try to change my personality.)

Scholars did not arrive at these five traits easily, though. Psychology is a young science—Harvard didn't have an independent department of psychology until 1936—and the modern concept of "personality" was little-discussed before the late 1800s. Much earlier, ancient Greek philosophers like Aristotle and Theophrastus pontificated on human nature in interesting but not very accurate ways. Theophrastus at one point outlined what he considered to be the thirty different types of "characters," including the "arrogant man," who "is not likely to admit a visitor when he is anointing himself, or bathing, or at table," and the "gross man," who "will spit across the table at the cup-bearer."

But then came early Christianity, and along with it a chilling effect on the study of human individuality. "The religious view of the human race held by the societies of that period was that it was intrinsically flawed—and had been since the original transgressions of Adam and Eve," writes Frank Dumont in *A History of Personality Psychology*. There was no point in probing human nature, since humans' reward was thought to be in heaven, not in personal betterment on earth.

That began to change with Enlightenment scholars like Gottfried Leibniz, who in the early 1700s speculated that people have subliminal thoughts—he called them *petites perceptions*—that motivate their behavior. The thing we now know as "personality" came later, with the rise of Freud, psychoanalysis, and a growing interest in differences between people.

Still, early psychologists tried—and often failed—to reliably measure personality. In the 1920s, the psychoanalyst Carl Jung argued that the world consists of different "types" of people—thinkers and feelers, introverts and extroverts. (However, even Jung cautioned that "there is no such thing as a pure extrovert or a pure introvert. Such a man would be in the lunatic asylum.")

Jung's rubric captured the attention of a mother-daughter duo, Katharine Briggs and Isabel Briggs Myers, who seized on Jung's ideas to develop that staple of Career Day, the Myers-Briggs Type Indicator. Though they lacked scientific training, they hoped to create a test that would help people pursue vocations that were best suited to their natures. "The more you know about what a man is like, the more effectively you can work with him or under him, or assign him to the right job," Isabel Briggs Myers wrote.

The test took off thanks to Isabel's job in human resources, as Merve

Emre describes in *The Personality Brokers*. But in time, it turned out to be virtually meaningless. Most people aren't ENTJs or ISFPs; they fall between categories. Personality traits aren't a "type," they're a spectrum. The organizational psychologist Adam Grant once compared the Myers-Briggs to asking people which they like more: shoelaces or earrings.

Others thought the best way to measure personality was by offering people a confusing picture and judging their reaction. The Swiss psychiatrist Hermann Rorschach asked people what various inkblots brought to mind, and along with a couch and an armchair, the inkblot became a trope of psychology. But many scientists now criticize the Rorschach test as being too subjective and inaccurate. Normal people, seeing a reflection or a cupcake in the blots, are wrongly deemed egotistical or dependent. One detractor even said psychologists would be better off reading tea leaves.

This is where Allport's view of personality as a constellation of stated attitudes, rather than of hidden impulses, gained momentum. Allport would later return to Harvard as a psychology professor intent on studying personality. Rigorous and dutiful, he perused the 1925 edition of *Webster's New International Dictionary* in search of words that might "distinguish the behavior of one human being from that of another." Eventually, he identified 4,500 such traits, including words like "airy" and "zestful."

A series of researchers later built on this work by winnowing these 4,500 down until they felt they had identified as few distinct, standalone traits as possible. (Some of the traits from Allport's list, like "taciturn" and "quiet," were basically synonyms.) This period, roughly the middle of the twentieth century, was a bit like Babel, according to Lewis Goldberg, a professor emeritus at the University of Oregon. "Each personality theorist had his or her own theory of personality. There was no unified theory," Goldberg told me.

Raymond Cattell, a British-American psychologist, narrowed Allport's list of traits down to 171, and then to 16. In 1949, he debuted his

Sixteen Personality Factor Questionnaire, which included traits like "privateness" and "perfectionism." In the decades that followed, Goldberg, the Oregon psychologist, and other researchers decided that really, Cattell's sixteen could be reduced to five main traits. Goldberg had been administering personality tests to his students and found they were basically describing "the Big Five," as they are sometimes bombastically known: openness, or how receptive you are to new ideas and activities; conscientiousness, or how self-disciplined and organized you are; extroversion, or how sociable and energetic you are; agreeableness, or how warm and empathetic you are; and neuroticism, or how depressed or anxious you are.

The traits can be remembered with the acronym OCEAN:

O - Openness to experience
C - Conscientiousness
E - Extroversion
A - Agreeableness
N - Neuroticism

When Goldberg presented that idea to other personality researchers, they seemed to agree. After all, things like "liveliness" and "tension," which appeared in earlier theories, sound a lot like extroversion and neuroticism. The fact that the Big Five took off, while other iterations didn't, suggests "there really is something to evidence," Goldberg told me. "And the others did not have much in the way of evidence."

Starting in the 1970s, Freudian psychoanalysis began to lose its shine, and the trait theorists—Allport's successors—ascended. Though he was in some ways a visionary, many of Freud's ideas about childhood psychosexual development—that personalities are orally or anally fixated—didn't withstand the rigor of modern research. Later studies showed that personality can't entirely be chalked up to childhood: Short of abuse or extreme weirdness, parents don't seem to shape their kids like lumps of clay. If they could, brothers and sisters raised together would resemble each other, but siblings often have no more in common than strangers chosen off the street. (I know this firsthand, as the allergic, aggressive, sun-worshipping sibling of an indoor-kid pacifist who loves cats.)

So what is personality? It's habit, but it's also reflex. "Personality is what you do habitually, automatically, without thinking about it, whether it's how you think about things, how you feel about things, or whether you do certain things," says Brent Roberts, a prominent personality psychologist at the University of Illinois.

Your personality affects how you approach life. Do you take small inconveniences in stride, or do you see them as a personal attack? When you come across a new idea, do you recoil or thrill to it? Personality encompasses your preferences, your mood, and your interaction style, and also the texture of your soul.

Roberts likens personality to a tapestry—an intricate composition in which every stitch matters, but pulling on just one thread won't unravel the entire creation. Your friends, your job, your marriage, your hometown, and your genes all shape your personality, but it's not the result of any one of those forces alone.

"I Radiate Joy"

One July weekend, Rich and I had gone to Ocean City, Maryland, for a short beach getaway. The city, which is named after its only redeeming quality, is crammed with mobile homes, mini-golf courses, and bright-red college students on their crab-and-beer Rumspringas. Most of the action sits alongside a single highway with the beach on one side and past-their-prime hotels on the other. There is one "nice" restaurant and many less-nice restaurants that will serve you a mix of vodka, Sprite, and orange juice in a sippy cup. Saint-Tropez this ain't.

It is also the closest beach to DC, and therefore all of Washington flocks there every summer weekend. We had paid $300 a night to stay in a run-down Best Western, in the kind of room where you try not to let your entire foot touch the carpet when you take a step. The first day, we sat on the beach for an hour. Then it started raining—hot, heavy droplets that sent everyone fleeing to the bars.

I wish I was one of those people who could enjoy rainy days during a beach vacation. Instead, I get mad at God, who never seems to respond by making the sun come out. Rather than find indoor things to do (Museum of Wildfowl Art?), I castigated myself for not checking to see if it was an El Niño year before booking a nonrefundable hotel room.

This all made me wonder whether my personality traits might contribute to my inclination toward senseless anger at things beyond my control. I decided to kill time by taking my first personality test, to get a baseline reading of my inner self. Sitting on the disgusting hotel bedspread, I logged into PersonalityAssessor.com, a personality-testing website created by the Southern Methodist University psychology professor Nathan Hudson. The site measures your personality by comparing your responses to the million or so other people who have taken its tests.

Clicking through a series of multiple-choice screens, I answered dozens of questions about whether I like poetry, whether I like parties, whether I "act wild and crazy," and whether I work hard. The prompt "I radiate joy" got a "strongly disagree." I also disagreed that "we should be tough on crime" or that I "try not to think about the needy." I had to "agree," but not strongly, that "I believe I am better than others."

The point of these questions was to identify where I fall on each of the Big Five traits. I scored in the 23rd percentile in extroversion—"very low," especially when it came to being friendly or cheerful. This seems plausible: I never say things I often hear other women say, like "I'm overjoyed for you" or "my heart is so full." Extroverts feel comfortable around lots of people and make friends easily. They like to be the center of attention, and to have sex. Enviably, they experience more positive emotions, and are always stoked about one thing or another. Introverts like me get stoked, too, of course—but about, say, reading a lyrical memoir or diving into a knitting project. We flinch whenever someone says "karaoke."

Meanwhile, I scored "very high" on conscientiousness and openness—my two strengths apparently being organizational skills and a general YOLO-ness. Conscientious people enjoy making plans and sticking to them. They are self-disciplined and goal oriented. You want a conscientious person to plan your vacation but not necessarily to tag along on it. Openness to experiences, the most nebulous trait, involves appreciating complicated art, being politically liberal, and feeling chills on the back of your neck when you see or hear something especially beautiful. Open people are creative, imaginative, and tolerant.

On agreeableness, I scored "average," my high levels of empathy for other people making up for my low levels of trust in them. Agreeable people are warm, altruistic, and often love children. They get along with pretty much everyone.

Finally, I came to the source of half my breakups, all my therapy appointments, and most of my problems in general: I was in the 94th percentile on neuroticism. "Extremely high."

Neurotic people are addled by stress and threats, real or perceived. "High neuroticism infuses everything with suffering," writes the behavioral scientist Daniel Nettle. (Neurotics' opposite, emotionally stable people, may not even be familiar with the sensation of anxiety at all, bless them.) Neuroticism is the advance runner on a whole relay team of disorders, from depression to anxiety to bipolar.

People tend to be happier and healthier when they're higher on all five traits—for the neuroticism category, this means higher in its opposite, emotional stability. Ideally, we would all be friendly, dependable, open-minded extroverts who don't carry around emergency Xanax. My results showed I was far from that paragon, on multiple levels.

The Big Five is, perhaps unsurprisingly, also not without its weaknesses. The framework only really applies in Western, industrialized countries, for example. But despite its limitations, the five factors at least form a common standard, a shared language for documenting our proclivities and penchants. Personality researchers have now replicated the Big Five in many different studies, and it's the personality model they use most often.

Rather than feel restricted by the five-factor breakdown, I was soothed by its regimentation. I liked that the Big Five would allow me to track each element of my personality over time, rather than pursue vague goals like "be happier" or "reduce your stress."

Taking the personality test reminded me of the first time someone told me that I have anxiety; that it's not normal to feel on alert all the time. Growing up, I was never diagnosed by a doctor. Instead, one day a high school teacher made fun of me in class for worrying excessively. ("I bet Olga's like, 'Oh no, I'm never gonna get this done on time!'" she said to my classmates with a wink. Texas is not very "trauma informed.") I had never considered that it was possible to worry *too much*. It felt like stumbling into a dark basement and flipping on a flashlight. Sure, what you see is dust-coated, and in desperate need of repair. But at least you can see it. Understanding yourself can be freeing, even if the first step toward freedom is realizing you're trapped.

The Plaster Softens

With that, I had my Big Five score—a B minus at best. But I still wanted to *change* my score, not just know it. And when you start to explore the idea of personality change, you quickly encounter a big, unyielding, 180-year-old stick-in-the-mud—one who influentially dismissed the idea that personality changes. His name is William James.

James, now known as one of the earliest American psychologists, was born into a wealthy and cosmopolitan New York family—you may have heard of his brother, the novelist Henry. But his early home life, in the mid-1800s, was chaotic. James's father, Henry Sr., devoted himself to writing long, mostly unread books, and he moved the family around constantly: By the time he was sixteen, James had lived in eighteen different houses, not including stays in various hotels.

In his early adulthood, James wandered, too. He first studied art, then went on an ill-fated expedition to the Amazon, then pursued medicine. He then fell into a severe depression ("nèurasthenia," it was called at the time), agonizing over the meaning of life and what it meant to be free.

Ultimately, James became more interested in philosophy than in medicine, and in 1890, he published an influential philosophical tome, *The Principles of Psychology.* The book takes, at times, a bleak view of humanity: "Habit is thus the enormous fly-wheel of society," James writes. "It keeps the fisherman and the deck-hand at sea through the winter; it holds the miner in his darkness, and nails the countryman to his log-cabin and his lonely farm through all the months of snow." We are all, he implied, frozen in the amber of our routines.

Perhaps his itinerant childhood prompted James to seek stability and fixedness. This might be why *Principles* also includes an idea of James's that has haunted personality science ever since. "In most of us, by the age of 30," he writes, "the character has set like plaster, and will never soften again." James seemed to think personality didn't change. Instead, it calcified.

For years, personality psychologists thought James was basically right about this. Important studies in personality psychology even used "set like plaster" in their title, tipping their hat to their depressive forebear. Researchers believed there was little hope for personality change once people reached adulthood.

But fortunately for people like me, the "plaster" hypothesis turned out to be wrong. This is obvious to anyone who has ever looked up a

Facebook status they posted ten years ago and found themselves staring at the words of a stranger. Personality *does* change over time—even if you don't really try to change it. And if you do try, it changes even faster.

People naturally grow less neurotic and more agreeable and conscientious with age, a tendency called the "maturity principle." When I learned about this, I was reminded of the times in college when I would begin writing a paper that was due the next day at midnight (a sign of low conscientiousness) and would then freak out that the resulting grade would tank my career prospects forever (a mark of high neuroticism). But in time, I evolved: Today, I get started on assignments as soon as I get them, and I only *sometimes* worry they'll doom my career. Maturity, in a way.

We change a bit during adolescence, a significant amount in our early twenties, and we continue to evolve as we marry and get jobs. One study that measured the personalities of American high school students in 1960 and again fifty years later found that 98 percent of the participants had changed on at least one personality trait by the time they were in their sixties. Another, which followed hundreds of Californians over the course of forty years, found that personality changes throughout a person's life, across all the traits. Yet another found that, on some traits, people change more *after* the age of thirty than they do when they're younger. Few of us, to paraphrase James, die nailed to the same log cabins in which we were born.

This new way of looking at personality comports with the Buddhist concept of "no self," or the idea that there's no core "you." To believe otherwise, the sutras say, is a source of suffering. As the Zen philosopher Alan Watts put it, "Ego, the self which he has believed himself to be, is nothing but a pattern of habits or artificial reactions." This belief in the flexibility of the self has percolated through various schools of Western philosophy, too. Jean-Paul Sartre wrote that "existence precedes essence," meaning that people decide what to make of themselves. "Man first of all exists, encounters himself, surges up in the world—and defines himself afterwards," Sartre explained. Or, as Nietzsche cryptically instructed, "Become what thou art!"

Much of personality change occurs because of something called social investment theory, or the idea that as we take on new social roles, we face new expectations and rise to the challenge. When they get jobs, twentysomething partiers start forgoing weekend keggers in order to polish up slide decks for work. Avowed ladies' men will deliver heartfelt odes to monogamy at their weddings. (Researchers have found that in cultures where teens take on adult responsibilities earlier, their personalities mature faster, too.) The people around us set the norm for our behavior, and we sculpt ourselves to meet it.

Some researchers even define personality as existing primarily within social relationships. "We all have multiple selves," writes the Stanford professor Brian Lowery in *Selfless*. There is no "stable, unchanging" you, he argues. Instead, "your self is a flux of interactions and relationships *and* your feeling of your self is created in that same flux." This view is sometimes called the "looking-glass self," implying we reflect the situations in which we find ourselves. This may be why I strayed so far, in my views and interests, from my own family: I left Russia when I was three, and I left suburban Texas when I was eighteen. Now most people who meet me say I'm "very DC"—a reflection of the conscientious, neurotic city in which I've spent most of my adult life.

This mutability of the self may explain why, especially in our twenties, we tend to become more like our friends and coworkers: Having more extroverted friends tends to increase extroversion, and working more tends to increase conscientiousness. You might have noticed this phenomenon if you went to college at a liberal arts school in the Northeast and gradually became more liberal, like your dorm-mates, or if you started working in sales with a bunch of extroverts and grew more outgoing. To a great extent, you are who you socialize with.

Falling in love can also shape personality. One study found that people between the ages of twenty-three and twenty-five who entered romantic partnerships became more conscientious, more extroverted, and less neurotic. We seem to become the brighter versions of ourselves that our partners see. "The process of coupling, and then committing, brings with it the fact that you can't just think about yourself . . . you have to think about and be responsible for somebody else," says the psychologist Brent Roberts. It's fortuitous, then, that I met Rich at twenty-four, the sweet spot of that study. Otherwise maybe I'd be even more neurotic than I already am.

Heritability and Malleability

The fact that personality changes can be a point of disbelief. In a well-known study published about a decade ago, the psychologist Dan Gilbert and his coauthors found that younger people predicted their personalities wouldn't change much over the next decade, but older people reported they had actually changed quite a bit. People find it difficult to imagine how they *might* change, so they think they probably *won't* change. This is the fallacy that keeps tattoo artists and divorce lawyers in business. "Human beings are works in progress that mistakenly think they're finished," Gilbert has said. "The person you are right now is as transient, as fleeting, and as temporary as all the people you've ever been." Even if you don't try to change your personality, that is, it might change anyway.

One reason why personality can seem permanent is that personality is, in fact, partly genetic. In the words of Philip Larkin, "they fuck you up, your mum and dad"—but mostly before you're born. Through research on identical twins separated at birth, scientists have estimated that about 30 to 50 percent of the differences between any two people's personalities are attributable to their genes. They chalk the remaining 50 to 70 percent up to "environmental factors," which includes the way you were raised, yes, but also your other life experiences and your peers—a combination of myriad small influences.

If something is even partly genetic, it can feel like you're doomed to be just like your parents—forever. But just because genetics explains between 30 to 50 percent of the variance of personality does not mean we "get" 30 to 50 percent of our personalities from our parents. We receive only half our genes from each parent, and those genes are shuffled, interacting with each other in unpredictable ways, explains Kathryn Paige Harden, a behavioral geneticist at the University of Texas. Therefore, though we inherit elements of traits from our parents, we end up fairly different from them. You may feel like you're becoming your mother, but, for better or worse, that's biologically unlikely.

Think of it this way: Say your parents are a pantry of ingredients. They contain milk, eggs, flour, baking soda, and if they're Russian like mine are, there's some dill in there, too. But they only pass some of those ingredients down to you. And whether you end up as quiche, pancakes, or an inedible goo depends on which ingredients you inherited and how those ingredients interact with your environment. How hot is your oven? Did you whisk the eggs or fry them? Just as you wouldn't look at a pantry and think, *This is definitely waffles*, you wouldn't look at a person and think they were predestined to have a particular kind of child.

Harden told me about an experiment in which mice who were genetically similar and reared in the same conditions were one day moved into a big cage and allowed to play with one another. Over time, these genetically similar mice developed dramatically different personalities. Some became fearful, others sociable and dominant. Living in Mouseville, the mice carved their own paths of existence, and people do that, too. "We can think of personality as a learning process," Harden says. "We learn to be people who interact with our social environments in a certain way."

Plus, genes and the environment interact. Our genetic predispositions may lead us into environments that then change our personalities. Happy people smile more, so people react more positively to them, which makes them even more agreeable. Open-minded adventure seekers are more likely to go to college, where they grow even more open minded. "Heritability," the Stanford psychologist Carol Dweck told me, "is not the same thing as malleability." Just because something is genetic doesn't mean it can't change.

This is something even William James might have agreed with. Posterity perhaps dwelled too much on his "set like plaster" comment. James occasionally adopted a more flexible take on habit, but these more broad-minded views aren't quoted as often by his successors. "James was almost obsessed with overcoming the limitations of habit formation," says John Kaag, a philosophy professor who has written about James. In his writing, James at times even praises people who act against their natures, recommending that one should "be systematically ascetic or heroic in little unnecessary points, do every day or two something for no other reason than that you would rather not do it." He argued that people do have natural tendencies, but that they can also override those tendencies—and sometimes should.

In fact, James himself became different after he turned thirty, the age at which people are supposedly "set like plaster." When he was around that age, he recovered from his depression by reading the work of the philosopher Charles Renouvier, who inspired James to believe that you could will yourself to be free. "My first act of free will shall be to believe in free will," James wrote, and soon after that he emerged from his "great dorsal collapse." (Would that we could all be so invigorated by an inspirational quote or two.)

Over time, James grew nicer in his writing, and more realistic. Later in his thirties, he got married, secured a permanent position at Harvard, and recommitted himself to his work. He produced most of his best writing after he turned forty.

William "set like plaster" James *did* change. I hoped I could, too.

2

Breaking the Flywheel:
The "How" of Personality Change

dentity, then, is not stagnant. The OCEAN of personality roils, sometimes casting us into unfamiliar waters. Where you began is not always where you'll end up, and this can be reassuring—especially if you, like me, spent your twenties believing that vodka could cure the common cold.

But even more encouraging is this idea: We are not helpless passengers on this ship. Instead, we can steer it. We can change our personalities, and by doing so, we can live happier, more meaningful lives. Though I realize it's unusual to frame self-improvement this way, many of the shortcomings that irk us—messiness, impatience—*are* elements of personality. You can't change yourself without changing your personality, too.

To find out exactly how personality changes, one recent December I traveled to Dallas to meet the Southern Methodist University personality psychologist Nathan Hudson, who has studied the concept of "volitional personality change"—the process by which people transform themselves intentionally. I also wanted to put a face to Personality Assessor.com, his personality-testing website that I'd been using for the past few months.

It was an odd, if convenient, experience, since I had spent my teen years in a suburb of Dallas, and my parents still lived there. This meant that I could pair the trip with a family visit, but also that I wouldn't have the preferred reporter's adventure of learning something fascinating in a dazzling new setting. It was more like being invited to meet the president and finding out he lives two doors down.

Still, Dallas is nothing if not a monument to change. Every time I return, I notice new subdivisions spreading across the metroplex. Out the car window I'll see another IKEA, another megachurch. Thousands of Californians had recently moved to Texas, and in my sleepy hometown, I did a double take: People were waiting in line for a trendy new pizza place. The city had long strained to become a destination and had, through the sheer force of giddyup, finally succeeded. "Anything that's beautiful in Dallas was either planted, dug, erected, or willed into being," Ellen Kampinsky, the former fashion editor of the *Dallas Morning News*, once said. I wondered if I could will a new personality into being, too.

I had, after all, already changed. In high school, I was shy, studious, and for a while, deeply religious. I had fallen in with some evangelical Christians and, never one to half-ass a project, soon became the most zealous among them. At lunchtime I terrorized the lone Hindu boy in school, as well as my atheist friend, Cait, warning them they were damned for eternity. I only rationalized watching the sinful show *Friends* because it was important to know what the godless were up to.

By college, I had largely discarded those beliefs, replacing the Christianity of Texas with the gods of dorm life: self-actualization and beer. I became fun-loving and boy crazy. My reputation was apparently so pronounced that once a classmate asked me if I had "four boyfriends." I guessed I'd be seeing Cait in hell.

Now I was basically a hermetic "pressure addict," as one former editor put it. It was time for yet another me to make her debut.

I found Hudson's office nestled in a high-rise beyond a maze of empty hallways, on an upper floor that towers over the roar of Highway 75 and, more pleasantly, the groomed SMU campus below. The man himself is bearded, soft-spoken, and extremely precise. If he had a catchphrase, it would be "That being said . . ." The most whimsical thing about him is the shelf lined with Power Rangers figurines on the wall of his office—like me, Hudson is a nineties kid. He has a good personality, scientifically speaking: average on extroversion, agreeableness, and neuroticism, and high on conscientiousness and openness to experience. It fits an even-keeled university professor.

Hudson's early interest in personality stemmed from a philosophical question: Why do people want different things out of life? To some, life is a playground meant for nonstop fun. To others, it's a race to acquire power and prestige. Hudson wanted to know why, exactly, we pursue such different paths. "I just find those questions fundamentally interesting," he mused. "What are people going for? What do they want? What motivates them?"

To Hudson, personality traits are the thoughts, feelings, and behaviors that serve some purpose in our lives. Agreeableness helps you form and maintain social relationships. Conscientiousness helps you stay productive. More than simply describing you, personality helps you get what you want.

Hudson is aware that people sometimes say they don't want to change their personalities—but, in the same breath, they might wish they were more organized or made friends more easily. But those are the *fruits* of personality traits. And, according to his research and that of others, changing your personality can help you achieve those goals.

Though Hudson doesn't take a stance on whether people *should* try to change their personalities, the case for personality change is, in short, that certain traits leave you better off. "Higher levels of all five of those variables are correlated with higher well-being," he told me, referring to the Big Five. You're more likely to be happy, healthy, and successful if you're more conscientious, extroverted, agreeable, open to experiences, and emotionally stable, as opposed to neurotic.

Each trait has different benefits, but some of the benefits are surprisingly substantial, accounting for a large percentage of life satisfaction, professional success, and even longevity. Conscientious people, for instance, are healthier, live longer, and are less likely to abuse substances. They tend to do well at school and work, which leads to even more money and even better health. A massive meta-analysis of 2,500 studies found that conscientiousness has desirable effects on 98 percent of variables related to job performance—including commitment, perseverance, and self-discipline.

And although introversion is not a flaw, studies show extroverts are happier, in part because they spend more time on activities that are challenging yet rewarding. Some of the strongest predictors of happiness are our social connections, and extroverts, through all their party-going and public speaking, end up befriending more people. As an introvert myself, I had to admit that, on the rare occasions when I was surrounded by a group of friends who knew me well, I felt a lightness that was never there when I was alone. It's a "joy to be hidden," the psychoanalyst D. W. Winnicott wrote, "but disaster not to be found."

Neuroticism, meanwhile, can really ruin your life. Despite the stereotype of the moody genius, neuroticism is correlated with *worse* cognitive function, in part because anxiety and depression undermine focus and concentration. When neurotic children and teens grow up, they don't perform as well at work or earn as much as their emotionally stable peers do. Neurotic people are more likely to get divorced— or to be less happily married if they do stay hitched. People who are high in emotional stability adapt better to aging: They are less likely to see middle age as a crisis or to be disappointed by retirement. Some research estimates that a small reduction in neuroticism feels like earning $314,000 more a year—a fact that helps explain some out-of-network therapists' fees.

It's not just *having* these traits that helps you thrive. People who develop these personality traits then go on to boost their salaries, health, and educational attainment. If you score low on a certain personality trait, in other words, you aren't doomed. You can still grow, and you can still reap the rewards of change. When people do successfully shift their personalities in the desired direction, they report feeling happier afterward. Science and history offer examples of people doing just that.

Fake It Till You Make It

One day in the 1940s, an inmate came to see Raymond Corsini, a psychologist at Auburn Prison in Upstate New York. The prisoner, a man in his thirties, was getting out on parole, and before he left, he just wanted to thank Corsini.

The inmate said that, before meeting Corsini, he had always hung out with "a bunch of thieves." He had a dead-end job in the prison kitchen, and he had long ago lost touch with his family and faith. His prospects for successfully reentering society were probably poor.

But, he said, after an encounter with Corsini two years prior, he had left feeling like he was "walking on air." That day in the yard, he started hanging out with a group of well-behaved guys instead of his usual crew. He began attending the prison high school, earned a diploma, and lined up a drafting job. He found religion and wrote to his family. "You have freed me," the inmate said later. "I now have hope." He said he felt like a new person.

Corsini wasn't sure what he was being thanked for. Perhaps embarrassingly, he didn't even remember talking to the man. His notes suggested he had once, very briefly, given the inmate an intelligence test. Corsini asked the inmate if he was sure it was him.

"It was you, all right," the inmate said. "And I'll never forget what you said to me. It changed my life."

"What was that?" Corsini asked.

"You told me I had a high IQ," the inmate said.

This experience, of course, is colored by the memory and interpretation of Corsini, who is deceased. But in the course of my research, I saw that this kind of sudden change does happen, however infrequently. Some people turn their lives around after a rushing realization—either one that's handed down from a trusted figure, like a therapist, or one that comes from inside themselves. The inmate explained to Corsini that people had always told him he was stupid and crazy. Corsini's offhand comment—"you have a high IQ"—thoroughly reshaped the man's self-concept.

The psychologist William R. Miller has studied fifty-five people who had these types of "sudden and profound" epiphanies that reoriented their lives—a phenomenon he calls "quantum change." A slight majority said they were in distress before the change, but many said nothing in particular was happening. One of Miller's subjects was cleaning the toilet when the eureka moment struck; another was smoking pot.

Then something shifted. Some of them heard a voice speak out of nowhere. They realized an important truth; they were relieved of a mental burden; they felt a wave of unconditional love. It was a "one-way door" through which there was no return. Afterward, they got divorces or stopped drinking. They found happiness and took control of their lives. They developed meaning and a desire to live. While this tiny study is more anecdote than science, it's worth noting that when Miller's coauthor, Janet C'de Baca, interviewed the study participants again ten years later, she found the changes had endured.

This type of quick transformation is what the phrase "personality change" calls to mind for many people. Change, in popular culture, is often depicted as an abrupt about-face—a baptism, a close call, a rock bottom. (Once, someone asked me if I was writing a book about stroke victims.)

But while these examples are interesting, they're also rare. They show that personality change *can* happen, but not how it *usually* happens. Typically, it takes months or years of concerted effort for someone's personality to swerve so dramatically. While a few of us might have a life-altering experience like Corsini's client or Miller's interviewees, most people experience personality change much more prosaically, by performing behaviors associated with the new personality over and over again. Absent a whisper from the heavens, the way to change personality is, essentially, by faking it until you make it. Virtually all researchers agree that the key to changing personality is to alter your daily thoughts and actions. The best personality-change interventions help people figure out what they want to change, tell them how to change, and remind them to continue changing.

Personality change may sound like an eerie, out-of-body experience—and as the quantum change stories show, it can be. But the science behind it is remarkably simple: You just have to remember to act how you'd like to be, consistently. And this is true even of remarkable-seeming feats. Corsini's inmate had to show up at the prison high school not just once, after all, but repeatedly. People who join Alcoholics Anonymous not only renounce drinking, they go to meetings for years. In journalism school, we learned that the best stories don't start with a brilliant mind pumping out five thousand words in one sitting. They start with a ream of boring documents that someone gathered from an obscure government office and logged into a database. Most incredible things are built, bit by bit, through persistence and repetition.

For a 2019 study, Nathan Hudson and three other personality psychologists devised a tool that would help people perform these types of personality-altering new behaviors. He and his coauthors created a website that would serve up a list of "challenges" to students who wanted to change their personality traits. Some of the behaviors required the involvement of other people, but others did not: For, say, extroversion, one challenge was "Introduce yourself to someone new."

To combat neuroticism, the website suggested, "When you wake up, spend at least five minutes meditating." Those who completed the challenges associated with a given trait saw changes in that trait at the end of the fifteen-week study, Hudson found. The participants faked it, and then they made it: Merely behaving in a more extroverted way, for example, caused the participants to grow in extroversion.

Hudson's study found that these challenges worked well to help participants change on the traits of extroversion, conscientiousness, and neuroticism, but they didn't really work for the traits of agreeableness and openness to experience. This could be because, as we'll see, openness and agreeableness can be harder to change, and in his studies, fewer people elected to try to change those traits. But, as we'll also see, there might be other ways to become a more agreeable or open person—or to at least address facets of these traits.

Other researchers have produced findings similar to Hudson's. Along with some colleagues, Mirjam Stieger, a lecturer at the Lucerne University of Applied Sciences and Arts, developed an app that reminded people to perform new behaviors to change their personalities. (An example for extroversion: "Let yourself be carried away by spontaneous ideas." For conscientiousness: "Prepare a to-do list every morning.") The app prompted the participants to learn from people who already possessed elements of their desired personalities, and to create a "change team" of friends who could keep them accountable. Stieger found that the study participants' personalities did, in fact, change, compared to a control group, and they stayed different for at least three months. Even the participants' friends and families reported that they had changed. If personality is, as F. Scott Fitzgerald put it, "an unbroken series of successful gestures," then apparently all you have to do is gesture in the right direction.

The idea behind these studies is that new behaviors eventually become new habits, and the habits grow entrenched. In the same way that you don't think about brushing your teeth in the morning, you would no longer struggle to talk to strangers or to hit the gym after work. Eventually, you'll break in the new personality like a stiff pair of loafers: What was once uncomfortable will become familiar.

These new habits then affect our attitudes about ourselves. When we see that we are acting a certain way—volunteering, joining a choir—we conclude that it must be because we just *are* that kind of person, a saint with a killer soprano. In that way, a new personality *state* can become a new personality *trait*.

In practice, this means that change requires doing things differently. You can't just say you'll start exercising or socializing; you have to commit. Personality isn't based on what we say we'll do. It's rooted in what we actually do, which becomes what we think about. Even though personality was then a hazy concept, this is something even the ancients implicitly understood. In his *Nicomachean Ethics*, Aristotle noted that "we become builders by building and harpists by playing the harp. Similarly, it is by doing just acts that we become just, by doing temperate acts that we become temperate, by doing courageous acts that we become courageous." By performing the acts of a different personality, you can change yours.

A New Mindset

When you're trying to change, it can be helpful to believe you *can* change. One of the most prominent lines of research on change in adulthood comes from the Stanford psychologist Carol Dweck's studies of people who have a "growth mindset," versus those who have a "fixed" one. Someone with a growth mindset believes in a person's ability to change and improve over time, through hard work and support, while someone who has a fixed mindset sees traits, interests, and skills as quantities that are set for life.

For instance, Dweck has found that people who believe they can cultivate empathy (a facet of agreeableness) do, in fact, display more empathy. In one 2014 study, she and her coauthors, Karina Schumann and Jamil Zaki, told one group of participants that empathy was malleable ("can be developed and cultivated") and another group that it was fixed ("hard, like a rock"). The participants in the "malleable" condition were more willing to read stories written by cancer patients, and they agreed to volunteer more hours in a support group that would require meeting with cancer patients face-to-face. Those led to believe empathy was malleable—who had a growth mindset—also said they *wanted* to become more empathetic. "People who know that they can change how empathic a person they are, are more inclined to try," Jamil Zaki told me.

These "mindset"-style interventions tend to have small effects—in the empathy study, it resulted in the participants volunteering for about two hours more—and their application to things like academic achievement is questionable. But when it comes to beliefs about ourselves, this kind of flexible self-talk can push us slightly closer to being the people we want to be.

Dweck isn't the only psychologist who has found it can be beneficial to believe in personal evolution. In the 1950s, a psychologist named George Kelly prescribed "roles" for his patients to play in order to overcome various phobias and hang-ups—hesitant wallflowers might be sent to socialize in nightclubs, for example. Afterward, his patients felt like they maybe weren't so shy after all. Kelly's goal was to help people experiment with their lives and assess the results. "No one needs to be the victim of his biography," he wrote. Far from dissembling, Kelly believed his patients were embodying their truest selves.

Much more recently, Jessica Schleider, an assistant professor at Stony Brook University, built on Dweck's work and found that kids aged twelve to fifteen who were introduced to the concept that people can change, and that the brain is malleable, showed greater improvements on depression and anxiety, compared to a control group. Yet another study found that people who had more of a growth mindset about anxiety—meaning they believed they could become less neurotic—were less likely to feel depressed or to use substances after experiencing stressful life events. The researchers Adriana Sum Miu and David Yeager also found that, among students entering high school, those taught that people can change showed fewer depression symptoms months later, compared to a control group. "The things you worry about and fret over now don't label you. They don't mean that you'll always be that way," Dweck told me. "And this potential for change is very heartening."

Back when I took my first personality test, I nodded knowingly, like a person seeing an X-ray of a fracture long after a bad fall. I'd always had a suspicion I could stand to be more extroverted, agreeable, and emotionally stable, but this confirmed it. Because it was still raining in Ocean City, I began brainstorming a list of activities and behaviors that would help me become my own version of Aristotle's harpist—a new and improved me. It felt like creating a syllabus for the discontented soul.

The best "program" for changing personality comes from a study by Hudson called "You Have to Follow Through"—named for one of the prerequisites for personality change, and not, as I thought, for a golf swing. The appendix of the study contains the long list of challenges that Hudson and his coauthors served up to their study participants to help them change, and I planned to use some of those same activities in my own personality-change program.

However, some of the assignments from that study were a little tame. For example, for extroversion, one of the suggestions was to smile and wave at someone new, something I already do regularly—not because I'm an extrovert but because I'm a Texan. I decided to combine the challenges from Hudson's study with other research-backed techniques to come up with a bucket list of sorts—a series of behaviors and activities that, when performed consistently, should help my personality transform.

"This will be fun!" I resolved that day in Ocean City, as the decrepit hotel air conditioner squealed. Ideally, in the end I would be happy, relaxed, personable. The screams of angry sources, the failure of my boyfriend to do the tiniest fucking thing—they would be nothing to me. I wouldn't cry at the disdain with which my fertility doctor says my biological age. I would finally understand what my therapist means when she says I should "just observe my thoughts and let them pass without judgment." Back at home, I attached the list of the personality challenges to my nightstand, because I'm very conscientious.

3

Dance Like Everyone Is Watching:

Extroversion

My journey into extroversion began solitarily, with me watching the improv show *Middleditch & Schwartz* on Netflix one night. The episode opened with two well-known actors, Thomas Middleditch and Ben Schwartz, spending an uncomfortably long time pulling a premise for their sketch out of a random audience member—a photography intern. Then, on a bare stage, Middleditch pretended to interview Schwartz for a photography job, making up absurd questions and requests like "Embody a gazelle."

The audience laughed along gamely, but mostly, the scene reminded me that I needed to file my expense report. I felt uneasy for the actors, like at any moment the crowd could turn on them, leaving them groping for laughs in ghostly silence. I wondered why they couldn't have just written out better scenes ahead of time. And even worse, I knew that soon I would be in their exact same position, except without the advantage of being a famous comedian.

For my personality-change project, I had decided to focus on each of the five traits intensively for a few months at a time, and I tackled extroversion first. In recent years my life had descended into a rut that I didn't particularly like, and extroversion seemed like the way out. Most days, I worked, made dinner, watched TV, and worked some more. Rich and I were planning to relocate, and it occurred to me that I would have both moved into and out of my house without having met any of my neighbors. A test in a self-help book reminded me that I have "high loneliness."

My "very low" extroversion score was probably not surprising to people who know me: My friend Anastasia once sentenced me to attending a party on pain of ending our friendship. But my hard-core introversion could turn pernicious, shading at times into loneliness and isolation. I have a career in which work can expand to fill every crevice of the day, and sometimes I thought that was a good thing, because I didn't have many hobbies or friends to otherwise occupy my time. (And say what you will about extroverts, but they have plenty of hobbies and friends.) I had always told myself I could focus on socializing after my life had stabilized, but the absence of social interaction was, itself, destabilizing.

Of all five traits, extroversion offers the simplest path to personality change: You just have to go out and talk to people. You don't even have to be particularly good at it, or to proclaim yourself an "extrovert" while you do it. You just go, and extroversion will find you, like the entire wedding follows the first intrepid dancer.

Coincidentally, this is also the ethos behind improv comedy: You just have to say something. Anything! For the uninitiated, "improv" is short for "improvisational theater." The idea is that two or more actors get up onstage without knowing what they'll say or do. They get to the "scene" by accepting and building on a partner's improvisations—a concept known as "yes, and." When this is done well, improvisers say there is virtually no difference between improv and scripted theater—a claim about which opinions surely differ.

I knew I needed a commitment device for extroversion—something to force me out of my house and into gregariousness. I decided to try improv, which seemed like the full-immersion extrovert experience.

It also felt like full-immersion insanity. Rich saw me entering my credit-card information into the website of Dojo Comedy, a cozy-looking DC improv theater whose logo includes a pair of mustachioed Groucho Marx comedy glasses. "You doing improv is like Larry David doing ice hockey," he said.

It's true. My general vibe is less "yes, and" and more "well, actually." I've never really liked improv as an art form. I don't find it particularly funny—it's more like an extended inside joke you're never going to get. I thought *Middleditch* would warm me to improv, but it only turned me off more.

Before the first class a few weeks later, I donned a Groundlings-ready black T-shirt and jeans, hoping to draw as little attention to myself as possible. I tried to shake memories of being so timid in middle-school drama class that I only qualified to be the understudy for the smallest role—Bob Cratchit's daughter. When I typed the address of the improv studio into my phone, I was relieved when the red snake of "heavier than usual traffic" indicated that I would have at least an hour to mentally prepare.

The improv class met in an old town house, in a room that was, for no discernible reason, filled with dozens of sculptures of elephants. Six of us novices sat in a circle on chairs that looked like they'd been salvaged from Victorian funerals.

The instructor, a short brunette with a brisk, friendly manner, opened by asking us about our past improv experience—none, in my case. One of the other women rattled off a long list of improv classes she had taken. *What kind of crazy person does improv multiple times?* I wondered. (Me, as it would turn out.)

Right after the instructor said "Let's get started," I prayed for someone to grab an elephant and knock me unconscious. That didn't happen, so instead I stood up to play warm-up games with a software engineer, two lawyers, and a guy who worked on the Hill. The games were meant to loosen us up for what was to come, which was "scene work," or acting out unscripted mini plays with one another.

First, we learned the improv standard Zip Zap Zop, which involves whooshing beams of energy at one another and taking turns saying "Zip," "Zap," and—you guessed it—"Zop." The point of the game is to stay unflustered enough to keep up the Zip-Zap-Zop sequence while still whooshing on to someone else in the circle.

I struggled for several reasons: Because of the pandemic, I hadn't been in a room with other people for more than a year. On top of that, I have poor reflexes, and, because we wore masks, you had to determine whether someone was about to Zop you solely by the angle of their eyes.

If someone messed up the sequence—said "Zip" to another's "Zip," for instance—we would all stop, clap, and say "Yay!," reinforcing the idea that it's okay to screw up in improv. The spirit of all this was so different from my job, where you can get fired for screwing up, that it felt like some sort of rehab for perfectionists.

Then we moved on to juggling various invisible items among one another, including an invisible ball, which we had to refer to as "invisible ball!" I sensed that the others were as nervous as I was, but this being DC, an air of try-hard overachievement subsumed everyone's true emotions. People, myself included, will behave ridiculously if they feel they have no alternative. I imagined all my fellow ball-jugglers back at work the next day, writing emails in which they promised to circle back and touch base. I wondered whether they would think back to this moment of whimsy at their brown-bag lunches, as they gravely discussed the situation in Burkina Faso. Maybe it would make the situation in Burkina Faso seem less chaotic by comparison.

Soon it was time to call an invisible hawk to my arm. I noted with gratitude that at least the blinds were closed, so no one could see us from the street.

The Extroversion Advantage

I looked to extroversion first for another reason: Extroverts are happier, research unfortunately shows. An exhaustingly chirpy series of studies have found that social connection is one of the strongest predictors of well-being, and extroverts are more socially connected. In lab experiments, extroverts tend to interpret ambiguous stimuli more positively, hearing the word "won" rather than "one," for example, or writing more uplifting short stories based on generic prompts. People who are extroverted as teenagers remain happier even when they're sixty.

I understand that introverts might not be thrilled to hear this—I wasn't, either. But Sonja Lyubomirsky, a psychologist who has studied this phenomenon, says it's worth focusing less on the "extrovert" part of this and more on the fact that these individuals are more enmeshed in community. "Connection is really the key to happiness," Lyubomirsky told me. And there are ways to square your natural introversion with the universal human need for connection. You don't have to mingle with everyone at the office party, for instance. You can just call a trusted friend for a one-on-one conversation. Even hanging out with others and listening more than you talk can be a form of "extroversion," Lyubomirsky says.

Though there's nothing wrong with being an introvert, several studies have shown that when introverts occasionally behave in extroverted ways, they experience more "positive affect"—science-speak for good feelings. "I started doing these studies because I didn't believe them," says John Zelenski, a psychology professor at Carleton University who has replicated this finding, and who himself is introverted. But "it absolutely seems correct that if you get people to act extroverted—and usually, that means socializing for a few minutes—there's a big mood boost there."

The reason for this twist is that behaving against our natures doesn't bother us as much as we fear it might. In one study, introverts even reported feeling *truer to themselves* when they were behaving like extroverts. That's because, as much as we might prize authenticity, we have other desires, too. We want to handle difficult situations appropriately, feel embraced by others, and accomplish our goals. Sometimes, achieving these things means going against our "natural" personality traits.

"Lots of things that we may not initially like doing actually really benefit us," says Lyubomirsky, who, as an example, offered that she now loves running but took a while to get into it. "A lot of things in life don't feel natural at first. . . . Just because it doesn't feel comfortable and natural doesn't mean it's not authentic." Authenticity can come from familiarity, and the only way to build familiarity is through experience.

This is an important point, because a desire to remain "authentic" is one reason people may balk at the idea of changing themselves—either through personality change or otherwise. But living authentically can also mean behaving in ways that feel, at first, uncomfortable, as long as those actions draw you closer to your values and goals. (More on this in later chapters.) Many of us, if we followed the North Star of "authenticity," would quit our jobs, neglect our families, and watch *Love Is Blind* all day. But what is instinctive is not always best.

This doesn't mean behaving like an extrovert constantly, just occasionally. I told Zelenski about a time I had to collect "man on the street" interviews—a horrible task that involves approaching random strangers and lobbing questions at them in an attempt to find a pattern of responses for your story. One freezing-cold night in New Jersey, I didn't conceal my misery well enough. As I mangled my words and rubbed my hands together, one woman looked at me with pity and said, "Don't worry, you're almost done."

"After a while, it does get old," Zelenski acknowledged. As Carl Jung might say, only a lunatic could be extroverted *all* the time.

Just Make a Choice

About two hours into the first improv class, we moved on from games to full-fledged "scenes," in which several of us would act out something spontaneously based on a suggestion from our instructor. But on my first few attempts at a group scene, I sputtered. I didn't know what to say, so I started asking my scene partners rapid-fire questions—*What kind of athlete are you? Why do you have a monkey as a pet?* You're not really supposed to do this in improv, since it dumps the creativity burden on the other person.

So I was relieved when one of my fellow improvisers made a bold choice.

"I'm a traveling salesman selling sulfuric acid!" he announced.

Suddenly we all had someone to lean on.

"As a scientist who specializes in sulfuric acid, I have to say this stuff is top-notch," one person added.

"And I'd love to buy some sulfuric acid," another person chimed in. We giggled, even though we were supposed to be serious solvent dealers. In improv, as in life, sometimes it helps to just make a choice, weird though it might be.

I decided to view navigating the awkwardness of improv as a kind of intellectual challenge—one with potential mental-health benefits. Though it's now closely associated with comedy, what's today called "improv" was born in the 1920s in an acting program at Hull House, a community center for poor immigrants in Chicago. Early improv was a type of "theater game" that was meant, in part, to help children overcome their shyness and for immigrants of different ethnicities to interact with each other. The research on improv's upsides is sparse, but one 2019 study did find that a ten-week improv class reduced social anxiety in teens.

Early on, I found myself especially drawn to Jewel, an improv classmate with a calm presence and warm amber eyes. Like me, she worked a job that involved health policy, and at breaks, we discussed the vagaries of the ever-shifting pandemic. During class, she would often jump in when I floundered, rescuing the scene and building on it. (If I was supposed to be Shakira, she'd be a Shakira superfan, and so forth.) Whenever Jewel volunteered to be in a scene with me, I felt my stomach unclench a little.

Jewel told me she had signed up for improv because, as the world tentatively reopened, she felt stiff, socially. She worked in communications, and she envied coworkers who could easily chat up a room full of strangers. She found herself overthinking social situations.

I felt the same way. At every gathering recently, I was silently thinking, *Oh my God, how do you do this again? What did people say in the Before Times?* When, post-lockdown, a friend of a friend introduced himself to me at a bar, in response I accidentally said "okay" instead of my name.

Some of the improv exercises reminded Jewel of therapy—like one where we had to name our scene partner's emotions—and she hoped it would have a similarly restorative effect. Growing up in an immigrant family, she told me later, she hadn't always felt very in touch with her feelings. "A lot of folks didn't learn about mental and emotional health growing up," she said. "I just saw so much value in getting practice in identifying my emotions."

I appreciated this, too—that within buttoned-up DC, we had a safe refuge in which to explore big, bold feelings. It was all just an act, after all.

As I sped home from my first class, I detected something that floored me. I was smiling. Wide! Without meaning to! Something about the whole exercise—even though I didn't condone it logically or, frankly, comedically—was just so *fun*. I'm rarely immersed in something that's meant to be light and exuberant, as opposed to correct or exacting. It had been months since I'd had a conversation about some-

the plate of
often, when
be. I seem-
ould simply
that some-

that matter,
e retreat to
. Gradually,
ollification
when you
my life was
mine was
ne than all
t in search

Anastasia,
t's hard for
s taller; she
vine. We're
ates where
like a lost
very action

ere intro-
ities. One
he had,
ours.
get

the vaccines would surely be. The elec-
d me, in spite of myself.

Lyubomirsky's adage, that sometimes
nd up feeling pretty good. The pioneer-
r said "You more likely act yourself into
action," and I had literally acted myself
, it seems, introverts should agree to do
ng them. Much like you sometimes have
ometimes you have to commit to social-
n the mood, you'll never go.
unwound by drinking one of my single-
e alcoholics.

e Elusive "Adult Friend"

m an introvert, I'm an introvert who at-
chools. For a few years my parents moved
rtment in the Dallas suburbs to another,
d on survival to worry about friendship,
cret rule book that I never possessed.
ed to be friendly by telling a boy—who I
football player—that I liked his shirt. His
spent the rest of the year mocking me for
the joke being that I was obviously too ugly
r not even bothering to argue; I just wanted
n chasing that sweet seclusion ever since. Ap-
: According to a study that followed more than
rican adults for ten years, introverts who moved
d fewer high-quality social relationships as adults.
se life satisfaction and psychological well-being, but

Ever since, I've viewed friendship like a garnish on
my life: nice to have, but no big deal if it's not there—and
you're busy and just throwing something together, it won'
ingly decided that since friendship is difficult for me, I sh
not have many friends. It's often less painful to conclude
thing we've never had is something we don't really need.

But of course, this mentality is not accurate—nor, for
healthy. Over the years I've watched older adults in my li
the suburbs and dismiss friendship as a silly extravagance
they replaced the rigor of human interaction with the m
of TV. I saw the anguish and conspiracies that take hole
don't talk to anyone other than your partner. I worried
on a similar track: The outside world was reopening, bu
still firmly shut. George Eliot called a friend "more divi
divinities," and in between waves of the pandemic, I wer
of salvation.

When one day I complained to my sociable friend,
about how hard it is to make friends in DC, she said, "No,
you to make friends in DC." Anastasia is my height but seem
has perfect skin and an encyclopedic knowledge of organic
both immigrants from Russia who grew up in fly-over st
no one understood us, and when she befriended me, I felt
toddler who'd finally been tracked down by her mom. Her e
says, *I've been looking all over for you!*

She and I met in that most Washington of ways: We
duced by a mutual friend to network about job opportun
after-work drink turned into another, and another—but
I'm being honest, initiated 80 percent of those early happy
h

Anastasia suggested I do group activities, where I coul
vor for lots of people at once and pick the ones I liked. Bac
I turned to the app designed explicitly for this use case, M
site where regular people hoping to meet other regular pe

nize gatherings and events. I scrolled through its long list of local book clubs, which included one for foodies, one for international-affairs professionals, several for conservatives, several for defending democracy, and many, many, many in which members read books recommended by Reese Witherspoon. One had a waitlist of "over 300 people." One suspiciously asked, "Are you looking for a Buddy in Washington with whom you want to Chat Online, Travel, Play, go for a Movie, Dinner, Outing, Event/Concert etc.?" I spent a few minutes trying to determine if it was a sex thing, then closed the tab. I signed up instead for the club that seemed the best-organized, which was geared toward young professional women. I also enrolled in some groups based around hiking and other vaguely social activities.

One Friday night in June, I realized that all week I had not seen any humans who didn't live in my house, and that one of my hiking groups was meeting up at a bar not too far away from me. My self-flagellating striver voice reminded me that if I was serious about this project, I had to go. But man, did I not want to.

"I just want to stay here and hang out with youuuu," I whined to Rich.

He helped expel me by letting out two ripe farts, putting on an action movie, and firing up his laptop to do some web development. I grudgingly grabbed my car keys and headed for the bar, blasting my nineties pump-up music the whole way.

The bar was in the basement of a high-rise in a soulless part of town. I kept my mask on and decided not to drink. Everyone was playing pool, and I felt in the way; immediately, I bumped into someone and spilled his Coke. Then I played a decent game of table tennis, which prompted some mild admiration from one of the other attendees, who said I was "good but needed to practice."

I chatted a bit with the organizer, who appeared to spend nearly all his free time creating and attending Meetups because it kept him from succumbing to depression. Another man I met said he had moved to

Northern Virginia during the pandemic, and that Meetups had been his primary source of social interaction. "Meetup was my savior," he said solemnly.

Until 2020, "hiking" was the number one searched term on Meetup, the organization's CEO, David Siegel, later told me. During the pandemic, though, it was "finding adult friends"—adult friendship being something that, paradoxically, anyone can provide but no one can find.

Meetup seems to work best in cities whose populations are big and transient, Siegel said, like Dubai or San Francisco. People tend to join Meetup when they move to a new city, or when they get divorced, or when they get depressed. The average number of people who attend each Meetup is fairly small—nine or so—and Siegel says it's better that way. After long rejecting online events, Meetup quickly began allowing them during the pandemic, and in the summer of 2022, the site's events were still about 20 percent virtual. One organizer was running a virtual Meetup group seven days a week, five hours a day, just to give lonely people someone to talk to.

That all sounded very heartwarming, but I soon found my own Meetups were a little hit-or-miss, and success depended largely on whether I had anything in common with others in the group. The hiking Meetups tended to attract dozens of people who would all squeeze onto the narrow paths, where we were forced to march two-by-two, as if bound for an ark that would rescue us from dying alone.

"You've got to be kidding me," whispered a man who was trying to hike back to his car when he realized he'd first have to let nearly a hundred Washingtonians ramble past.

I would usually end up falling beside someone and, after covering travel, movies, food, and mild office complaints, run a little dry. I found myself saying bland, stilted phrases like "Do you miss the weather in Vietnam?" or "I do enjoy baking, but it can be quite complicated," like I was performing a CIA dead drop. In an effort to switch hiking buddies,

I'd madly eavesdrop and then yell a noun I overheard back at the group. "Are you guys talking about AllTrails?! The app?! I love it!"

Once, I went on a sweltering four-hour trek during which I was sucked into a long conversation with a woman who kept wildly misunderstanding everything I said.

"What's your last name?" she asked.

"Khazan," I said. In English, I pronounce it with a silent "K," like huh-zahn.

"Oh, that's not how I say it," she said.

"What?"

"I say hoh-zah," she said, as though we were talking about "jif" versus "gif."

"I mean, I guess people can say it however they want," I said.

"Oh, you do not know how to say it?" she asked.

"Um, no, I mean I do know . . . it's . . . my name," I said as politely as possible. I didn't think these were the seeds of bosom friendship.

Being Yourself versus Being Included

Sometimes I think it's a miracle anyone socializes at all. "We look at any other person, and there is an entire universe in their head," says Matthew Lieberman, a UCLA psychologist and the author of *Social*, about the neuroscience of connection. "You are trying to figure out how to make your universe and their universe coalesce and make sense together." We're always guessing whether a certain anecdote will appeal to someone, whether a comment will come across as funny or abrasive. Each interaction ricochets between the opposing goals of "being yourself" and saying whatever will get you social validation.

To be sure, humans evolved to be social—we need one another to survive and succeed. Our skin is very easily puncturable, and independently, we are not particularly strong. An adult human can barely outrun a wombat. "Primates can hunt together and do various things together that are hard to do on your own," Lieberman says.

But socializing has risks, too. Groups shield us, but they can also drain us. "When you get primates together, and they are more social, you also get things like food being stolen and mate poaching. So the key to successful socializing is knowing how to get that balance," he added.

Togetherness, therefore, requires constantly weighing the group's needs against your own. The trick is to be sufficiently yourself as to feel seen and heard, but not so much that you scare off other people. In every interaction, writes the linguist Deborah Tannen, we obey two contradictory commands: the need to be connected to other people, and thus avoid dying, and the need to be independent, and thus avoid dying *as individuals*. "The needs and wants of others can be imposing, or even engulfing," Tannen writes in her book *Conversational Style*.

The difficulty of this trade-off between extroversion and introversion is one reason why your personality can congeal into a dysfunctional status quo. Maybe you had some interactions in which the needs of the group overwhelmed you, so now you mostly keep to yourself. Maybe you went to a few house parties that proved boring; afterward, you arrived at the conclusion that you were a hard-core introvert—no parties for you!—rather than the conclusion that your fellow partygoers might have also struggled with interaction. You might find conversation annoying because you aren't having the right kinds of conversations.

The "you" in each of these cases is absolutely also me, to be clear. From my days as an aggressively bullied middle-schooler, I found that staying quiet was a good way to keep the peace—and at times, to hide from view. No one could make fun of you if you never said anything. I held fast to my individuality, yes, but I was cut off from my fellow primates, wandering the wilderness alone. I wanted to learn to relate to others without losing myself.

To figure out how to get better at the kinds of small-dose social interactions I was having on Meetup, I called up Gillian Sandstrom, a senior lecturer in psychology at the University of Sussex in the UK. More importantly for my purposes, she talks to strangers—on the street, on vacation, even in the sacred space of the London Tube. She researches the power of "weak ties," casual acquaintances with whom we interact, but usually only briefly. People who have lots of weak ties, who make eye contact and idle chitchat with baristas and neighbors, feel happier than those who don't, her studies find.

When I read some of her research, though, it felt alien to me. I had stopped working in an office when the pandemic started, and I didn't miss it at all. I live in the suburbs, so I don't interact with many people unless I make a point to—and I usually don't.

Sandstrom told me she's the same way: She's an introvert and tends to avoid demanding social situations. But she uses talking to strangers as a coping mechanism of sorts. If she's in a big, crowded room, she finds someone who's off by themselves and starts a one-on-one conversation. When she's on public transportation, she'll test the waters by complimenting the person sitting next to her. (She recommends remarking on something other than their looks.) Or, she'll comment on something in the environment—if they have a suitcase, she'll ask where they're going. One time, she was walking in a park and noticed a man smiling at some ducks. "Aren't they cute?" Sandstrom said. She and the man ended up chatting for half an hour, since they were walking in the same direction. It turned out he was visiting London, and he hadn't spoken to anyone in days. At the end of her conversations, Sandstrom just says something like "Thank you, it's been nice talking to you" and walks off.

I told Sandstrom that I don't miss my weak ties much, and I'm not really one for small talk. We either have to get to the bottom of your childhood trauma, or we're not talking at all.

The thing is, she pointed out, most weak ties probably aren't going to become long-term relationships. I needed to set the stakes way lower. Her conversations tend to last just a few minutes, and sometimes, they're nothing special. But just like a mediocre movie wouldn't make you swear off cinema forever, one bad conversation shouldn't keep you from trying again.

Over time, these weak ties do benefit us, even if we don't especially notice them. They make us feel woven into the social fabric, Sandstrom says, like we're part of something bigger. "When I do talk to people, I feel better," she told me. "It's almost always at least an average experience." And when a conversation is unusually engaging, "it feels awesome, because I wouldn't expect there to be anything coming from it."

Weak Ties in a Strong Wind

During that same Summer of Extroversion, I joined a sailing club that Anastasia was also part of. She billed it as a low-pressure group activity that, despite the name, didn't require any seafaring skills. When I signed up, I figured we could go together, and I could say nothing and do nothing and hide behind her while she did all the emotional and physical labor.

The marina was near a hip new development dotted with breweries and loft apartments; I found it by following a trail of office workers carrying life jackets and hurriedly tapping out their last few emails of the day. The first time I came, I realized I had forgotten my life jacket and had to ask to borrow one. "Or maybe I could just drown," I muttered, but no one heard me.

While it's true that extroverts enjoy talking, sex, attention, parties, and people, they also enjoy activity, period. They're more energetic, adventurous, and cheerful, even when they're by themselves. Those days when I would rather just sink into the couch for some Netflix, extroverts would rather be doing *something*—anything. Including climbing aboard a small boat with strangers and propelling themselves around a highly polluted river by harnessing the power of the wind.

Per the rules of the sailing club, I had to be on a boat with at least two experienced people. Anastasia and I persuaded a group of seasoned sailors to make room for two newbies, and we gingerly stepped aboard our vessel. Then we were off.

I immediately noticed that one woman had a joyful face and a soothing aura of expertise, attributable, I would later learn, to eight years of experience. She did none of the steering. Instead the boat was alternately steered by a college-sailing-team type with a need for speed, an aggressive older guy who liked to order the other people around, and a quiet older guy who did a great job suppressing his rage at the aggressive guy.

I guess I'd always thought sailing meant being on a yacht—sipping Moët and listening to Avicii while you worked on your tan. Instead, sailing mostly involves being screamed at not to "backwind the jib" while teetering over the starboard side of a nineteen-foot Flying Scot. More people would probably take up sailing if the terminology made any sense, like if the "sheet" was the sail and not the rope.

My first trip was also my most terrifying. Our skipper said the sailing club didn't go out when the wind was over fifteen miles per hour, and that time it was "just at fifteen." We rocked violently on the choppy water, our hair whipping our faces; few of us dared check our phones. The reason why sailors in the Olympics are always leaning precariously out of their boats, I learned, is not only because this helps you go faster but because it *keeps the boat from flipping over*. Anastasia took pictures of me looking petrified, but we didn't talk much—your eyes should always be forward! She said that next time I should take pictures of her for Tinder.

Still, I kept coming back—once again, I was surprised to find that I enjoyed it. DC is not known for its weather, but summer evenings on the water caught the city at its finest. By then, the air had shed the day's humidity, and a pale iridescence veiled the river's surface. I loved the feeling of drifting away from the city and seeing it as an observer would, the way I had when I first saw the ivory crowns of the monuments twenty years ago. Back then, I thought it was so regal and exciting—a shining city where I'd construct my future. The mood on the boat, too, reminded me of the languid end-of-semester days in college, when exams were done and we would sit outside drinking beer, letting our forearms burn after the long winter. I felt awash in nostalgic tenderness for this place that, most days, I actively disliked.

When Anastasia was busy, I would go without her; it turned out I didn't need her as a security blanket after all. On the boat, there was always plenty to discuss. I'm convinced more people would talk to strangers if bars had a complicated series of ropes and pulleys that needed sorting out. I noticed people often said they almost hadn't come, but once we were out on the water, they didn't feel so tired or busy after all.

Whenever I skipped, I detected the faint prickle of FOMO. Over the years of working weekends and overtime to get ahead, I had trained myself not to care when people hung out without me. I often saw time spent on social engagements as robbing from my career. (I remain confused as to how some people manage to have both active social lives and great jobs in journalism.) But each sailing excursion felt special and rare. Unlike a bland happy hour, an afternoon of sailing didn't make me worry I was sacrificing precious work hours. Sailing felt like the *point* of all that work—a chance to live a little.

At the sailing club, you had new people in your boat every time, and you talked just enough to feel connected but not so much that you'd hang out outside of sailing, per se. The dynamics were those of a relaxed group work project—a couple hours of light banter that lifts everyone's mood and gets the job done. It was the "weak tie" sweet spot that Sandstrom was referring to. I must have found all of our maritime microconversations so delightful precisely because I hadn't been expecting them at all.

One time, toward the end of the sail, the sky cleaved open and poured pent-up mid-Atlantic rain all over us. "It could be colder," one woman said as we tacked back to the dock, drenched and shivering. "It could also be warmer," I said, characteristically.

It was the first time I had made someone laugh, in person, since the pandemic started—and only then did I notice how much I had missed that sound. I had been wearing my "introvert" badge so consistently for the previous two years that I had forgotten how it feels to be audibly appreciated by other people. All day, I wrote tweets that earned likes and sent Slack messages that merited "joy" emojis. I lived like an astronaut on a solo Mars mission, entertaining myself in perfect solitude. But the laugh linked me to Earth once again.

"Right, And"

About halfway through the eight weeks of improv, we arrived in class to find we had a substitute teacher. It was the owner of Dojo, a big, red-haired actorly guy named Murphy. We were in awe of him because unlike us, he was naturally funny and had theories for how to make other people funny, too.

During our warm-up games—the familiar Zip Zap Zop, the outré Big Booty—Murphy bounced from foot to foot, as if unable to contain himself. When we performed scenes, he would hoot "Oh yeah!" for whoever volunteered, like he'd been waiting for exactly those two people to pop up.

Apparently, Murphy had determined that by this point we had progressed from being comfortable enough to do improv at all to being capable of doing improv better. He sat in the corner to offer some "side-coaching," or feedback on how to improve.

At a suggestion that might have been "bread" or "bakery" or maybe "annoyance," one day I found myself depicting a French baker who made up absurdly high prices for my bread loaves.

"I'd like to buy a baguette," said my scene partner, the customer.

"It costs one 'undred, s'il vous plaît," I said in my best Pepé Le Pew. The idea was that the customer would then get angrier and angrier, and I would get more and more French and incorrigible. Get it?

By then, even though I was invariably happy after improv, I was still jittery during it, in part because of scenes like this. After a few iterations on "zis cwa-ssoint is seventy dollairs," I ran out of material, and my scene partner and I got stuck in an unfunny loop. I silently thanked Christ that our French classmate wasn't there that day.

Watching from a chair off to the side, Murphy seemed to detect my anxiety. "You have to embrace the imperfection of it," he said. "I'm just proud of you for being here and trying."

Behind my N95 mask, I smiled appreciatively and whispered, "Thanks."

"Now," he added, "I want you to really commit to that French baker impression. Really *hon-hon-hon* it up, okay?"

It was this ennobling attitude of his that explains why, when the first level of improv was over, I signed up for level two—the level taught by Murphy. The class was, at that point, my only source of serotonin. It was January 2022, everything had shut down again because of the Omicron variant, and DC was brown, wet, and freezing. We were a forgotten people, smote by our maker. One entry in my journal from that time reads, "I feel like nobody really knows me." I was ready to concede that I was an improv skeptic who needed improv to function.

Level two of improv was more for people who wanted to do improv, instead of people who felt they had something wrong with them. Several people came prepared: They'd been practicing other forms of comedy on the side. My classmates' heightened ability made me feel like I should try harder, too, and I grew more competitive, even though that's not very "improv."

At one point, each of us did a "solo scene"—one in which we had to play both characters. I played a drunken White House aide begging her boss, the president, not to embargo Russian vodka (you know, because she wants to drink it). I found it to be unsettlingly reminiscent of the time I had to do a "humorous speech" in college speechwriting class—one meant to poke fun at the hoity-toity shoppers at the fancy stationery store where I worked. No one laughed, but I had to deliver my entire five minutes anyway to pass.

The solo scene was supposed to be a stress test for when you're up onstage and no other improvisers join you off the back line. And, I suppose, for when you're in a social gathering and other people aren't picking up your line of conversation. At those times, "just play the other fuckin' characters," Murphy said. It was, at least, a good demonstration of the fact that if you're trying to be funny and you're simply not, the world goes on, people look at their phones, and nobody remembers it but you.

This was the point in improv at which two important things happened: First, I stopped being nervous in improv. Through sheer repetition, I had taught my brain that on Wednesday nights, I acted like a total buffoon for a few hours and then went home to look at Zillow and make salad.

Second, I learned a useful interpersonal skill. Recall the infamous "yes, and" principle—that you should say "yes" to whatever your scene partner is doing and add something else. We still used "yes, and" often, but Murphy also taught us a more sophisticated way to maneuver through an improv scene—one that doesn't involve just agreeing with whatever's happening. And you can apply it in real life.

Let's say someone comes at you with an insane statement: "Washington is run by a cabal of Satanists who drink the blood of children." Instead of saying "yes," you can say "right." "Yes" implies agreement, but "right" just signifies that you understood. Then try to figure out *what the other person wants* from the fact that they told you this. You're listening for the *intent* behind their words, rather than for the content. It's possible they want you to agree with them about the Satanists, but underneath that, they probably just want to feel understood. Then say *what you are going to do* in response to this need.

In real life, this might look like, "Right, you're telling me this information about the Satanists because I'm a trusted confidant of yours and you want to share important news with me. I appreciate that—I'm so honored that you consider me a friend! And I'm going to change the subject, because I want our budding friendship to instead be about our mutual love of prog rock." This strategy can be useful when your improv scene partner is doing something you don't quite get—or when your new friends are saying things you can't go along with.

Toward the end of my time in improv, I interviewed Murphy in a park not far from where our class met. I wanted to learn more about him and to understand what regular people could get—or were getting—from improv.

He arrived carrying an enormous jug of water, his voluminous mane rebelling against the damp July air. Murphy told me he started out doing stand-up in college, but after he joined an improv group, he realized he liked team-based comedy even more. When he was doing stand-up, Murphy would freeze if he stumbled over his words. But since there are "no mistakes in improv," that was no longer a risk. He isn't naturally sociable, but improv pushed him to collaborate, and he found it thrilling. By his senior year, he realized he wanted to do improv for the rest of his life.

He said he only wished he had discovered improv even earlier.

I told him there's no way I would have done improv before my midthirties.

"What would have kept you from doing it?" he asked.

I was scared, I said. Plus, I added, "journalism is such a self-serious profession. It doesn't even have the silliness of, like, 'an accounting firm that just loves to have fun.'"

"The kind where everyone's got a wacky calendar?" Murphy asked.

"Yeah," I said. "Exactly."

I was correct in my assumption that most people who sign up for his beginner improv classes are not planning to be professional improvisers. They're lawyers who want to loosen up a bit, or office workers searching for a diversion. The attrition rate from the first level, to the second, and then the third and fourth, is steep. Still, Murphy has noticed that, even if people only dip into improv for a short time, they gain confidence and empathy. They bond with other people. They learn that, as in improv, sometimes in life it can be helpful to state your intentions clearly so that people understand you better.

Murphy loves the feeling of walking up onstage, not knowing what's going to happen, and having it all work out anyway. This is similar, I realized, to what happens when we talk to strangers. Previously, I would panic in social situations because I didn't have a script ready, and I worried the other person couldn't or wouldn't do their part to move the conversation. But improv taught me I can rely on others to supply their side of the interaction. It allowed a control freak like me to trust-fall into other people's brains, knowing I'll be caught.

I came to agree with Viola Spolin, the Russian-Jewish "mother of improv" who worked with immigrant children at Hull House. (Her son, Paul Sills, cofounded Chicago's Second City improv theater.) Explaining her approach in 1963, Spolin wrote, "Through spontaneity we are re-formed into ourselves. It creates an explosion that for the moment frees us from handed-down frames of reference, memory choked with old facts and information and undigested theories and techniques of other people's findings." The spontaneity of improv had, finally, freed me from my own and other people's undigested theories about what my personality was "really" like. It allowed me to make up my own personality—to improvise it, in fact.

Improv had provided a safe space in which to practice being outgoing—a dress rehearsal for a play that would never be staged. But, I wondered, how would my new people skills perform in the real world?

Overlapping at Home

I decided to test my newfound extroversion by having a party at my house. After all, to host is to invite guests, but also judgment. In a bar or restaurant, a boring evening isn't really your fault, but in your home, there's no one else to blame. Having people over with the promise of fun felt like an appropriate raising of the stakes.

I had thrown exactly one party before, but I'm not sure it qualified as such. Ten years prior, when Rich and I moved into our first "nice" apartment, we had a housewarming. I spent days trying to make it look like we owned less crap, and at the last minute I sprinted to the store to buy a tablecloth. When people showed up, I got the sense—and this is colored by my negative, neurotic introvert glasses—that they didn't have a good time. A few people seemed to stay for exactly an hour and then desirously eye the front door. I had invited my coworkers, but in the moment, their presence made me anxious rather than happy. (*Do they think my apartment sucks? Are they gonna talk later about how poor I am?*) After it was over, I made Rich reassure me repeatedly that it was fun, and I vowed never to do it again.

"Again" was now, though, and the night before the party I couldn't sleep. At three a.m., I curled up on my couch and cracked open Deborah Tannen's book *Conversational Style*, which is an examination of two hours and forty minutes of conversation at a Thanksgiving dinner in Berkeley, California, in 1978. The dinner guests comprised Tannen, a born-and-bred New Yorker, and some of her friends and family: two other New Yorkers, two Californians, and a Brit. Tannen transcribes snippets of their conversation, then breaks down patterns she noticed, such as whether the friends tended to draw on personal or impersonal topics, and how many words each person spoke per "episode."

Reading a close sociological analysis of a party is a good way to psych yourself out about hosting a party. The book reveals in almost comical detail how easily misunderstandings can happen, even among people who know one another, and even before the Internet super-charged our ability to take offense. Upon analyzing the conversation, Tannen realizes that during the dinner she repeatedly asked someone a question and interrupted him before he could answer, a tactic she calls "overlapping." But she didn't mean to talk over him; she expected him to talk over *her*.

She compares it to a type of argument she had witnessed in Greece. Two men would start shouting loudly at each other, and often, one of them would raise his hand as though about to strike the other man. But invariably, another man nearby would grab his arm, holding him back. The man only wanted to show that he was angry enough to get violent, not to actually hit his friend. He knew a bystander would intervene before he could. It was the kind of secret rule of interaction people everywhere take for granted: Tannen was relying on her interlocutor to talk louder and overpower her.

In general, Tannen notices that the New Yorkers tended to be louder, faster talkers who asked "machine-gun" questions, interrupted, and persisted in introducing new topics, even if others didn't pick up on them. "The non–New York participants had perceived the conversation to be 'New York' in character," she writes. (Putting a, uh, finer point on it, one California participant said he felt the dinner had been dominated by "the New York Jewish element.") The others, who preferred to wait for a silent moment before saying something, didn't manage to say much at all.

Though I grew up in a loud, "overlapping" family, I reminded myself that not everyone sees talking as a competitive sport, and that I should keep this in mind the next day. Then I went back to bed.

In the morning I began scrubbing and chopping for six furious hours. I cleaned our house to make it look like no one lived there, like it was merely haunted by ghosts who make charcuterie boards. I hid away all my IBS medications and begged Rich to stop sitting so hard on the couch cushions.

Four p.m., the party's start time, came as I was still violently slicing fennel. Fifteen minutes later, the doorbell rang, and this is it! This is the party! It's people talking. The COVID risk made it more exciting. It was a combination birthday party (for me) and Bastille Day party (for France), since it was halfway between the two days. "It's not really Bastille Day," one woman said as she walked in. I threw her a death glare and offered her a macaron. Another woman handed me a small cactus. "You know, because you're prickly," she said.

A former coworker seemed confused, asking, "So is this for the book or for you?" It was admittedly hard to tell. Maybe these things were working because they were both for the book *and* for me. I couldn't back out of a Meetup because I knew it would be good for the book. But it was also good for me. I decided to apply this attitude in the future, after the book was done: It doesn't matter if people think my furniture sucks; *this is good for me.* It's okay if I blunder through my attempts to meet new people; *this is good for me.*

Between all the frenetic drink refilling, I wove between groups of people, trying to make connections. Because of all my activities, I was in a better mood than usual and had lots to talk about—extroversion building on extroversion. Mentally, I praised myself for creating the right mix of journalists and normal people—journalists to ask the questions and normals to relish being asked. I did drink way too much. I think I overheard one of my new friends say, "I might just be an experiment for Olga." *Maybe,* I thought, *but the experiment is working.*

That night, I woke up to my heart pounding, wondering if I had hugged people too much or said something weird. Probably yes and yes. But there's some evidence that I was judging myself more harshly than people were judging me. A concept called the "spotlight effect" suggests we overestimate how much other people notice everything we say and do. For one study that illustrated this phenomenon, researchers asked students to pop into a crowded room while wearing a T-shirt with the singer Barry Manilow's face on it. Then the researchers asked the students how many people they thought would remember the unusual wardrobe choice. The students thought about half the room would remember, but only a quarter did. As the authors of one spotlight-effect study write, "Many of the details of our appearance or performance are likely to be lost on the audience whose opinions we so assiduously court."

In that case, maybe I could ease up on my assiduous courtship of everyone in the DC area. It's likely that people remembered the night as just another sweaty house party. Even if they did notice a stray bottle of Beano or some wall art that was very obviously from Urban Outfitters, as Buddhism teaches us, everything ends. Including parties.

A couple of days after the party, after the mess and hangover were gone but before the glow of company had faded, I took another personality test. I was now talking to people on more days than I wasn't—a major reversal from before I began my project. At one river-tubing Meetup, the organizer praised me for being "someone who can talk to anyone." Underneath the surface, I kicked my legs frantically as I tried to think of more things to say.

Some of these interactions were uncomfortable or dull, but as Gillian Sandstrom suggested, most of them were fine, maybe even pleasant. I often learned something, and even during the most uninteresting exchange, I at least had the chance to practice being attentive and supportive. When I had nothing in common with a new acquaintance, I just tried to explore the universe that is another person's mind.

When I logged into Personality Assessor this time, I still answered truthfully—like that I "strongly disagree" that "I am not easily annoyed"—but this time I was neutral as to whether "I love life"; maybe not always, but I certainly don't hate it.

I had changed my answers on enough of the exuberance-related questions to also change my score. I was now in the 42nd percentile on extroversion—about average, up from "very low" before I began.

I had been telling myself a deceptive story, about how I'm not good with people, and that people, generally, would prefer it if I wasn't around. But I tested this hypothesis in dozens of Meetups and improv classes, and I proved it false.

I still identify as an introvert, and I still need our well-known elixir: quiet time to myself to recharge. But I don't *only* need quiet time to myself to recharge. I need the variety and spontaneity of conversation. I need a glimpse into people's lives that isn't mediated by interview questions. Extroversion did help me get out more, and it also taught me it's okay to *want* to get out more, and to prioritize pleasure, sometimes even at the expense of work.

Through all this activity, I found that occasional extroversion can be a tool. It pauses the broken record of the depressive mind: Nothing rescues you from endless rumination like social interaction, even when forced. It's a bulwark against loneliness and an implement of connection. Trying on extroversion allows you to understand others, I found, and also to understand yourself. Because sharing our thoughts clarifies them, Emerson wrote, "sincere and happy conversation doubles our powers." Like a superhero, when I cloaked myself in extroversion, I felt my powers heightening, readying me for a leap into the unknown.

Emboldened, I moved on to face my biggest foe: neuroticism.

4

From Overwhelm to Om:

Neuroticism

I t's ironic that 2022 was the year I decided to quell my intense neuroticism, the trait marked by anxiety and depression, because 2022 was one of the most stressful years of my life, one during which I would have to quickly make several crucial and lasting decisions. This is not the strong suit of the neurotic.

For years, Rich and I had gingerly walked the prime meridian between having and not having kids, usually leaning toward the no side. Having a baby had always seemed unaffordable, and, for a journalist, undoable. On days when I left the office at eight p.m., the thought of procreating made me laugh, then shudder.

Recently, though, I'd been thinking that it might not be worth forgoing one of life's greatest joys (and pains! I know, I know) for a slightly higher midyear performance review. Just as the window to do so was sliding closed, we finally resolved to try to start a family. But I had health problems that made me suspect this wouldn't be easy, to say nothing of my age, which in a less delicate time was called "geriatric" for pregnancy. My doctors had taken to telling me that I was born with all the eggs I'd ever have, a disgusting phrase that brought to mind a baby with a swollen belly full of yolks.

To determine if any of my eggs were still serviceable, that spring I ordered a fertility test online that said it would give me fast results with just a few drops of blood. The videos on the test's slick website featured a smiling blond woman jumping up and down and then effortlessly dribbling blood from her fingertips all over a little strip of test paper. (The jumping is intended to stimulate blood flow.) All I had to do was be just like her: Joyful. Sanguineous. Fertile.

In the bathroom, I unwrapped the test's glossy white box. The instructions said the test would take twenty minutes. The only trick was that the blood had to come down in big droplets, as opposed to a wet smear like the kind a paper cut would produce. I grabbed a lancet and stabbed it into my geriatric forefinger.

Two hours, five used lancets, and a graveyard of gauze and alcohol wipes later, I still couldn't squeeze a single, intact droplet out of my fingers. While I was jumping and flinging blood all over my bathroom, my boss messaged me to ask when I might be filing my story. With my less-bloody hand, I typed "Soon! Sry!"

That day was the beginning of the unrelenting stress, doctors' appointments, sleeplessness, and uncertainty that marked the better part of my year. Because the at-home test had failed, I had to visit an actual fertility doctor. This process took hours upon hours since, if you see a fertility doctor and check "Ashkenazi Jewish" on any of their forms, they will run you through every cutting-edge genetic scanner because—and they say this nicely—your ancestors boinked their cousins. No matter how many tests they did, they never had any good news for me. "We're on a complicated journey," one doctor told me.

I had always assumed that I would simply get pregnant one day when it was convenient for me—like after I had finished enjoying my thirties, and when work wasn't too busy, and when there wasn't a global pandemic, and I was having a good hair day, and there was a sale on baby clothes at Target. That my body might prefer some other, less-optimal timetable felt like a betrayal. Why wouldn't my ovaries prize efficiency as much as I do?

Perversely, even as I worried I wouldn't be able to have a baby, I was also scared to death of having one. I worried that, with a baby, I wouldn't have time to read, and I would lose my clammy grip on the journalism industry. I worried that my relationship with Rich would suffer, and that the occasional squall that disrupted our smooth sailing would turn into a lethal typhoon. I worried about sleep deprivation, and that my baby would know me primarily as a zombie who cries all the time. I felt torn between my lifelong conviction that people shouldn't create problems for themselves and my (apparent) desire to do just that.

Soon, I was waking up in the middle of every night, my heart racing. In an attempt to soothe my worries, I would google things like "percent miscarriage pregnant while 36?"; "anxiety pregnancy miscarriage causes"; "Diet Coke fetal defects"; "pregnancy brain stops working hands stop working." These searches surfaced random, horrific anecdotes, but never any conclusive answers.

All these anxieties caused me to put off the baby decision even later. Every time I read an article about how older moms and their babies experience more medical complications, I got so scared that I would put off trying for yet another month—thus making myself an *even older* potential mom. I was approaching the point of no return, running out of fuel and weighing whether to press ahead or turn back. Here was another reason to try to conquer neuroticism: I wanted to make a clear-sighted choice about whether to commit to motherhood or not—and be satisfied either way.

The other ordeal we were staring down was the Florida real estate market, which was unusually "competitive," to use the euphemism favored by my new home pages, Redfin and Zillow. After I, and my seasonal affective disorder, had endured seventeen winters in DC, my job had given me permission to relocate. I was elated—but for the neurotic, happiness is always tinged with the suspicion that you'll screw it up somehow.

My house-hunting and my neuroticism seemed to feed on each other, such that I would get anxious unless I had Redfin open, but then I would get anxious as soon as I opened Redfin. Neurotic people often have trouble with decision-making, including the kind where you plow your life savings into a random building in another state and hope not only to live there, free of termites and mold, but also to somehow make a profit in the long run. Our home-buying was further complicated by the fact that every day nearly a thousand people were moving to Florida, many of them boomers with Buicks full of cash. These were not good odds.

At night, we hovered our cursors over a map of Florida, wondering which coast we could afford to move to—and, after Hurricane Ian smashed into the state, if we should even bother. "Anxiety does not necessarily mean trembling and running away," wrote the early Austrian psychologist Alfred Adler. "It can be revealed in the dragging of one's feet over a problem, approaching a situation hesitantly, or looking for an excuse to avoid it." "Anxiety," in fact, stems from the ancient Greek word for "choke."

When I told my liberal friends that I was planning to move to Florida, they reacted like I was heading off to Kabul. "Ugh, Florida," said people who had lived under actual authoritarian regimes. "Don't you realize there are hurricanes there?" And then, more quietly, "Don't you realize there are Republicans there?" They asked me why not LA instead—apparently failing to calculate that if we could barely afford Florida, we could absolutely never afford California. These conversations did not inspire confidence in my choices, but they did prompt me to withdraw from my friends. Instead, I kept the moving talk to myself, and my brain gradually spun out, conjuring ever wilder worst-case scenarios.

That summer, Rich and I went on a real-estate scouting mission to the South Florida suburbs, during which we learned that we were between two and thirty years too late to buy anything there. We could only afford the bleak, blistering tracts near the Everglades, so we spent our days driving past Outback Steakhouses to creepy homes that Rich described as "perfect for a family of four or a religion of eleven." At each stop, I tried to determine, by the level of disrepair, if the house's owners had suddenly died or been shipped off to a retirement home by a relative.

One day, we met with a Realtor who appeared to think that Rich was my dad, that I was deeply stupid, and that, if we wanted to move to Florida, we should be prepared to pay twice as much for our new house as we did for our current one, along with tens of thousands more for all new appliances, flooring, paint, and something called "appraisal gaps." When I questioned the wisdom of paying this much for the poorly maintained home of a colorblind eighty-six-year-old, the Realtor interrupted me. "You have to remember," she said sharply. "You're. Moving. To. South. Florida."

I told her we'd be in touch. Then we went to the airport and I threw back a mini bottle of wine—the only thing, at that point, that reliably diluted my stress.

While we were waiting for our flight, the FBI raided the Mar-a-Lago Trump mansion a few miles away.

"Do you want to stay and cover it?" Rich asked.

"I want to get out of here," I said, "as quickly as possible."

Learning Not to Fear

Neuroticism is a personality "trait," sure, but for me, it was a heavy shroud that obscured my vision and smothered me slowly. According to Hudson's test, I was more neurotic than almost anyone.

Neuroticism encompasses anxiety, depression, and irritability—a feeling that the world is a dangerous place, and there's no way to protect yourself. At our core, we neurotic people hate uncertainty. We're flattened by the "have a second?" email from the boss and the slight frown from the ultrasound technician.

Though our parents don't directly pass their personalities down to us, neuroticism is one trait in which our upbringings can imprint themselves. Adverse childhood experiences—stressors like abuse, poverty, or a parent's death—are all associated with higher levels of neuroticism. Being plucked from the sanctuary of childhood too soon can predispose you toward worry and woe.

As though it weren't enough to live every day like you're under invasion, neuroticism is also linked to a variety of mental, physical, and substance-abuse disorders—including a higher risk of dementia. The trait predicts whether someone will be "anxiously" or "avoidantly"—as opposed to "securely"—attached to their significant other. For whatever reason, we neurotic people tend to have more bad things happen to us (or maybe we just perceive more things that happen as bad), and our health and quality of life are worse.

Neuroticism was also the trait that seemed most rooted in my identity. On my father's side, my Jewish ancestors spent their lives evading first the Russians, then the Germans. My grandma recounted lying face down in a frozen potato field as a girl, her brown coat camouflaging her from Nazi snipers. My mother's parents, meanwhile, survived prisoner-of-war camps and abject poverty on the fractious border between the USSR and Finland. In *their* midthirties, my parents did the most nerve-racking thing imaginable, renouncing their Soviet citizenship and immigrating permanently to America. All this persecution might have etched itself into my cells, sending them on a never-ending search for potential threats.

Growing up, I got the sense that my parents had exhausted their capacity to take risks. The food stamps, fast-food jobs, and other immigrant indignities had left a permanent bruise, one they were careful never to touch. My family regarded anything slightly unsafe—my decision to become a journalist, my travels to countries where you can't drink the water—like an attempt to free-solo the Burj Khalifa. *Why risk it?*

As people do with the transmissions of childhood, I internalized the idea that it's often better not to risk it. In some people, neuroticism primarily takes the form of depression, but for me, it's defined by worry. (Though, in the winter, depression visits me, too, in the form of seasonal affective disorder.) One of my signature phrases as a toddler was "I won't like it. I'm going to be uncomfortable." As an adult, I've lived my life snapping between worrying about things that have already happened and worrying about things that are about to happen. I've wasted some of the best years of my life being anxious about mean emails and B minuses. In studies, neuroticism is the trait that most people say they want to change, and it was the trait I most wanted to change, too.

Unfortunately, my gender was undermining my quest to achieve neuroticism's opposite, emotional stability. "There is no greater risk factor for anxiety disorders than being born female," writes Andrea Petersen in her book about anxiety, *On Edge*. Girls and women are far more likely than boys and men to develop anxiety disorders.

The reasons for this anxiety gender disparity are speculative and manifold. Women might actually experience more stressful events, such as sexual assault, and therefore be more stressed out for good reason. (Some researchers even say women have the correct amount of anxiety, while men have too little.) Or it might start from childhood: Parents tend to praise the bold, assertive behavior of boys, but not that of girls. The hormone levels that fluctuate throughout women's menstrual cycles might also cause fear and anxiety to spike.

I, too, often feel punctured by fear. In fact, if I had to describe my 2022 mental state, it would be that I was afraid of not being able to get pregnant, but also of getting pregnant. I was afraid of moving, but also of not moving. I was afraid of making a decision that would make my life worse, and of having no one to blame but myself. I was just afraid.

I wanted to overcome neuroticism not just for this book's sake but for my own. In case Hypothetical Future Child ever did materialize, I wanted to sleep through the night while I still could. I wanted to make decisions without worrying myself sick, and to cast off my heavy yoke of dread. To paraphrase the poet John Berryman, I wanted to travel in the direction of my fear.

Buddhism for Newbies

When you so much as whisper the word "anxiety," people will pop out from behind bushes, they will rush over to your brunch table, they will drop down from the rafters on flying rigs, they will grab you by the hands, and they will ask you if you've tried meditation. Meditation is, alas, the most commonly suggested technique for cultivating mindfulness, supposedly the hidden, neuroticism-fighting potion inside all of us.

Here's the oversimplified explanation: Mindfulness is an impartial awareness of the present moment, the ability to observe our thoughts without deeming them wrong. It's focusing on the here-and-now, not the what-next. Meditation, which often (but not always) involves sitting silently and following one's breath, is often (but not always) the best way to achieve this lofty state. If thoughts do come up during meditation, you're supposed to let them pass without dissecting them. Training your attention in this way supposedly helps you better handle difficult emotions, like depression and anxiety, when they do arise.

Regular meditators speak of the practice as though it's a magical glow-up for their lives. But for me, meditation has always ranked alongside root canals in the category "great that it exists, but preferable to avoid."

Nathan Hudson's "You Have to Follow Through" study recommended meditation to reduce neuroticism, but, in the early months of my experiment, meditating felt like a fifteen-minute opportunity for my anxieties to replay themselves on loop until my iPhone sounded its little gong. On almost every page, my journal reads, "meditating sucks!"

Eventually, I remembered that once during an interview a source recommended meditating in something called a "float spa," otherwise known as a sensory deprivation tank. These large, dark tubs are supposed to relieve anxiety and improve sleep—two things I desperately craved. Plus, their lack of light and stimulation, along with their gallons of sloshing water, make it impossible to glance at your phone mid-meditation. I booked my session for $100 and with dreams of a holy hot tub delivering me unto Zen.

The spa itself resembled any generic relaxation establishment, all gleaming countertops and beige tones. A spa employee guided me through a hall lined with enormous bags of Epsom salts and to my room, where she sped through some instructions that I mostly missed. I was distracted by the tank—a giant ceramic oyster that would be my moist home for the next hour.

The attendant left. A faint speaker crackled on with some Muzak, and I figured it was time to climb into the oyster. Inside was about a foot of salty warm water, into which I slid myself like a chicken breast into buttermilk. Immediately, my picked-at cuticles and shaving nicks began to sting. Then that stopped, and the boredom started.

The idea is that you should be able to lie flat and feel weightless, but my pendulous Slavic backside, which is designed for fieldwork and not relaxing, kept dragging me down into a parabola shape. Periodically, I'd have to thrust my pelvis upward in order to stay afloat. Whenever I tried to meditate, I'd realize I was sinking.

After a few minutes, it felt like too much floating. I had the urge to curl up or to wrap my hands around my head. I bounced off the walls, literally. Since I couldn't get truly comfortable, my thoughts turned to rising real-estate prices. I felt like I was waiting in a wet airport terminal, listlessly wondering when I'd be free to go.

Then, disaster: I got cold. The room-temperature air raised goose bumps on my skin, and I shivered. I tried folding my arms, but it didn't really help. Whatever ethereal illusion the tub had strained to create dissolved instantly. I had no choice but to acknowledge that I was just a thirtysomething woman bobbing around in a lukewarm sitz bath. I was born with all the eggs I'll ever have.

Then it was over. I took a shower and blow-dried my hair. As soon as I stepped outside, the rain made it wet again.

———————————

One day, I tweeted about my failure to control my rumination while meditating, and Dan Harris, the former *Good Morning America* weekend anchor, replied, "The fact that you're noticing the thoughts/obsessions is proof that you are doing it correctly!" I picked up Harris's book *10% Happier*, which chronicles his journey from a high-strung reporter who had a panic attack on air to a high-strung reporter who meditates a lot. At one point, he was meditating for two hours a day.

I was drawn to Harris's work because his profession—and therefore his struggles—are so similar to mine. Journalism is an intensely unpredictable industry that seems to attract almost exclusively neurotic people. "I'd seen so many careers soar or sour based on seemingly random things," Harris writes. He compares journalists to lab rats whom researchers feed food pellets at unpredictable intervals. "Those rats went crazy," he notes. Meditation helped his inner lab rat relax a bit, and I was hoping it could help mine do the same.

When I called Harris, he said that it's normal for meditation to feel like "training your mind to not be a pack of wild squirrels all the time." Very few people actually clear their minds when they're meditating. The point is to focus on your breath for however long you can—even if it's just a second—before you get distracted. Then do it over and over again. Occasionally, when Harris meditates, he still "rehearses some grand, expletive-filled speech I'm gonna deliver to someone who's wronged me." But now, he can return to his breath more quickly, or just laugh off the obsessing.

Harris suggested I try loving-kindness meditation, in which you mentally beam affectionate thoughts toward yourself and others. This, he said, "sets off what I call a gooey upward spiral where, as your inner weather gets balmier, your relationships get better." In his book, Harris described a loving-kindness meditation in which he focused on his two-year-old niece. As he thought about her "little feet" and "sweet face with her mischievous eyes," he started crying uncontrollably on the floor of the meditation hall.

What a pussy, I thought.

Nevertheless, I downloaded Harris's meditation app, Ten Percent Happier, and pulled up a loving-kindness session by the meditation teacher Sharon Salzberg. I liked how, in her cozy voice, she asked me to repeat calming phrases like "may you be safe, may you live with ease"—an improvement on chimes, nothing, or my breath. Then she asked me to envision myself surrounded by a circle of people who love me, radiating kindness toward me. I pictured my family, my boyfriend, my friends from college, my professors from grad school, all arrayed around me, emitting beneficence from their bellies like Care Bears. *You're good; you're okay*, I imagined them saying. Before I knew what was happening, I had broken into sobs.

The Great Unwinding

Inside me there are two wolves: one who hates the Unwinding Anxiety app, and one who thinks it might actually be helpful.

In addition to meditating, I had downloaded Unwinding Anxiety, a mental-health app featuring Jud Brewer, a Brown University psychiatrist and author of a book by the same name. The app consists of videos in which Brewer delivers his anxiety-reduction techniques, exercises meant to reinforce the videos' teachings, and a community forum where users share their experiences. It also consists of lots and lots of analogies, including a version of the highly parodied proverb about how "inside you there are two wolves." Which will win? "The one you feed," Brewer says.

In the book, Brewer makes the case that anxiety is a "habit loop" in which the emotion of anxiety triggers the behavior of worry, which may temporarily alleviate the anxiety but makes it worse in the long run. Worrying, to him, is like drinking too much or bingeing on potato chips: It may seem comforting in the moment, but it takes a toll. Chronic worrying, according to Brewer and other researchers, escalates and reinforces anxiety.

Reading all this made me admit that I do use worrying as a coping mechanism, even when it doesn't serve me. It makes me feel like I'm doing *something*, even if I'm just twirling through the same old nightmares. I would worry about a hurricane hitting our future house in Florida, then do something about it, like research flood insurance, then find myself worrying about the same thing again a few minutes later.

To stop the worry cycle, Brewer tells people to ask themselves, "What do I get from this behavior?" He then advises treating your brain like a dog you're house training, rubbing its nose in the "poop" of the behavior (worry, in my case) to show it how "stinky" (or unrewarding) it is. You might notice how awful worrying feels, how it seems to accomplish little but stealing your attention. By doing this, you are supposed to get "disenchanted" with worry.

Whenever a moment of worry or panic does arise, Brewer suggests you get curious about its effect in your body. You should ask yourself, "Am I feeling tightness? Pressure? Contraction?" He also recommends mindfulness techniques like paying attention to your breath, as well as "noting" whatever's happening in the moment.

So, dealing with a typical anxious episode in the Unwinding way might involve recognizing and allowing the wave of anxiety to crash over you, investigating what it feels like in your body, and noting what's happening with short, simple words, like "thinking," or "tingling," or "clenching."

Brewer seems to have a lot of satisfied customers. According to his data, people's anxiety goes down by 67 percent after two months of using the Unwinding app.

But to put it mildly, I had trouble following Brewer's guidance. I found the exercises too cerebral, requiring me to think about my anxiety in esoteric ways at times when I wasn't really anxious. At times when I *was* anxious—like when I was running late for something or fighting with Rich—I could never quite remember what the exercises even were.

One day, I kept falling over in yoga class because I was worried about a problem at work. My balance always suffers when I get anxious—a very direct example of anxiety exerting itself on my body! But instead of helping me, noticing this just made me lose my balance even more. In the locker room afterward, a hot twentysomething chided me that if I was brand-new to yoga, I really shouldn't be on the end of a row, because I was throwing everyone off.

"I've been doing yoga for twenty years," I told her. I grabbed my mat and fled to the parking lot in shame.

About halfway through my work on the app, I called up Brewer for an interview to clarify all of this. It turned out I had been doing pretty much everything wrong.

I told Brewer that worrying did seem to help me plan my complicated real-estate transactions. Anxiety reminded me that I needed to call some loan officer, or to look into rental comps. What would prod me to perform the trillion tedious tasks of adulthood if not for anxiety?

Brewer told me I was conflating planning with worry, and that I could just try planning things out without the worry, or without revisiting the plans over and over.

Then I made the mistake of asking Brewer about the "curiosity" aspect of his program.

"Are you supposed to get curious about . . . why you're anxious?" I asked.

"No!" he said adamantly.

I felt the same way I did the time in college when two pages of my constitutional-law textbook got stuck together, and in class the next day I gave a great answer about the Watergate scandal to my professor's question about the Pentagon Papers.

The "why" behind the anxiety doesn't matter, Brewer says. It's best not to get hung up on it. Instead, you're supposed to get curious about its effect on the body.

"I don't really feel anxiety in my body," I told Brewer.

"You can focus on, how's my head feel when I worry a lot?" he suggested. "Does worry make your brain feel rested and relaxed and ready to go to solve problems?"

"Yeah, definitely not," I said. Instead I tend to feel stuck and, eventually, sick of myself. According to Brewer, noticing those sensations might help me reach the ultimate goal: getting disenchanted with worry.

Most importantly, I was, at least subconsciously, resisting Brewer's view that anxiety is unhelpful. Like many anxious people, I secretly believed that anxiety was beneficial. Hell, when people asked me how to get more writing done, I sometimes suggested having an anxiety disorder. Many neurotic people treasure our anxiety, thinking it powers us.

Some research suggests anxiety has a bell-shaped influence on performance: No anxiety can hurt, a little can help, but too much can paralyze you. Brewer, though, disagrees with this, and writes in his book that any amount of anxiety inhibits performance. To Brewer, worrying impedes planning for the future, because it locks you into fear and dread.

At one point, Brewer told me, "It sounds like you're still pretty identified with the worrying"—meaning I still saw it as an indelible part of me. I had to agree with him there.

With that, Brewer pointed out the knot that kept my anxiety wound up tight. Though I knew I needed to become less anxious, I was in some ways reluctant to do so. One of the biggest obstacles to changing personality is this kind of ambivalence: a sense that yeah, maybe you should get around to being less angry or drunk or chronically late, and maybe one day you will, but not today. After all, you're a fun drunk, and you get angry for a reason, right? In my readings about Buddhism, I was struck by the Zen teacher D. T. Suzuki's insight that "the ego-shell in which we live is the hardest thing to outgrow."

My newfound extroversion was easier for me to accept because introversion had never done anything for me. Aloofness in social situations has held me back, not propelled me forward. But sometimes I didn't know how I'd live without anxiety—a sentiment I seem to share with many self-abnegating workhorses. "In many ways, anxiety has fueled my work," writes Andrea Petersen in *On Edge*, adding that "insecurity and paranoia can be useful qualities."

I saw anxiety as a net for my high-wire life, proudly recalling times when my hair-trigger spidey sense jolted me awake at three a.m., just in time to correct a factual error before a story went live in the morning. And I still cringe at the time in college when, sick with love and senioritis, I slacked off on a documentary assignment and left our team with a mediocre grade. Our professor, a journalist of some renown, said our project "didn't even make sense." I had been laid-back about it, and it showed.

But I also look back at vacation photos where, having nervously planned everything to the fifteen-minute interval, I look stress-addled, not relaxed. And I lied to Brewer: My body does carry the scars of worry. Multiple times, I've suffered severe infections in my fingers from tearing at my cuticles. What I wanted, it seemed, was to reduce my level of neuroticism without compromising the meticulousness on which I had built my career.

Unlike some other traits, Hudson has found that to change on neuroticism, you have to *want* to change. For it to work, you've got to "do the work," to borrow the therapeutic line. Reading an anxiety-busting book, rolling your eyes, and continuing to obsess apparently won't suffice.

————————

That summer, my college best friend had a baby shower, which Rich and I drove to a country club near Harrisburg to attend. It was a humid, ninety-five-degree day, and I felt insecure about the fact that, though we were the same age, my friend was very pregnant, and I was very not. I arrived just before food was served to avoid the possibility of being asked if we'd started "trying."

During the brunch portion of the shower, I took a bite of some sort of Pennsylvania confection made of caramel, butterscotch, and pure glucose. The sugar drew every drop of moisture from my body, and I started to feel faint and queasy. *That was so sweet,* I thought. *Why am I so thirsty? Why is it so hot?* And then, ominously, *My heart is beating so fast.*

I don't normally experience panic attacks. Typically, my anxiety is more free-flowing, a venom that seeps into every vein. But right then, immediately before the unwrapping of the onesies, I felt the unmistakable throb of panic coming on. In seconds, my thoughts spiraled from normal to horror show: *I'm so thirty-six and so not pregnant. What's wrong with my body? I'm sitting next to my boyfriend; we're not even married. Her whole family probably thinks I'm an urban fuck princess. My heart is pounding. Why is my breathing so shallow? What if I pass out? If I pass out here, everyone will hate me even more. What if I die and all I leave behind are blog posts instead of actual human children?*

Without being sure I was doing it right, I tried Brewer's curiosity and noting strategies. *Wow, my heart is beating really fast,* I told myself. *It feels like I just ran several miles or drank a bunch of coffee. I wonder how fast it will go. And yeah, my breath feels like I'm climbing a mountain. These are some of the symptoms of a panic attack, but I've also done all those activities before and been fine. Most people don't die from panicking, and since I'm sitting down it's unlikely I'll faint.*

I ran to the bathroom to dab myself with water—once, twice, then finally a third time during gift bingo. I probably made the waiters think I was having sympathy barfs, and I missed a long explanation by my friend's other best friend's boyfriend about how to land a Cessna in low visibility.

But in about twenty minutes, the panic subsided. I never passed out. I doubt anyone even noticed. I didn't unwind my anxiety completely, but I noted it, and then I sent it on its way.

Full Catastrophe Meditating

By summer, my neuroticism had assumed the form of insomnia, a problem that has stalked me since childhood and strikes whenever it sees an opening. After staying up all night, I was barely making it through the day. I had trouble forming sentences; I was afraid I'd crash my car. When I thought about the future, I saw only horrors and traps. Even more than sleep, I craved freedom from my thoughts.

When I was little, I could go to sleep if my parents put on a vinyl record of a Soviet children's story; I'd drift off to some fairy tale about a little girl who was eaten by wolves because she wasn't industrious enough. As an adult, nothing seemed to work.

One night, I had a nightmare that I was in a paragliding accident and was free-falling to the ground. I flailed my limbs around, which sent my weighted blanket flying, and I woke up to it pouncing on me like an animal. Wide-awake at night, I'd alternately ruminate and stress-google. (I now know of some very good appliance repair technicians in Miami-Dade County.)

I thought about the possibility that we would hate it in Florida, and Rich would blame and resent me. I thought about the logistics of recording podcasts with a baby at home. I remembered the time I had drinks with a reporter friend, and we spotted another female journalist walking back and forth down the sidewalk. She was pushing a stroller, trying to get her baby to sleep.

"She had a baby by herself," my friend whispered disdainfully. "And now, look at her. She just walks back and forth."

I thought maybe Rich and I should just stay the way we were, childless and dissatisfied. *Why risk it?*

Some people find relief for anxiety—and other elements of neuroticism—through Lexapro and other antidepressants. (Indeed, one small study found that two months of taking paroxetine, the generic form of the antidepressant Paxil, led to decreases in neuroticism and increases in extroversion, over and above improvements in depression scores.) For me, though, the side effects of SSRIs have tended to outweigh the benefits. Though I completely endorse their use generally, I had recently gotten off antidepressants and was trying to stay off. I was riding my anxiety without a saddle.

For the weeks in which I had strung together one too many sleepless nights, I also had Xanax on hand. Nothing will get me eight uninterrupted hours of shut-eye like my bottle of generic alprazolam. Xanax and other benzodiazepines help the neurotransmitter GABA, which is already relaxing, relax you even more. It's like "alcohol in pill form," as one researcher put it to me. That must explain why I love it so much.

However, I had been trying to take Xanax less often after learning that, over the long term, Xanax and other benzos tend to stop working and can even make anxiety worse. "You have people who are taking the benzos to sleep better, and they do sleep better for about three months. And then after six months, they're sleeping worse than ever," says Keith Humphreys, a professor of psychiatry at Stanford University. At that point they up their dose of benzos, which eventually stop working again, and the cycle repeats itself. When I asked Humphreys what I could do instead of taking Xanax, he said "mindfulness." Hrm.

I interviewed a few sleep doctors who speculated that I simply live close to the "insomnia threshold"—that it takes little to push me into poor sleep. Most of the time, insomnia is waiting on my front porch, but then something happens—stress at work, relationship woes—and it steps right in and gets comfortable. One night of poor sleep turns into another, and another. People who are high-strung, with tendencies toward perfectionism, tend to be especially susceptible. (In studies, neuroticism is associated strongly with sleeplessness.)

The worst part was that I knew all the tricks of good "sleep hygiene." I kept my bedroom dark and cool. I cut back on caffeine and alcohol. I didn't do anything in bed but sleep and have sex—and that second one I hadn't had much energy for lately. I took a nightly dose of the sleep supplement melatonin. When I did wake up in the middle of the night, I got up and went to another room to read. You're supposed to spend a few minutes reading, then go back to bed once you start feeling sleepy. Instead, I would plow through the better part of a novel, never get tired, then realize it was eight a.m. and I should probably "wake up" formally. I even tried to stick to a routine wake-up time, but realistically, I was grabbing a few hours of sleep whenever I could get it.

Most of the time, whether you do or don't do something about it, short periods of insomnia go away by themselves. But 10 to 20 percent of people end up missing several nights of sleep a week for months, and I soon found myself in that unfortunate minority.

———

One night at four a.m., once again completely alert, I took stock of my adventures in mindfulness. I had come to love Sharon Salzberg, the meditation teacher on the Ten Percent app, and in trying times I'd turn to her guided meditations like a lonely Jerseyite turns to Springsteen. But it felt strange to be so emotionally tethered to a ten-minute audio track. Eighteenth-century Buddhist monks didn't have iPods, after all.

Still, I'd learned that too much unstructured mindfulness time, such as an hour spent floating naked in water, made me feel uneasy. And though the curiosity elements of Brewer's program were interesting, I found them most effective for panic attacks, which I don't often have.

In desperation, one day I enrolled in Mindfulness-Based Stress Reduction, or MBSR, an eight-week mindfulness program conducted over Zoom. Developed in 1979 by a molecular biologist named Jon Kabat-Zinn, the program combines weekly two-and-a-half-hour-long classes on mindfulness-adjacent concepts with daily forty-five-minute meditation "homework." A few weeks in, there would be a seven-hour meditation "retreat," also held over Zoom.

MBSR is nothing if not established; it's mentioned in a 1986 *New York Times* article whose headline screams, "RELAXATION: SURPRISING BENEFITS DETECTED." Meta-analyses stretching back decades have shown MBSR can improve both physical and mental health, including by slashing depression and anxiety. A recently published study even found that MBSR worked as well as Lexapro for anxiety reduction. Perhaps because of this evidence base, it's the mindfulness class that smart, driven people will direct you to. There are now hundreds of MBSR classes to choose from; I selected one taught by a veteran instructor whom I'll call Louise.

In the introductory session, Louise explained that mindfulness allows us to make friends with our minds, but also to interrupt where our minds are going by pausing. This is helpful because, she explained, "sometimes things happen that you don't like." *It's true*, I thought.

A surprising number of the things that happen, I do not like. I wrote that down and underlined it. Later, I would find myself muttering this phrase to myself regularly.

One of my classmates said she was overwhelmed by the amount of daily homework, and Louise told her to "respect the overwhelmed feeling." In fact, over the weeks I spent in MBSR, it seemed like every time someone said there was something they didn't like about MBSR, the response was that you're supposed to embrace not liking it. One of the "five hindrances" of Buddhism is desire—including the desire for things to be different.

The homework the first week was to do a daily "body scan," or a forty-five-minute guided meditation in which you pay close attention to the sensations you feel in your body. Louise told us that we aren't supposed to fall asleep while we're doing it, but just in case, to not do it while we're driving.

That night, I sat on my bed and positioned my laptop next to me. I strapped on my Muse meditation headset, which supposedly reads your brainwaves to determine when you're truly in a state of "calm." On our MBSR class website, I clicked on Louise's body-scan recording. Her voice invited me to focus on how just my big toe felt, then just the bottom of my foot. Then just my ankle. I felt like I was on the Magic School Bus, floating through the human body with an eccentric woman as my guide. I thought about my shins, then all the tissues underneath them, then my kneecaps, then . . . I'm not sure what happened, because it was an hour later, and Rich was shaking me awake.

"Babe," he said. "What happened? You were snoring so loud."

I looked around groggily. All the lights were on. My laptop, having finished playing the body scan, was sitting open next to me on the bed, and my Muse headset was still stuck to my forehead. At least I was "91% still," according to the headset. Somewhere between the left kneecap and the groin, I had collapsed into sleep.

I soon learned that the body scan—which I had dismissed when

Brewer suggested it—*really* helped me fall asleep. It was the Soviet fairy tale of my youth, but a strange and boring one narrated by a woman with a thick New England accent.

In class a few days later, I admitted that the body scan had this soporific effect on me. Louise responded that if I fall asleep, I should do the entire forty-five-minute body scan again the next day, when I wasn't so sleepy. Apparently, mindfulness means being aware of the present moment, not unconscious during it.

There was only one problem: I soon found I *couldn't* stay awake during the body scan. Right around the time the recording said "it's important to stay awake" is when slumber really overtook me. Once, I did the scan sitting up, on a busy train, in the middle of the afternoon, and woke up to the conductor shouting, "Wilmington, Delaware!" *Well*, I thought, *at least I have my Xanax replacement.*

Otherwise, MBSR often filled me with anxiety, giving me yet another unpleasant task to fail at. I sometimes skipped doing all the homework, which was just long meditations, body scans, and yoga sessions that were creepily slow—I like fast LA yoga for hot people. ("The slowness is on purpose," Louise said.) My class was in the morning, and I always slept poorly the night before, feeling like a C student unprepared for her midterm. Sometimes I was upset that I'd spent hundreds of dollars on a woo-woo class that was both a last resort for my neuroticism and did not appear to be working. It grated on me to spend so much time doing so little. Other people were winning National Book Awards, which was an insult to me, personally. I knew I had willingly signed up for MBSR, but in the moment, my ego-shell was hard, and there was no cracking it.

In a private phone call, I confessed to Louise that I hated meditating.

"Maybe you should be kinder to yourself," she said, and I held back tears.

Over the weeks, she would often reference a parable about the "double arrow": When something bad happens, don't make it worse by dwelling on how bad it is. If, say, you didn't get as much work done as you meant to, don't harangue yourself for failing. You've already been struck by the arrow of misfortune; don't then impale yourself on the arrow of self-blame.

Gradually, I made peace with the arrows of MBSR: that I was wasting time waiting for Louise to load her PowerPoint slides, or that I'd spent a twenty-minute meditation rehashing a conversation from five years ago. I tried to avoid salting the wounds by imagining everything I could be accomplishing instead.

Our all-day Zoom meditation "retreat" finally arrived, fittingly, on an October day so overcast it looked blank. I showed up hungover, having figured that since I would be miserable all day, I might as well have fun the night before. For the retreat, Louise was joined by some other MBSR instructors, and together they led us in various meditations, some yoga, and a body scan for which I remarkably stayed awake. I felt lazy and bored. At one point, I tried to recall some old train schedules.

We did a short loving-kindness session, including the part that always makes me weep, in which you tell yourself that "you can search throughout the entire universe for someone who is more deserving of your love and affection than you are yourself, and that person is not to be found anywhere." I thought about why, exactly, being nice to myself always makes me cry. *Is it because I so rarely am? Does it pain me, a bad bitch who pretends to be above it all, to admit that I need love, too?* Maybe I was crying because I was flung sideways by this uncommon burst of self-compassion. Maybe I was crying because I wished I felt it more.

During the lunch break, we were instructed not to read or watch anything—the day was supposed to be about letting in whatever came through our "sense-doors." I mindfully ate a Subway sandwich but cheated by reading part of a *New York Times Magazine* article. When we reconvened, we entered breakout rooms to discuss our thoughts on the retreat so far. One man in mine said he'd already attended several all-day MBSR retreats.

"Why would you do this more than once?" I asked.

He said MBSR had helped him tremendously, and he saw this as a refresher. He always felt better afterward. "You might not notice anything today," he said, then added mysteriously, "but in the coming days, you'll feel it. Just wait."

In the afternoon, we were supposed to take a silent, mindful walk outside. During this, I cheated again and listened to music—mostly upbeat oldies that seemed harmless. It felt so delicious to hear something other than my own regurgitated thoughts that I was late coming back for yet another silent meditation.

During question-and-answer time, my mild annoyance with MBSR spilled into outright hostility. "I enjoy listening to music on my walks," I said. "Music is a big part of my life. It makes me feel less negative and less stressed. I'm wondering why it's not advisable to listen to music during the mindful walking."

"There's a subtle striving in what you shared," one of the other MBSR teachers responded. "Maybe you want for it to be relaxing and not challenging. But that's not the reason we practice. We practice for the sake of practicing and to meet with whatever is arising."

I could have thrown my laptop across the room. *What does that even mean?* Obviously I'm striving! Everyone is always striving! My only secret to securing my place in the world has been to work harder than everyone else. I studied maniacally in high school in order to get a full scholarship to college. I studied maniacally in college in order to get a full scholarship to grad school. At various points in my career, when I asked editors for advice, they said I should "get up earlier and work weekends." Striving was the very reason I hadn't had kids yet—they seemed like an expensive luxury for people with time on their hands. Life, as it had been portrayed to me, was a slog in which you work eighty hours a week, deny yourself every earthly pleasure, and maybe watch a movie on Fridays. *How dare these hippies tell me not to strive.*

At the end of the retreat, we made a word cloud of our feelings, on which "gratitude," "calm," and "peace" were the largest, meaning the greatest number of people had selected those. A couple people, though, had written down "angry" and "sad"—which did not seem to bother our instructors one bit.

Striving Not to Strive

A pillar of Mindfulness-Based Stress Reduction is, in fact, this principle of "not-striving." People who come to MBSR are often told *not* to try to make their anxiety go away. In his book *Full Catastrophe Living*, Kabat-Zinn writes how, in meditation, "the best way to achieve your goals is to back off from striving for results and instead to start focusing carefully on seeing and accepting things as they are, moment by moment."

Intellectually, I understood that. But inside, I felt the tug of resistance again. Stripped of my Muse meditation headset, I'm just an anxious little immigrant who thinks you should, in fact, be striving. If you're not careful, some deeply buried shtetl gene tells me, you can mindful yourself to sleeping on a park bench. If personality change meant no longer striving, I wasn't sure I wanted it.

Dan Harris, the *10% Happier* author, ran into a similar problem in his meditation practice. He eased up on the striving, and at times he became so serene that his work began slipping. After all, if you're not striving, you're probably also not achieving much.

He writes that he resolved this conundrum by working hard, but also by loosening his attachment to the outcome of his hard work. You can do everything within your power to be successful—you can, in effect, strive—but mindfulness means acknowledging when the results are out of your hands. Harris quotes another guru of sorts, the Democratic operative David Axelrod, on how he thinks about political campaigns, which involve striving furiously for months and then, come Election Day, letting go. "All we can do is everything we can do," Axelrod says. You can do your best, but you can't do *more* than your best. I decided that's all I could do, too.

After the class was over, I continued practicing elements of MBSR: the shorter meditations, loving-kindness, and the body scan. I accepted that these techniques often might not feel, in the moment, like they're relieving my anxiety. I conceded that worry is a fickle friend, one who takes credit for my successes while subtly undermining me.

Most of all, I tried to recognize the times when I was doing everything in my power to secure a good outcome, without punishing myself for the existence of uncertainty. I tried to follow the housing market but not obsess about it, and to track my fertility but stop rereading the same article about how fertility drops "right around a woman's thirty-seventh birthday."

It appeared to be "working," to the extent such a thing is possible in the world of mindfulness. During some of the longer MBSR meditations, my Muse headset reported that I spent more time in the "calm" zone than was typical. And the body scan continued to usher me into unconsciousness, which was no small thing after my struggle with insomnia. I capitalized on the fact that, like a toddler, my brain would only go to sleep when someone told it not to. If I couldn't stop striving in life, I could at least stop striving for sleep.

Everything Changes

On an especially good day in November, after an especially relaxing week, I tried to make myself as calm as possible. I went to yoga. I journaled. I did a fifteen-minute meditation with Sharon Salzberg, who once again asked me to wish myself health and happiness. I tabled, for the moment, thoughts of babies and houses. I fixed my mind on the Buddhist monk Thích Nhất Hạnh's admonishment that "Life is available only in the present moment."

I finally figured out why loving-kindness meditation always makes me cry. Many natural-born strivers feel we only deserve love when we've accomplished something. But loving-kindness forced me to consider, even if only for a few minutes, that love and achievement can be untangled, and that living itself merits recognition. Waking up and trying again is as amazing as anything. The idea that you might be enough, just as you are, is a heartbreakingly nice thing for an honor-roll student to hear—especially from herself.

Still, as I prepared to take another personality test, I girded myself for a high neuroticism score. I prepared to write a paragraph about how, well, meditation can't fix everything, trauma is intergenerational, and you can't expect bone-deep neuroses to clear up overnight. Then, apprehensively, I filled out another of Hudson's questionnaires. When the score came up on the screen, I thought there must be some mistake.

My neuroticism had fallen so much as to now be considered "low"—in the 39th percentile. And strangely, it was not because of the part of neuroticism I thought I'd been working on. My anxiety level did decrease, but it was still considered "high," according to the test. Instead, my depression score had fallen off dramatically, to the 27th percentile. The test was telling me that "compared with other people, you feel low amounts of sadness and like yourself to a high degree."

I searched my life for what might have buoyed me so significantly. I was working on this book, which did make me feel happy and capable. Through the lessons of Buddhism, I had accepted that my future was uncertain; I couldn't wring a guarantee from the universe that moving and parenting wouldn't sometimes be grueling. I knew my only choice was, as the Bhagavad Gita instructs, to act without attachment to the fruits of my actions. I could be careful, but things I didn't like would still happen.

My new, lower level of neuroticism meant I might not grind away at every conceivable achievement. That year I broke with tradition and didn't bother submitting stories to a bunch of small-time awards that I never win anyway. Even a podcast that features more-famous-than-me journalists had seemed less irritating lately. I would clock the rising wave of jealousy and think, *So what?* I did everything I could do. I made a mean cacio e pepe. Maybe I did deserve love and kindness. So does everyone.

Maintaining this score longer than a day, would, I predicted, be a constant battle. After a while, the body scan never helped me sleep as reliably as it had those first few weeks. And without the accountability mechanism of a class, eventually I found it hard to remember to meditate. I even slept fitfully the night before I took the personality test that registered my new, lower neuroticism score.

My neuroticism might billow back up, and it will likely dissipate again, too. Louise liked to say that "this too shall pass" can be both soothing and sad. Misfortune is ephemeral, but so is luck. Everything changes, including our moods—as Freud put it, like landscapes before a passenger on a train. While I could, I tried to enjoy the view.

5

Down for Whatever:

Openness to Experience

Many years ago, at a party in Los Angeles, I wandered outside for a break from socializing. On the back deck, people smoked weed as the faint synths of MGMT leaked out from the living room. I took a few gulps of the brisk LA night air. Then I noticed something: This was a Craftsman house in a nice area; even partitioned between several roommates, I guessed the rent was substantial. I couldn't suppress my Washingtonian urge to determine what the party's hostess did for work.

I walked up to her and asked that classic DC question, "What are you working on?"

The hostess, a woman with an asymmetrical haircut and an age that could have been any number between seventeen and thirty-seven, gave me a bemused look.

"Well, right now I'm working on a portrait of my grandma with pork ribs shooting out of her eyes," she said.

And *that—that* is openness to experience.

People who are open to experiences love art and music, and they tend to be politically liberal, "spiritual but not religious," and sexually adventurous. They have dreams they can more easily recall. They seek out novelty in books, art, movies, and activities, and when viewing a painting or listening to music, they have more tolerance for "disfluency," the scientific term for something that's difficult to understand. They'll venture off to some obscure wing of the Louvre while everyone else waits in line for the *Mona Lisa*. Open people can be "sensation seekers," craving new adventures and thrills. They spend lots of time on the Internet but relatively little time watching TV.

People who are very low in openness, meanwhile, are likely to be conservative, traditional, and rigid. They like things in a very specific way, and they allow little deviation from the tried and true. They might even see new ideas as best ignored, even dangerous.

Open people are keenly sensitive to the marvelous and the awe-inspiring. One sign you might be open is if, when you see or hear something especially magnificent, the hairs on the back of your neck stand up and shivers go down your spine. The trait is usually measured by asking people, among other things, whether they like to engage with abstract ideas and in philosophical discussions, and whether they enjoy poetry and plays. Of all the traits, openness is most closely linked to creativity, and it also seems to correlate with verbal, but not mathematical, intelligence. If you have ever taken a class from a yoga instructor wearing bohemian culottes, smelling of natural deodorant, and recounting her recent psilocybin retreat, you have stared openness to experience in the face, and she has smiled back and said, "Do you want to come to the sound bath later?"

Because psychologists tend to be liberal and open themselves, the studies on openness can start to make it seem like everyone should be as open to experiences as possible. But you can, in fact, be *too* open. High openness predicts involvement with the arts, but also involvement with psychiatrists. Openness tends to be high in people who have a mild form of schizophrenia called schizotypal personality disorder, and in people who harbor unusual or paranormal beliefs, like that they might be telepathic. For especially open people, ideas can trigger a "broad raft of associations," as Daniel Nettle puts it, and on this raft floats the gift of creativity but also, sometimes, the curse of delusions and hallucinations. Very open people can become captured by false patterns, even at times breaking from reality.

Teenagers might chafe at the rigid ways of parents who are low in openness, but parents who are overly open can fail to provide sufficient structure and stability. In her memoir, *Hello, Molly!*, the *Saturday Night Live* star Molly Shannon describes the consequences of her father's extremely relaxed approach to parenting. When she was a little girl, he encouraged her to steal, and when she was thirteen, he dared her to try to "hop" a flight by herself. (This was before 9/11, when such a thing was possible.) Shannon took a train to the Cleveland airport, and, when the plane landed in New York City, called her father from a pay phone. "He was definitely worried," she writes, "but he was also kind of excited because he liked crazy stuff." "Liking crazy stuff" is a hallmark of the open-to-experiences—and it's a tendency that can delight or disrupt, depending on the situation. (Indeed, it seems like Shannon's upbringing both scarred her and pushed her into a career in comedy.)

Openness is unique in that it doesn't predict health and wealth as much as some of the other traits do. Despite its relationship with verbal intelligence, it doesn't correlate strongly to academic performance. Open people tend to perform well in certain types of creative or investigative jobs, but not in all jobs. I, a person who scores "very high" on openness, was bored out of my mind when I briefly worked as a secretary at a mail-order mailbox company. (Yes.) Because I was physically incapable of caring about mailboxes, I skipped work often and almost got fired. But at my creative, analytical journalism job, I'm one of the best-performing employees. Reporting suits my openness perfectly.

Openness has upsides, but they're subtle. The trait predicts "humanistic flourishing," or a sense of knowing who you really are, says Ted Schwaba, a personality psychologist at Michigan State University who has studied openness. Open people are alive in the world, excited about discovery and tolerant of difference. The openness sections of personality questionnaires tend to spotlight reflectiveness and imagination—qualities that are "intrinsically valuable," Schwaba says, "but they're not necessarily things that I can point to and be like, 'Oh, I became more open, and now I make six thousand dollars more a year.'"

But what's $6,000 when you're flourishing in other ways? Or so an open person might say.

Donald Takayama and Me

Research suggests that to purposefully increase in openness, you can indeed sample new experiences, like visiting art galleries or museums, going to concerts, traveling, and engaging in physical activity. One study that compared college students who studied abroad with those who didn't found that those who traveled became more open to experiences—especially if they made friends while visiting the foreign country. To the authors, the study "showed that hitting the road has substantial effects on who we are. The difference is made by the international people we meet on that road." Then again, if you can't afford a plane ticket, maybe you can just introduce some "international people" into your life: Another study found that exposing college students in Arkansas to people, traditions, and food from other countries led to increases in openness and reductions in prejudice.

But, as any exasperated parent of a picky eater can tell you, it is really hard to get other people to try something new. This is the essential struggle of openness to experience: People can likely increase in openness if they try new things, but people who are low in openness often don't *want* to try new things. They'll have the same old PB&J with crustless white bread, thank you. "So much of openness development is people becoming more who they are," says Ted Schwaba. "People who aren't open, they don't want to be more open, and people who are really open want to increase more on that trait."

In fact, when I looked to increase my own openness levels, I soon ran into a related problem: I already did everything open people are supposed to do. Most of the activities that are meant to increase openness—like reading novels, asking people about controversial topics, and going to concerts—were how I already spent my time. I'm a journalist who loves live music and modern art. A few books I read suggested that you can increase openness by watching foreign films, but I'm already always dragging Rich to movies in which French lesbians stare at each other meaningfully for hours.

So in an attempt to hike my openness score even higher, I decided to seek out what psychologists call a "peak experience." Initially described by Abraham Maslow, of hierarchy-of-needs fame, peak experiences are oceanic, ecstatic moments that elicit clarity, euphoria, and harmony. They zip you into the universe's warm jacket and inspire a personal metamorphosis. Falling in love, finishing a marathon, or giving birth to a child are all examples of peak experiences. These moments "involve absorption in the moment, a sense of timelessness and spacelessness, feelings of profound awe, and experiences of unity," according to one study for which researchers interviewed people who'd had peak experiences in nature. Though the researchers didn't measure openness specifically, they found these experiences allowed the study participants to unearth new parts of themselves. One woman they interviewed, Lital, was so shaken up by a trip to the Arctic that she left her factory job, lost twenty pounds, and got to work on a play. Peak experiences at least meet the barest definition of what it means to be open: They require doing something new.

I opted to focus on the "oceanic" part of the definition and take to the ocean. I would try surfing, something I had always wanted to do but had always been afraid to try. I've lived in Southern California and have stared, mesmerized, at surfers gliding through the water in their black wetsuits, like sexy orcas. But whenever I mentioned to my twitchy family the idea of surfing, they reacted like I was suggesting majoring in theater dance or failing to contribute to my 401(k). My dad and brother brought up the likelihood of sharks, as well as the likelihood that the board would crack me on the head and impede my ability to make a living as a knowledge worker. We Khazans are not an aquatic people, and nurture, heretofore, had always won out over adventure.

But openness often involves separating from your younger self. It requires saying, "yeah, I am the kind of person who does that," even if you suspect that you are not. Many of us do simply repeat the patterns of our childhoods: Political orientation, one element of openness, is to some extent passed from parents on to their kids. But a fair number of people—about 20 percent—reject their parents' politics as adults. They become more or less open, even if they weren't raised to be, and never previously were. Some people *choose* openness, rather than inherit it.

I thought trying a scary new sport would be a good baby step in facing my fears about larger life decisions—like, well, the baby step. No one from high school or college or even my California grad school would have pegged me for a promising surfer—or a promising parent, for that matter. But what if I was?

Rich agreed to try surfing with me, perhaps because he's also very open to experiences. Openness is a trait that's often shared between friends and lovers: Tidy people are friends with messy people, but open people are mostly only friends with other open people. As the personality psychologist Robert McCrae put it, "Open people are bored by the predictable and intellectually undemanding amusements of closed people; closed people are bored by what they perceive to be the difficult and pretentious culture of the open." Open people always want to try new things—*with* other open people.

One recent November, we forded our rental SUV across a small creek in Playa Grande, Costa Rica, and drove up a winding dirt road to a cheap "surf hotel." This meant that the hotel was convenient for surfers, not that it would in any way assist you with the surfing. I tried to prepare for what surfing would demand of me—upper body strength? balance?—by drinking lots of juice in the open-air café and by practicing yoga under the skeptical gaze of spider monkeys. A few yards from our hotel was a wide beach with soft, beige sand, inviting waves, and driftwood reaching for the heavens. My winter coat, which I had worn in a sleet-soaked airport parking lot just a day prior, looked in my room like a bizarre and unwanted interloper.

As our first day of surfing approached, I felt myself close off to experiences a little. I kept waking up at three a.m. and googling for updated counts of shark attacks, rationalizing that one more or one less arm ripped off would guarantee my safety, because it would mean the sharks were either nonexistent or already full from other people's appendages. When Rich sleepily asked what I was doing on my phone in the middle of the night, I said, "Did you know that two hundred people a year drown in Costa Rica's rip currents?"

Our surf instructor, Andy, was a Southern California guy who one day twelve years earlier quit his job as an accountant and moved to Costa Rica to surf—a profile in openness to experience and also my dad's worst nightmare. I had thought, or perhaps hoped, that the first day we would be mostly practicing "popping up" on dry land. Instead, we did that for about two minutes before Andy said, "Okay, let's get wet!"

We waded into the tourist-friendly turquoise water, and as instructed, I pointed my board's nose over the cresting foam of the waves. With each step, it became harder and harder to see my feet. Real surfers had mounted their boards at that point, finding it faster to paddle. My paddling, though, was still highly inefficient and far inferior to walking.

Finally, the water was lapping at my chin, and it was time to mount the board ventrally, my knowledge-worker ass dragging down the tail and my lips stopping just short of the board's small red logo: SURF BOARDS BY DONALD TAKAYAMA. "Keep and protect me, Donald," I whispered.

After trying to catch a few waves under Andy's tutelage, I grew impatient and lunged for one without his go-ahead. At first, everything went according to plan: My board raced forward with me atop it, paddling and yogically breathing. Then, in an instant, I was somersaulting through water. The wave had smashed into me, knocking me off my board. As the swell held me under, my hips scraped sand and my board leash yanked my leg rightward. When I surfaced, something sharp grazed my left hand.

Andy gave me the "Are you okay?" signal, tapping the top of his head. I wondered if maybe all my limbs had been severed by shark teeth and I couldn't feel the injury yet because of the adrenaline in my veins. This happened a lot, according to my nighttime googles.

But after a brief inventory, I had to admit that I was okay. I raised my left hand to examine what was surely the shark bite my family had warned me about. It turned out to be a one-inch welt left by a baby jellyfish. I groaned and climbed back on my board.

That first day, Rich and I both managed to stand up occasionally, but usually for barely a second before we'd sink or fall off. By evening, alongside the jellyfish sting, I had somehow abraded both hips, flashed the beach, liquified my biceps, cut my left quad, and bruised both knees, even though my knees were not supposed to be involved at all. But Donald Takayama and I would try again. Rich and I spent part of every day of the vacation thusly—being open to surfing but finding it was not quite open to us.

On the final day, though, Andy was barely watching when I maneuvered myself into the right position, paddled ahead of a two-foot wave, and pushed up like a proud graduate of the 1993 Presidential Fitness

Test. My legs somehow found their way to the center of the board. I rode for a good three seconds, a surfing sea nymph in command of my board, the wave, the ocean and all its creatures, and definitely my own fear.

I'm still probably a long way from taking up surfing as a hobby. But every one of those flailing days in the water, I was thankful that surfing required an all-consuming, physical attention—a reprieve from a life defined by scrolling and sitting. I'm never embodied, but while trying to surf, I was *only* embodied. I was astride earth's largest wilderness, a beast among beasts. I was reminded—however briefly—that I'm an incarnate being, and that I, too, seek food, pleasure, and a challenge. No matter how much I struggled, I withstood the pull of the undertow.

Shaking the Snow Globe

You might have noticed from my surfing story that all too often people chasing openness run straight into a brick wall of anxiety. My florid *Blue Crush* fantasies blurred into unrealistic catastrophizing—a fear that not only would I not surf, I'd die. But wait, aren't we talking about openness, the fun Picasso trait, not neuroticism, the skittish, anxious trait?

It occurred to me that the two traits might be intertwined. Low openness can be veined with fear; you can be closed to something because it scares you. Increasing openness, meanwhile, sometimes requires muffling neuroticism's high-pitched shriek. And occasionally, to reduce neuroticism, it helps to be open. Sometimes, neuroticism and closedness can pick away at the mind in concert, digging a hole deeper. This, in fact, might be how the mysterious trait of openness pulls off its biggest magic trick: The trait might be an important intermediary when it comes to healing brains scarred by trauma, depression, and anxiety.

Perhaps nothing illustrates the relationship between neuroticism and openness better than the psychedelic drugs—like "magic" psilocybin mushrooms, ayahuasca, and MDMA—that have emerged as potential therapeutics for people suffering from depression, trauma, and other ills. Most of these drugs remain illegal nationally for now, and they've shown benefits mainly only when taken under the watchful guidance of therapists and researchers. Still, psychedelics appear to cause substantial increases in people's levels of openness, possibly for the long term, and they also seem to reduce neuroticism alongside it. They reveal how low openness can braid itself into neuroticism, and how when you change one trait, you often change the other.

An organization called the Multidisciplinary Association for Psychedelic Studies, or MAPS, has run several trials for which they treated post-traumatic stress disorder with MDMA, the hallucinogenic stimulant also known as ecstasy. The group found that MDMA-assisted psychotherapy both reduced the study subjects' neuroticism and increased their openness, and that the subjects who increased on openness the most also showed the greatest reductions in PTSD symptoms. "Individuals scoring higher on Openness tend to seek out new experiences and be open to self-examination, factors that can serve to enhance therapeutic change," write the study's authors.

In studies of psilocybin, the active ingredient in so-called magic mushrooms, healthy participants who had "mystical experiences" while on the drug likewise made huge leaps in openness, and their new personalities stayed that way for at least a year. The psilocybin increased openness even more than antidepressants or intensive counseling.

This openness boost pops up in research on all kinds of psychedelics. In one small study, openness increased in a group of healthy adults who took a dose of LSD. Ayahuasca, a ritual drink made from two Amazonian plants, often provokes elaborate visions and profuse vomiting—and it also sparks changes in neuroticism and openness, compared to control groups.

Psychedelics have also been shown, in some studies, to decrease authoritarian political views, which can be seen as a form of low openness. In one unusual episode, an avowed white supremacist who took

MDMA as part of a study went on to reject his bigoted beliefs. "Love is the most important thing," he told the study's research assistant. "Nothing matters without love." Though bigotry and authoritarianism are not identical to low openness, the two mindsets share a certain inflexibility and insularity. In this case, MDMA seemed to open up a closed, hateful mind.

Psychedelics seem to rearrange their users' core beliefs about the world, prodding them to see their circumstances in new ways. The drugs relax attitudes about the dangerousness of other people or the bleakness of the future. In lab rodents, psychedelics appear to promote neuroplasticity, or the growth of new connections between brain cells. In mice, they reopen so-called critical periods of learning—times of heightened impressionability that are typically only open during childhood—which may foster a powerful receptivity to new ideas and narratives. Researchers don't yet know if these same neurological changes appear in humans—that would require killing the, uh, "specimen"—but they think it's possible. If it does occur, this plasticity may help the brain learn new ways of thinking. One prominent psychedelic researcher, Robin Carhart-Harris, has likened taking psychedelics to shaking a snow globe or lubricating cognition, smoothing the way for fresh thought patterns. The drugs seem to summon a long finger from the stratosphere that clicks "reset" on your brain.

Curiously, the increased openness spurred by psychedelics seems to bring with it a reduction, if not in neuroticism outright, then in the depression, substance abuse, and other conditions often associated with neuroticism. Psilocybin paired with psychotherapy has been shown to decrease not only neuroticism specifically but also depression for at least a year, and to help with smoking cessation and potentially other types of addiction. MAPS has found that after taking MDMA, about two-thirds of participants in their studies no longer met the diagnostic criteria for PTSD.

Genesee Herzberg, a therapist in the Bay Area who uses the psychedelic drug ketamine alongside therapy in her practice, says that among her patients she sees "a decrease in neuroticism, and an increase in openness in the moment, and possibly in a lasting way." (Though some don't consider ketamine a true psychedelic, it is currently the only drug of this kind approved by the FDA for the treatment of depression.) Her patients don't necessarily become more interested in art museums and experimental music. "It's more like a shift out of these deeply ingrained ways of thinking," she told me.

Though this might all sound miraculous, some skepticism is warranted here. The psychedelic studies are small and fuzzy on the mechanism of action. Researchers aren't completely sure that some of these aren't placebo effects. Because the psychedelic experience is so powerful—the people taking them often hallucinate for hours—it's impossible to blind people to whether they are taking a placebo or a psychedelic. The FDA recently rejected MDMA as a PTSD treatment because it's not yet clear that the drug is safe and effective.

And like all drugs, psychedelics carry risks. The therapeutic doses tend to be large, and some people who have taken psychedelics have reported negative side effects, which can range from headaches to, much more rarely, a psychotic break or suicidal ideation. "They're not concert doses," says Matthew Johnson, a prominent psychedelics researcher. If you were to take a dose this big at Burning Man, he said, "I'd find my tent and zip my ass up until morning."

Just how, exactly, an increase in openness might lead to a decrease in depression and PTSD is also still unclear. Johnson says that while it's not yet proven that openness is behind psychedelics' healing powers, it's likely playing a role. Issues like smoking and depression involve a rigidity of thought, he says. People know that smoking isn't good for them, but they'll return to it anyway because they can't imagine life without cigarettes. On psilocybin, people seem to have realizations about themselves that may have seemed obvious before, "but now they really, really get it," Johnson says. The drug helps people imagine themselves changing.

Weirder still is why the changes in openness persist long after the psychedelic trip has ended. It might be that, once you take in the revelations of psychedelics, your brain remembers what it saw. Johnson likens it to taking a helicopter ride over a beautiful mountain. After you glimpse the gorgeous views from the skies, you might be inspired to take the arduous hike up the trail, since you now know how you'll be rewarded in the end.

Psychedelics seem to help people immerse themselves in challenges, rather than hide from them. As I learned from a woman named Lori, the drugs can help you not only confront your demons but also see them for what they are: false, fleeting, outmatched by your inner hero.

Opening the Dam

Lori Tipton was a college student in New Orleans when her brother Davin, who was living in New Mexico, came for a visit. The two had always been close; growing up, they knit together as allies within their dysfunctional family. They even looked alike. Now he had come to celebrate his twenty-second birthday.

That night, Lori stayed in to study for an exam, and Davin went out drinking with friends. He came home drunk; Lori remembers feeling annoyed that Davin woke her up when he returned. The next morning, Lori went to class as usual.

On her way back, she got a panicked call from her boyfriend: Davin was unresponsive. In the night, he had died from an overdose of alcohol and pills.

In the months after, Lori worked to ignore her emotions. She moved in with her mother, who struggled with a severe mental illness, and tried to manage her mother's grief. She didn't allow herself to truly miss her brother. "I would just act like it didn't happen," she recalls. She eventually moved out on her own.

When Lori was in her midtwenties, six years had passed since Davin's death. One day, she called her mother's house, only to get no answer. Lori drove over and found a horrific scene. Seemingly in the midst of a psychotic episode, her mother had murdered her former lover and a family friend, and then shot herself through the heart. She had been sleepless and unmedicated, and "she couldn't see her way out of something," Lori says. Lori called 911 and told the police her mother was dead. All she remembers feeling is shock. "It was almost like watching a movie," she told me.

Lori scrambled to find money for the funeral and to get her mother's affairs in order. She couldn't get through a night without terrifying dreams. More than feeling sad, she remembers being angry with her mother, even hating her.

At the time, Lori was still living in New Orleans and working as a physical therapist's assistant. About six weeks after her mother's death, Hurricane Katrina pounded the city, and Lori and many of her friends had to evacuate. She returned to find that seven feet of storm surge had sloshed through her home, destroying most of her belongings. At her new place, she didn't have gas or water for weeks.

A year later, Lori was at home with a cold when a friend called her from a bar, drunk and upset. She went to the bar, retrieved her friend, and helped him walk home. When they reached his house, he leaned over and kissed her, which Lori allowed, thinking it was the easiest way to end an awkward situation. But then, she says, he raped her. As soon as she could, she grabbed her things and ran to her car, where she threw up in disgust.

A few weeks later, Lori learned she was pregnant. She decided to get an abortion, a challenge in the very abortion-unfriendly South. *Is there a fucking curse on me?* she thought. Lori felt trapped in a life that would always be painful. She was exhausted and her body hurt. In Katrina's wake, New Orleans wailed in anguish—everyone was traumatized in some way. "It allowed me to really fall into substance abuse, and hating myself, and it was socially acceptable because everybody else around me was doing a similar thing," Lori told me.

For a while, Lori didn't think she had PTSD. She held down jobs, working as a disaster-recovery consultant and the manager of a bar. She had friends. But though she had been a free-spirited and confident child, as an adult she would double-check door locks. At work, whenever someone clapped their hands or slammed down a shot glass, she jumped. She was always on high alert, scanning the room for potential threats.

Despite her troubles, Lori felt the urge to care for a child, and in 2013 she got pregnant again. She and her partner, Andy, decided to raise the baby with the help of a gay couple they were close with. The presence of three dads lightened the load, but Lori still had awful postpartum anxiety. On the rare occasions when she went outside, she'd imagine that a neighbor's dog might break free of its chain and maul the baby. She never took her child—who has since come out as nonbinary—to restaurants or on trips by herself.

Lori took antidepressants and antianxiety medications, but she nevertheless swung between brief periods of functioning and stretches of panic attacks and night terrors. "My brain was always either in the past being traumatized by intrusive memories, or it was moving into the future and predicting all the horrible stuff that could happen," she told me. She drank too much and took Xanax and Vicodin. Sometimes, she wondered if on some level she deserved all that had happened to her. Other times, she questioned whether she might ever again experience joy.

In 2017, Lori heard about a study that would treat trauma survivors with MDMA. The drug seems to rev up the brain's prefrontal cortex and turn down the fear-oriented amygdala, the combination of which allows people to revisit their past traumas and process them. MDMA might also strengthen the person's connection with their therapist, who in turn helps them work through their trauma more effectively.

To prepare for her treatment, Lori met with therapists to talk about her past and what she wanted out of the experience. In all, Lori had three MDMA sessions, each about a month apart. She would arrive at nine a.m., take the drug, and spend the rest of the day with her therapists, alternating between crying, talking, and sometimes laughing.

On the drug, Lori would flip through a mental Rolodex of memories. She revisited the elation of seeing snow for the first time as a little girl, and the aroma of a good cup of coffee. Every memory felt real in her body, like she was experiencing it in the moment. But she wasn't just blissed out. She also felt safe enough to finally feel the pain tied to her traumas. "It was like opening the dam on a lake of grief," she told me.

During these MDMA sessions, PTSD patients recall traumatic memories in a setting that's unusually warm, empathetic, and reassuring, says Matthew Johnson. Harmful narratives can become encoded with our memories, but under the drug's influence, memories become more pliable and open to recontextualizing. The amygdala is less activated, so old traumas don't stir their usual fight-or-flight response. While taking MDMA, patients might pull up and refile their troubling memories, creating a picture that's less triggering and less critical of themselves. (This blurring and softening of old traumatic memories is similar to what happens in some other forms of trauma therapy, such as eye movement desensitization and reprocessing.) "You're learning how you can respond differently," Johnson says. "How you can think about this situation, and how you can think about yourself, in a different way."

Lori then had a series of small epiphanies. She realized that her body could feel joy and free-spiritedness after all; it was like a favorite song came on the radio long after she'd forgotten it. She felt intense empathy for herself. She saw her mother as both an incredible woman and a horrible murderer. Lori hadn't realized how much she had been blaming herself for what happened—for not sounding the alarm about her mother's mental illness sooner. But on MDMA, she forgave her mother, and she forgave herself.

On the clearheaded morning after taking the drug, Lori would have an "integration session" with her therapists about her trip, which would help her internalize her epiphanies. She saw that her self-talk was extremely negative—a warped view of a woman just trying to survive.

After the study, Lori felt a swell of courage. She left the bartending job she had wanted to quit for a while. The dense coil of dread that had inhibited her parenting gradually unspun. One of the biggest differences, she says, has been "having a much more beautiful, open, capable relationship with my child."

Today, Lori is in her early forties, with apple-red hair and a frank self-assuredness about her. She spends her time writing, doing yoga, and teaching others about psychedelics. She says her friends describe her now as more relaxed, less angry, and more open to adventure.

For a while, Lori worried it would be like "some *Flowers for Algernon* shit, where I heal, and then I slowly regress back," she said. But the experience has stayed with her—a "grand remembrance" of her best self. The healing powers of MDMA were put to the test a few months before we talked, when she saw a man lying dead in the street near her house. There hadn't been any gun violence; he died of a heart attack. Before, Lori would have reacted with hypervigilance, locking herself up in the house and worrying about her kid. But today, she recognizes that his death doesn't mean the entire world is unsafe.

Some of these changes in Lori sound like decreases in neuroticism, and indeed, they might be. The researchers at MAPS, who connected me with Lori, have found that neuroticism did decrease in people with PTSD who were treated with MDMA—but neuroticism also decreased among those who simply got therapy along with a placebo. The big difference between the two groups—MDMA and placebo—was that MDMA increased openness to experience. And the openness was what correlated to a decrease in the patient's PTSD score.

The two traits—openness and emotional stability—might be amplifying each other, a call-and-response that creates a steady rhythm. It could be "helpful to have both the reduction in neuroticism as well as the increase in openness so that the therapy can be more effective," says Berra Yazar-Klosinski, the chief scientific officer for the MAPS Public Benefit Corporation, now known as Lykos Therapeutics. "I think MDMA is opening people up, reducing the fear response."

Michael Mithoefer, a psychiatrist who leads much of MAPS's MDMA work, told me that our trains of thought can resemble toboggan tracks on a snowy hill. As you slide down over and over, you cut a groove in the snow, from which it soon becomes impossible to deviate. PTSD is a lot like a groove, or a rut: When you're stuck in one, all new places look dangerous; nobody can be trusted. MDMA can create freshly fallen snow, allowing people "to take a different track down the mountain," Mithoefer says. "Suddenly they have a new perspective. And they're able to respond in a new, more creative, and more realistic way."

To Lori, the MDMA reduced anxiety and *made room* for openness. Previously, she had been so preoccupied with survival, she couldn't be open. "Not being afraid means I can interact with the people around me," she says. "And by interacting with them, I can understand them and care for them."

Lori's move to greater openness in her late thirties is unusual: Most people tend to increase in openness during their late teens and early twenties and grow *less* open later in life. As we age, we lose the desire to meet new people, try new things, or adopt new points of view. The emotional calluses of middle age shield us from the unfamiliar and the risky. (This later-life decline in openness may help explain the common trajectory in which liberals become more conservative as they age.) But it was almost like Lori redrew the boundaries that had marked her young adulthood. She had every reason to doubt the world, but she found a way to open herself to it instead.

It might be a while before most people who have PTSD, or who just crave more openness, can access MDMA—as of this writing, the drug still isn't approved as a medication. In the meantime, people who have depression and anxiety can try to re-create those small epiphanies with the help of a therapist or a more accessible drug, like an antidepressant or ketamine. "We really believe that each individual has their own ability to connect to their own wisdom and intuition," says Shannon Carlin, chief of therapy training and supervision at MAPS. She calls this ability the "inner healing intelligence"—the mind's innate potential to restore itself after adversity. The MDMA helps people find that intelligence, but it doesn't invent it from nothing.

And while it might not be as easy without a drug like MDMA, anyone can access their own joyful memories. Anyone can change the way they talk to themselves and the stories they've convinced themselves are true. Anyone can open up and let life rush in.

At one point, Lori remarked to me that "there's always this chance to change and do something differently." She seemed to have compassion for the person she once was and also a sense that she's become someone new. After always being the parent who would stay inside and lock the door, Lori teared up when one day her child turned to her and said, "You're so fun." The snow had settled into a new path, and now, it shone brighter than ever.

Every Living Thing Matters

To be honest, Lori's story made me want to do psychedelics. Though I am fortunate not to have experienced her level of trauma, I wish I could dry-erase all my cognitive distortions and fill my mental whiteboard with cool visions instead.

A few years ago, I did take a small dose of psilocybin mushrooms. Rich procured them, and I did not inquire too much about their provenance. But unlike Lori, I didn't have a guide or a therapist to lead me through the experience. Instead, I implored Rich to monitor me as I sipped the small cup of hot water in which my mushroom slice had steeped. About twenty minutes later, I got dizzy and took to the couch. From there, I had a perfect vantage point from which to stare at our colorful, abstract wall art, which suddenly seemed to be throbbing at me.

"Outside," I whispered.

Gently, Rich walked me to a nearby park, gripping me by the arm to keep me upright. We passed some roses that exploded off their stems at my arrival. Nature had never before seemed so . . . *real*. I reached out and stroked the leaves of a boxwood like a little country girl in a movie trailer.

At the park, I unfurled a blanket and lay down in the grass. I had brought an old issue of the *New Yorker*, which I placed in my lap so that passersby would think I was reading instead of tripping.

I stared up at the trees, and I noticed they were undulating, their branches pulling closer to me, then retreating. No, they were *waving*. At *me*. They were trying to tell me something. *What was it?*

"What is it that you want me to know?" I said quietly.

A woman walked by with her dog, who started barking excitedly in my direction. "Calm down!" the woman yelled. "She's just trying to read!"

I, deep in conversation with the trees, ignored them.

Rich picked a dandelion and held it out to me. This made me deeply sad, since I now knew the Secret Truth: Every living thing matters. Solemnly, I said goodbye to the trees, since I knew what was coming. About three hours after it started, my high had ended, and the most painful headache of my life began. The next morning, I was the same person I always was.

My mushroom voyage would probably have been more transformative had I both taken a larger dose and worked with a therapist. And I thought about finding a toboggan-toppling dose of psychedelics and ending this chapter with a long description of me high off my gourd, laughing at my own hand. Then I'd of course be cured of all my problems, and I'd proceed through life confidently popping out children, buying houses, and sitting for performance reviews with nary a sweaty palm.

But though it seemed promising, MAPS's MDMA work also gave me pause. Months after I connected with Lori, some other subjects in studies conducted by MAPS's related company, Lykos Therapeutics, said that their therapists seemed biased toward the benefits of MDMA, and that they felt pressured not to report the suicidal thoughts they experienced after taking the drug, the *Wall Street Journal* reported. (Lykos has said it reported any increases in suicidality to the FDA.) I started to think that maybe this stuff wasn't quite ready for prime time.

In the end, I failed to do drugs for this book for the same reason I failed to do drugs in high school: I like to follow rules. MDMA was not legal, and I didn't know a guy. If I did procure MDMA in a back alley, I probably wouldn't trust it, since it could be laced with something else. I definitely wouldn't feel safe enough to take a life-altering dose. I also didn't have access to a drug-friendly therapist, shaman, or even a lab technician who could help me find my own personal Jesus. If I did psychedelics again, I risked just repeating what happened last time. I'd have to be satisfied with my weak little microtrip.

Saudade and Sardines

Instead, I decided to travel to foreign lands—something suggested in the scientific literature as a way to increase openness. If there was any hope of raising my openness score even higher, I thought it might lie in immersing myself in a new culture. Lured by photos and stories from a friend who had recently gone, I booked a ticket to Portugal.

I've often used travel to break through periods of restless inertia. Once, I was stuck on a difficult story, but on a flight to Dubai for a *different* story, insight suddenly swept over me. I rewrote the entire draft in eight hours while wedged between two snoring businessmen. Now I was mired in a similar morass: I wasn't sure what to do about moving, which we had made no progress toward, or about my fertility, such as it was. Whenever I sat down to write, I would instead research the cost of IVF, then send Rich a text ordering him to learn to change a diaper, then google idiotic lists like "best places to live in Florida" (number one is Sarasota) or "how to calm a screaming toddler" (the toddler who didn't exist), then start the process all over again. I needed to cut the motor.

Portugal was one of the few countries in Europe I had never visited, and I hoped that, as with the surfing expedition, I would have my mind at least marginally blown. I remembered some of my early reporting trips, in which I would arrive in a remote village with a tape recorder and a camera and feel like I was shaking my long-held assumptions with every interview. Maybe it would be like that. I landed in Lisbon feeling ready for this hilly place to absorb and remake me.

The first day, I circled the limestone cloisters of the sixteenth-century Jerónimos Monastery, which crops up like an enormous vanilla cake in the Lisbon suburbs. The church was financed by the pepper trade and is named for the Hieronymite order of monks, which the Portuguese king Manuel installed there so they could pray for him daily. I gazed out through its ornamented arches, wondering what it would be like to spend my life here.

I lunched on a pile of grilled sardines, then rambled along the Tagus River and peered up at the Monument to the Discoveries, the striking—and somewhat problematic—stone tribute to early Portu-guese explorers. (Monument to Plundering may have been more accu-rate.) Then I skipped the Belém Tower, the L-shaped structure Portugal is best known for, because my jet lag had finally caught up with me.

I had gone there by myself in part because Rich hates vacations, and I hate playing tour guide for a man who hates vacations. I thought I would have the rare chance to entertain private musings without constantly having to ask if he was okay with a given restaurant or making sure he was having fun. I hoped to enter my own preferred kind of meditation: a long stretch of alone time in a place where I couldn't understand a soul.

What I had failed to consider was that twelve years of continuous cohabitation had made it so I no longer *have* private musings. I have a running monologue whose audience was suddenly absent. I felt lonely and discombobulated. Who was I even taking all these photos for? I ended the day FaceTiming Rich on my hotel Wi-Fi and asking what he was doing.

The next day brought a ferocious rain that filled my sneakers with water as I walked the declivitous streets. I went to a performance of doleful Portuguese fado music and ate more cheese than is probably advisable. I guess I don't look like I would steal an iPhone, because six or seven different couples asked me to take their photo.

I noticed that I was efficiently checking off every sight from my *Rick Steves' Europe* guidebook. But, after a couple of days, I also noticed with dismay that everywhere I looked, I was surrounded by my fellow tourists—a trend to which I was obviously contributing.

Travel seems to foster openness when it forces you to interact with the locals. But in truth, I met very few Portuguese people during my trip. Blame pandemic stir-craziness, a strong job market, or Instagram, but everywhere I went in Portugal, I saw people from countries other than Portugal. I saw Dutch teens on Bird scooters. I heard two Russians plotting to cut the line at the Pena Palace. On the beach, I saw a German guy apparently very much in need of Vitamin D drop trou and begin sunning his butt cheeks.

An Uber driver I had was a local, but he spent the whole ride listening to Portuguese rap and talking on the phone to his buddy Miguel. At the end, he scraped together his best English to ask me for a big tip. Being open to Lisbon felt like being open to Disney World— you weren't observing an authentic culture so much as floating along in an ersatz economy created specifically for you. The difference between traveling and surfing was that I had, albeit badly, communed with the ocean. But I felt like I barely met Portugal.

Not long after I returned, another personality test showed my openness score had gone up a bit, from "very high" to "extremely high." Given that I had spent the week wedged between Czech girls and their selfie sticks, I was happy to see even this minor increase. Perhaps it happened because I had, in small ways, discarded some preconceived notions of myself, like that I wasn't sporty or that I could only vacation with a partner.

In the end, the Lisboan I connected with most was Portugal's most famous poet, Fernando Pessoa, whose bronze statue I passed outside the A Brasileira café. Pessoa, who lived and wrote in the early 1900s, embraced the theme of this book: that identity is flexible, and that within each of us plays a symphony, as he put it. He wrote under more than one hundred different pseudonyms—Álvaro de Campos, Alberto Caeiro—and considered each to be a different persona entirely, with his own style, point of view, and even identity. "Each of us is several, is many, is a profusion of selves," Pessoa wrote.

Much of Pessoa's writing can be read as celebrating openness: "Literature," he famously argued, "is the most agreeable way of ignoring life." However, his openness didn't extend to wanderlust. He found the thought of traveling nauseating, and he had a dim view of people who sightsee for fun. In one essay in *The Book of Disquiet*, Pessoa points out that existence, itself, is a form of traveling: "Life is what we make of it," he writes. "Travel is the traveler. What we see isn't what we see but what we are." To find openness, he seemed to say, you don't have to look at sixteenth-century monasteries. You can look inside yourself.

Being open, I realized, means understanding that a place can't be both universally beloved and a hidden gem. New experiences aren't always unquestionably good; they can be complicated or underwhelming. Sometimes the banal might appear wonderous, and the exotic kind of a letdown. True openness means accepting those possibilities. It requires seeing ambiguity clearly.

6

Plays Well with Others:

Agreeableness

On my original personality test, the one I took in the rank Ocean City hotel, I scored about average on agreeableness, the trait whose paragons are "people people"—selfless, cooperative, modest, sympathetic, trusting, and nice. Though I was trying to improve on agreeableness, part of me accepted my middling score. I belonged to that great horde that doesn't stop for the Greenpeace clipboard people but doesn't give them the finger, either. My life's motto was to neither a chump nor an asshole be, and I was living by it.

As the pandemic wore on, though, my agreeableness level flagged. I spent too much time alone, brooding about people's flaws, searching for evidence they had wronged me. In normal times, the good and bad interactions I had with people evened out, such that my overall impression of humanity was that it was basically fine. Now, since I never saw anyone, I never heard the joke that tempers the backhanded compliment, never reveled in a boozy reassurance session after a difficult day. I had Zoom happy hours, and then I sat by myself and kicked every sarcastic remark around my mind. *What did they mean by that?* This was not agreeableness-inducing.

My disagreeableness surges when someone does something stressful, disrespectful, or just rude. I will get mad at them. But also, and crucially, I will get mad at myself for the decisions that led me to that point. *Why am I still with a guy who puts my $100 swimsuits in the dryer? Why didn't I try harder to make friends in college? Why didn't I become an actuary so I could have a nice house in a warm state and not be so stressed out all the time?* Then I issue the inevitable verdict: *My life would be better if I wasn't such a fucking moron.* That conclusion, perhaps predictably, makes me feel even more disagreeable.

Internally, I'm screaming at myself. But externally, in these moments I'm usually and paradoxically screaming at the person I love, my boyfriend. It's like I can't yell at myself enough, so it spills out onto him—and only him. Sometimes I yell at Rich for real war crimes, like playing the guitar instead of putting away the camping stuff like I told him to. But I also yell at him for minor infractions, like the time he complained that the Shake Shack to which Google Maps had directed us was inside a large and complicated shopping mall. ("Then you fucking plan something for a change!") Often, my anger toward him is displaced anger at people I *can't* yell at, such as the people who write to scold me for saying "like" on the radio.

I learned this style of conflict management from my dad—or, possibly, I inherited it, some chromosome whispering to both of us that your disappointment will feel less suffocating if you expel it as rage. My dad was a Russian immigrant operating with two kids and broken English in backwater Texas, and his nervous system strained under the load. He's reaped the upside of disagreeableness: I've heard people say he is the funniest person they've ever met. But he has a voltage to him, and so do I. Especially in my teenage years, our house often became a chorus of screams.

Growing up, I hated my dad's yelling, so it's ironic that I now replicate it exactly, but in English. Normally, Rich and I speak in a sappy private language—the kind where you intentionally mispronounce "pizza" because you did it once accidentally ten years ago. But every few weeks, something sets me off, and I get sweary and insulting, at a deafening volume. If they overheard me, those couples therapists who say contempt is the most glaring sign of a failed relationship would probably advise us to start divvying up our furniture.

Rich, by contrast, comes from a family that said things like "bless your heart for trying." In Montessori kindergarten, his teacher asked the students to name a trait that describes them, and five-year-old Rich said, "likes to be nice." In more than a dozen years, I've heard him raise his voice maybe twice. Usually, when I'm yelling, he pretends he can't hear me, which is somehow even more infuriating. Afterward, I always apologize, and he always accepts my apology. But one time, he said, "You know that with a kid, that's not really something you can take back, right?"

He's right. Kids remember screaming, and they learn from it. To be a loving, supportive parent, it helps to be both conscientious and agreeable. I had down conscientiousness—the orderly, organized trait—but I needed to develop my agreeableness before I brought additional life onto this already very disagreeable planet. Studies suggest agreeable parents are warmer and less prone to overreacting. They view their children more positively, support them more effectively, and have a smoother "transition to parenting." If I was going to become a parent, I wanted to be an agreeable one.

Agreeableness is the saintly trait, the one that allows you to react calmly to a raging client and to collect a bridal party the size of a basketball team. The agreeable are likable, help people in need, and forgive people who wrong them. They tend to have better relationships with their romantic partners and friends. They laugh, nod, and smile more at other people; they're kinder and less offensive. Think Mr. Rogers, not Mr. T.

Being slightly disagreeable, or disagreeable on occasion, can be useful. Certain times call for us to negotiate ruthlessly, to point out

BS, or to stick up for ourselves and our loved ones. But high levels of disagreeableness can assume the form of hostility, aggression, and callousness. The *very* disagreeable are psychopaths. Women tend to be more agreeable than men, perhaps because when we aren't, we're called bitches and told to calm down.

Agreeableness is another trait that doesn't, when maximized, promise riches. Agreeable people aren't more financially successful than the disagreeable, on average. They have less of a "results emphasis" in life, and they're often so busy helping others that they forget to climb the ladder themselves.

But the agreeable are rich in other ways: They're happier, less likely to get divorced, have a better quality of life, and cope better with adversity. A study that tracked hundreds of people who became disabled over a period of four years found that the more agreeable among them bounced back psychologically much more quickly than the disagreeable ones did. The agreeable aren't martyrs; they're resilient.

I wanted to be more like that, and for the right reasons. I wanted to increase my agreeableness so that I could one day be a good mother, but also so that I could connect better with sources, empathize more with others, and improve my writing. I wanted more and better friendships, and for Rich to feel as loved and safe with me as I do with him.

I once had a session with a hilariously bad online therapist who, after I told her that a family member had just died, decided to say, "I think, underneath *alllll* that, you're a good person." This story has become a favorite of mine to tell at parties—what a psycho!—but I'm still nagged by the possibility that she detected my disagreeableness too easily. What did she see that made her say that? I had a feeling I *was* a good person, but I wanted to be sure.

Agreeableness can be hard to change, though. Part of disagreeableness, it seems, is not wanting to be agreeable. In personality-change studies, people don't often report wanting to change on agreeableness, and so they don't tend to change. (The trait is similar to openness in this way.)

This might be because agreeableness, can, frankly, feel like drudgery. Unlike extroversion, it's not an actual nonstop party. Unlike reducing neuroticism, it doesn't involve yoga, meditation retreats, or spa days. Agreeableness, in fact, has no fun points. It's the arduous march of empathizing with your enemies, managing your anger, and putting others first. It's doing things for other people, usually at your own expense, and often with no thanks in return. (Some readers might register how much this description sounds exactly like parenting.)

A big part of agreeableness is empathy, and empathy is easy enough when it comes to people we like. But when we face opposition, empathizing can feel like losing an argument. Agreeableness can resemble giving in, so when we're challenged, we often prefer to stand our ground, even if it means being disagreeable. Americans tend to cluster along political lines in part because it's easier than constantly straining to be agreeable toward your ideological foes. As the personality psychologist Donn Byrne put it, "Disagreement raises the unpleasant possibility that we are to some degree stupid, uninformed, immoral, or insane."

Therefore, attempting to grow in agreeableness is a test of how you'll react when it feels easier and better *not* to change your personality. Agreeableness asks what you'll do when change feels hard, and you're tempted to give up. It challenges you to speak softly when all you want to do is scream.

Playing the Lyre

My first foray into agreeableness was through a Zoom anger-management class. Though "anger" is technically a facet of neuroticism, it is also one of the most visible signs of low agreeableness: Agreeable people tend to get less angry in the first place, and they don't think about their anger as much as disagreeable people do. They don't tend to swear at their boyfriends over Shake Shack. Agreeableness seems to help people soften their fury whenever it does emerge.

I had picked an inexpensive course offered through my county's social services department, which consisted of eight sessions. In the first meeting, my classmates and I took turns introducing ourselves and describing why we were there; I quickly learned that I was the only person who hadn't been court-ordered to attend.

Then we described how anger had affected our lives. I said it made my relationship worse, such that it sometimes operated less like a partnership and more like a toxic workplace. Other people seemed genuinely worried their anger was hurting their families. One guy shared that he didn't understand why we were talking about our feelings when kids in China and Russia were learning to make weapons, which I deemed an interesting point, because you're not allowed to criticize others in anger management.

The sessions were led by one kind, no-nonsense instructor and another who served as her hype woman of sorts. After each of the leader's remarks, Hype Woman would nod deeply and say "Yes!"

The early meetings did not exactly inspire hope: "Next time you get angry, try a grounding exercise," our instructor said.

"Yes!" said Hype Woman.

That wasn't the only suggestion of its kind. The course contents would be familiar to anyone who has ever killed thirty minutes in the self-help section of a Barnes & Noble. We learned the familiar diplomatic entreaty from couples counseling: "When you X, it makes me Y." We learned about taking deep breaths. We learned that our thoughts are not always accurate. Yes!

Still, I wasn't a star student. In one session, I mentioned how when someone makes me angry, I like to ask them lots of questions. It makes me feel like I can expose their stupidity without *technically* doing anything wrong. It's hovering your hand an inch from someone's face while chanting "I'm not touching you"—but for adults.

"That's not a coping mechanism that I've heard of," the instructor said, her voice quiet with concern. Hype Woman said people might find that triggering—which, to me, is precisely the point. Child Weapons Guy said that sounds like a good way to get yelled at or fired. He seemed like he would know.

We all get angry, of course, but we're not supposed to show it. This wasn't always so. At various points in history, the expression of anger was thought to be justified. Moral thinkers in the Edwardian era discussed the benefits of "righteous indignation," especially for boys and men. "The strenuous soul must fight or grow stagnant or flabby," asserted a representative piece of parenting advice from 1906.

Since then, American culture has pivoted toward anger suppression as the righteous ideal. The notion that we shouldn't express anger at work, for instance, was practically invented by early, Dale Carnegie-esque HR experts. The twentieth-century mandate to "stay cool" symbolizes "our culture's increased striving for restraint," argues the historian Peter Stearns in *American Cool*. In the early 1900s, corporate overlords and other authorities began urging Americans to just grin and bear it. "Cheerfulness, turning the other cheek, became part of a new-style work personality designed to subordinate personal reactions in the interests of moving goods," Stearns writes. The idea that "the customer is always right" smirked itself into being. Industrial psychologists hoped smothering anger would make the workplace "more machinelike," resembling "a smoothly running engine." This new style of work, Stearns writes, was "impersonal, but friendly."

I was reluctant to submit my emotional life to capitalism. Don't I already own an entire wardrobe of Banana Republic cardigans, watch what I say on social media, and use phrases like "circle back," all in order to appease corporate America?

But in my case, anger doesn't trickle out at work. It oozes out at home, all over Rich. Sometimes when I'm yelling, it feels amazing to be so mean—as though finally, I've engulfed Rich in my distress. When he can't smell the smoke, I open a door and show him the leaping flames.

But a few minutes later, I can still see myself, nostrils flared, eyes glassy, screaming things that I don't quite mean and that Rich doesn't deserve. When I yell, he sits back and stares at me in bewilderment. Sometimes I wonder if he's envisioning Hypothetical Future Child sitting on the floor next to him, watching me lose it.

The writer Elissa Schappell encapsulates my fear in an essay she wrote for the collection *The Bitch in the House*. One night, after what sounds like a blitzkrieg of a bedtime routine, Schappell's three-year-old son throws a book at her head, hitting her in the brow bone. Schappell then yells at her kids with "an otherworldly bellow of hell and doom," she writes. When they yelp that she's scaring them, she screams, "Good! You should be scared!" But, she admits, she's scared, too, "scared of hurting my children, of not being able to protect them from myself."

Reading this, I identified a lot more with Schappell than with all the "gentle parenting" influencers that social media had been feeding me of late. I couldn't see myself telling a tantruming toddler, "I know you are feeling so frustrated right now." But I could envision spitting out a "you should be scared!" I didn't need to manage my anger for work, I figured. I needed to do it for love.

One of the main reasons some people get angrier than others is "inflammatory labeling," or the tendency to view people and situations more negatively than is realistic. Inflammatory labeling is calling a co-worker who made a minor mistake a "total idiot," even if it's only in your head. Instead of making you feel better—*That person, sorted!*—these labels do the reverse, giving you cause for even more anger. You wind up in a toxic spiral in which you see someone as completely worthless, get angry that you have to interact with them, and then label them even more inflammatorily. Thoughts can lead us to anger in other ways, as

University of Wisconsin-Green Bay professor Ryan Martin writes in his book *Why We Get Mad*, but inflammatory labeling is one of the major divides between inveterate rage-aholics and people who can manage their fury.

Psychologists' call to resist inflammatory labeling is similar to the stoic Seneca's recommendation not to look for ways to be offended. In guidance that might be helpful for modern-day users of social media, the Roman philosopher once wrote that you should try *not* to determine whether someone spoke ill of you, or whether something was done with malice. Just assume that it wasn't. "It is well not to see everything, not to hear everything," Seneca wrote. (His other anger-management techniques included not getting too busy, avoiding frustrating people, staying well fed and hydrated, and playing the lyre.)

In his book, Martin similarly warns against "misattributing causation," or assuming someone slighted you on purpose, rather than unintentionally. Like that of many psychologists, Martin's research is "me-search": His father's anger frightened him when he was a boy and came between them in adulthood. Martin describes his father snapping at waiters and honking angrily as he drove. "I was never comfortable enough around him," he writes.

He told me it makes sense that I'm mostly only angry around Rich—family can feel like a safe space to express anger. A lot of people bottle up their rage all day and pop the cork when they walk through the front door. In the twentieth century, we chased anger out of the workplace, but in doing so, we sent it home.

Changing Expectations

The anger-management sessions, remedial though they seemed, did contribute to my arsenal of anger-fighting tools. Anger is sparked when people and events in our lives fail to meet our expectations, our instructors said. You expected your kids to do the dishes, but they didn't, and now you're angry. Instead of setting expectations for other people, they said, we should try setting "goals," which have an air of fallibility. As in, the *goal* is for Rich to call the property-management people today—and his failure to do so is akin to a soccer ball swerving too far to the right: disappointing, but it happens.

Ironically, tactics like punching pillows or breaking things don't reduce anger, Martin says. They make you angrier, prompting your brain to hunt for reasons why your body is smashing plates and stomping around. Instead, Martin recommended anger-relieving techniques like switching from stewing to planning, which can make you feel like you have some control over the situation. (*Okay, traffic is bad so I'm going to be late to the dinner party. How can I make it up to my friends later?*) If you regularly enter situations that make you angry, you can practice in advance—when you're not angry—how you'll maneuver your way through them.

A few weeks into anger management, I had a rough day at work and complained to Rich about it.

"Why don't you just march into your boss's office and tell him exactly what you want, or threaten to quit?" Rich said. A solution dreamed up by a computer programmer, whose LinkedIn page gets spammed with job offers daily.

"That's the dumbest fucking thing I've ever heard!" I yelled. "How would we pay our mortgage?"

Rich paused. "You're just like your dad," he said tersely. That only made me yell more.

When I shared this episode in anger management, the instructors said I should be clearer about what I need from Rich when I'm in a bad mood—which is typically listening, not advice. I had never thought to do that.

One week, I blew off anger management to go see Kesha in concert with some friends, because the concert was a group activity, which is good for extroversion. The next time the class gathered, we talked about forgiveness, which Child Weapons Guy is not big on.

"Instead of forgiving someone, I'd rather invite all my enemies onto a bridge and light the bridge on fire," he said.

I thought he should get credit for being honest—who *doesn't* sometimes want to light all their enemies on fire?—but the anger-management instructors were starting to look a little angry themselves.

In the last session, though, Child Weapons Guy seemed contrite, acknowledging that he uses his anger to deal with life, which was a bigger breakthrough than I think anyone expected. I was praised, meanwhile, for an unusually tranquil trip home to see my parents, which my instructors said was an example of good "expectation management." "Be picky with your energy and time," they advised me. It is well not to hear everything, but not to dwell on everything, too.

———————

Ultimately, it was something my therapist said that helped me learn to manage my anger toward Rich. I complained to her about how, lately, Rich was refusing to do any tasks related to moving—like consolidate his belongings or research neighborhoods. He seemed to be dumping all the extra work on me, which made me fume.

I've found that most therapists' advice leans toward self-care and boundary-setting, so I was surprised when my own shrink, a serious young woman who went to Bible college, told me I needed to express more empathy toward Rich. "Try to see it from his perspective," she said. "Why might he be doing that?"

Her advice reminded me of a story one of my anger-management classmates had once shared. My classmate, a gruff middle-aged woman, explained that she had a friend whose chronic lateness had always made her angry. One day, she finally asked the friend why she was never on time. The friend explained that she had once been in a house fire, and now, she couldn't bring herself to leave until she had checked to be sure every appliance was unplugged. By the time she was done checking, she was running late. As she told this story, my classmate's harsh demeanor relaxed a little, as though even the memory of it invited compassion.

Maybe my own frustration would abate if I better understood the people who enrage me. People high in agreeableness tend to pay attention to the mental states of others, and they factor those states into their own actions. They appreciate other people's motives, and that appreciation calms them down. Low empathy and irascibility may seem like two different elements of disagreeableness, but they're related after all.

After weeks of simmering resentment over moving logistics, in the middle of another argument, I finally took a long, penetrating look at Rich.

"Do you . . . not want to move?" I asked.

"No," he admitted. "Not really. I'm willing to do it if you really want to, but I have no particular desire to."

I probably could have guessed this by how he had been acting: setting impossible standards for our future home and refusing to do anything to help find it. But asking gave me the house fire—the secret motivation behind his actions, which all suddenly made more sense. When he grumbled about a house-scouting trip that I had planned, or when he put off sorting through his musical instruments, he was telling me, without telling me, that he had no interest in actually moving. Acquiescing to the move was an extension of his own agreeableness—a concession made for someone else, for the sake of serenity.

The other way to view this, of course, is as passive aggression. I wish he had just told me directly that he didn't want to move. Even so, the admission made me less frustrated that he wasn't helping. Each time I would assign him a moving-related task and he would conveniently drop the ball, I thought to myself, *Well, he did say he didn't want to do it.* Empathy—"made of exertion, that dowdier cousin of impulse," as the essayist Leslie Jamison put it—was what boringly, gently, talked me down from the high of anger.

This empathetic exertion will probably always drain me, benefitting my loved ones at the expense of my own catharsis. This doesn't look very triumphant, but maybe it's not supposed to: Anger grabs attention, but agreeableness moves slowly, to the extent that you hardly notice it.

Anger management had helped me avoid torpedoing my relationships. But I also wanted to *improve* my relationships. I wanted deep, abundant friendships. I wanted to be in the "favorites" of people's phones. And so, I went looking for another benefit of agreeableness: Its ability to help you make an ally out of just about anyone.

Two a.m. Conversations at Noon

Georgie Nightingall has the unusual job of helping people have better conversations, and I was hoping she could show me how. From our first video call, I noticed that Georgie, who has caramel-colored hair and is in her early thirties, is like a cross between an old British anthropology professor and a spunky summer-camp counselor. She dispenses deep truths, but with a whole-face smile.

Georgie started her organization, called Trigger Conversations, in 2016, when she grew tired of having the same kind of exchange over and over again: *What do you do, where do you live?* She wanted to have those two a.m. dorm-room debates about the meaning of life, but to have them as an adult, at networking happy hours while clutching a tiny slice of quiche.

For the extroversion chapter, I had learned to talk casually with strangers, and sometimes even to get them to have coffee with me. But

I still felt a stabbing unease in one-on-one conversations that weren't interviews. I wondered if I was too boring; I wondered if the other person was too boring. I wondered what people even talk about. I rarely left a conversation feeling more agreeable toward my interlocutor, let alone transformed or refreshed.

I hoped Georgie could teach me how to have not just *more* conversations, like an extrovert, but *more meaningful* conversations, like an agreeable person. Many people can grit their teeth through a five-minute chat by the breakroom microwave, but agreeableness involves caring about other people—and showing it in the way you talk to them. Conversation is, as Vivian Gornick argued, "the most vital form of connection other than sex."

People consistently underestimate how much both they and others will enjoy discussing deep topics—having two a.m. conversations. We think it will be awkward; we can't fathom that other people would rather know our motivations and values, rather than how our flight was. I'm someone who has researched this phenomenon extensively and whose job essentially requires having deep conversations. Still, when I get together with friends, I can't help but run through a laundry list of upcoming vacations, work complaints, and homeownership woes. It feels safer. How do I know what they're into? What if they think I'm rude?

Yet in a study by the University of Chicago psychologist Nicholas Epley, people felt more connected after asking each other things like "For what in your life do you feel most grateful?" rather than "How is your day going so far?" "I've now done this with well over a thousand people in experiments," Epley said. Participants, he told me, often say, "'I was surprised by how open the other person was, and that when I opened up to them, they opened up back.' Psychologists respond to that by saying, 'No duh.' That's the way reciprocity works. . . . You earn intimacy by showing intimacy to somebody."

People miscalculate how well these deep interactions will go because we tend to evaluate our own behavior in terms of competency: *How well am I doing this?* But others evaluate us in terms of our warmth: *How kind is this person?* When we obsess about being agreeable "correctly," we underestimate how important it is to do it at all.

Georgie invited me to come to London to participate in a workshop centered on having these kinds of deep conversations. I signed up, figuring I could combine it with my trip to Portugal. In truth, though, Georgie is so persuasive and charismatic that had she told me the workshop was underwater, on Jupiter, and cost $1 million, I would have signed up anyway.

Before we left the Zoom room, I asked Georgie a question that had nagged me ever since I began experimenting with extroversion. Georgie prides herself on starting conversations with strangers, sometimes by making a statement about the other person, like "Cool hat." But that move, in this day and age, felt risky to me. One of the reasons I hesitate to start conversations with men, casual or otherwise, is that if the man decides he doesn't like me or the *Atlantic*, he can post online that I flirted with him and, potentially, get me in trouble. I thought about the time I asked a former colleague to have drinks with me so I could get some career advice, and he kept interrupting our conversation to ask, suspiciously, "What is this about?"

I asked Georgie if people ever think she's hitting on them.

She said you should be aware of boundaries, personal space, consent, and so forth. She doesn't recommend pestering people who react badly to you. But also! "Humans are sexual beings," she said dreamily. "You can't get away from the fact that there may be attraction at some energetic level."

I pictured myself completely misreading British social cues and inadvertently coming on to someone. I decided to wear a fake wedding ring to London just in case.

At Heathrow Airport, I rolled my suitcase to the snaking line of visitors that always makes you feel suspicious, even if you have nothing to hide. When it was my turn, the burly border officer asked me why I was traveling to the UK.

"I'm going to a workshop," I said.

"What kind of a workshop?" he asked.

I turned bright red. "It's on how to have better conversations!" I declared. I would rather have admitted to being in Al-Qaeda.

He laughed and said, "Seriously? You seem to talk nicely to me." Then he waved me through, into England and my new life as a sparkling conversationalist.

That night, suddenly famished, I didn't bother changing out of my rumpled airplane clothes before walking to dinner at a restaurant down the street. As I ate my soup, I noticed the bartender talking and laughing boisterously with one of the other patrons.

I swiveled around—my head instinctively pivots toward loud talking because it could turn out to be newsworthy.

"Hello!" the bartender said to me. He was rail-thin and about a decade older than me.

"Hi!" I said back.

"Are you alone?" he asked. I did not expect this follow-up, since I clearly was.

"Uh, I mean yeah," I said. I mentally scolded myself for giving such a dumb, honest answer. I bet this is how the girl in *Taken* got taken.

The bartender waited a beat, scrutinizing me.

"Are you . . . always alone?" he asked. His voice welled with pity, like he was talking to a soot-smeared orphan on Christmas morning.

Oh, what the hell, I thought. Disagreeableness roared up inside me. *Why didn't I put on eyeliner before I came here? Why are people always trying to fuck with me?*

"I'm on a business trip," I said pointedly, turning back around. I said the words too slowly, on purpose. Maybe I needed this conversation training more than I thought. Maybe everyone does!

———————————

Georgie had asked us to fill out a questionnaire before the program about our motivations, our struggles, and the "baggage" we bring to interactions. On the Tube the next morning I pulled it out and began writing out my responses.

What are you struggling with?
The line between being myself and not being offensive.

Are you carrying any excess baggage into the programme that can be dropped?
People don't like me. I'm a second-tier friend.

How will you celebrate your successes on the programme?
Hopefully an improved score on my personality test.

A little after nine, I arrived at a conference room inside Park Crescent, a gleaming, nineteenth-century Regency building in central London. The others in Georgie's workshop were mostly office workers seeking to connect better with their colleagues, or just with other people. One was an eighteen-year-old savant who was preparing himself for the social experience of college. Though we were supposed to be building friendly warmth with one another, out the window I mostly saw heavy rains, a cadaverous sky, and, strangely, a bright blue portapotty.

One thesis of the workshop was similar to the theme of this book, which is that identity is made up, and that you can experiment with behaving differently to see if it suits you better. Since you wrote the story of who you are, with time you can also rewrite that story. "You can create the kind of reality you want to have," Georgie told us. "And if you don't like it, you can bin it."

Georgie doesn't frown on small talk, per se, but she explained that we can use it to "create avenues, and go down the avenues," like by asking people open-ended questions. Asking what a city someone recently visited "was like," for example, is better than asking them which airline they took to get there.

Mercifully, we also discussed the tactful ending of conversations. The upshot is that it's okay to end them, even by saying something brief like "I really enjoyed this conversation. Let's stay in touch on Twitter." Or as one Italian participant delightfully put it, "I liberate you from myself!"

On the second day, Georgie had us try out longer conversations, for which we paired up and listened to a story our partner told us, then pointed out the feelings and needs they expressed. I talked about my friend who recently had a baby, and how much admiration and respect I felt for her. Her strength and resilience as a new mom inspired me; it was like watching her reveal a talent that had been hidden inside her all this time.

"It sounds like you're feeling wonder. Is that right?" my partner asked. It *was* right. How nice it was to have someone hang on my every word! I was saving a fortune on therapy.

Part of better conversations is better listening, and this was where I always thought I excelled, given my profession. But listening is a delicate art, and it's harder than it seems. As Kate Murphy writes in *You're Not Listening*, much of what people do in conversation is interrogate. We ask rapid-fire questions like "What do you do?" and "Are you married?" that make people feel put on the spot, not connected.

Instead, you should ask questions that encourage elaboration on what the person has already said, Murphy writes, getting at the deeper reasons behind *why* they're telling you something. This will help draw out their emotions and allow them to feel truly understood. For example, if a friend told you they just got laid off, rather than quickly assuring them, "You'll find another job soon," it might be better to say something like, "So now you have to break the news to your family? That's rough. How do you think they're going to react?"

Similarly, Georgie suggested we try listening for the *meaning* behind people's stories, rather than collecting facts. Sometimes, that literally entails asking someone what a certain experience meant for them, and why that meaning was important. We paired with a different partner to discuss a recent vacation in this more feelings-oriented way.

"Tell me about your recent vacation," asked my partner, the eighteen-year-old.

I had already told the group about my trip to Portugal several times that weekend, and I was feeling a little sick of it, but I pressed on.

"I went to Portugal, to Lisbon and Sintra," I said, smiling, knowing he had heard all of this already.

"Who did you go with?" he asked. (We were told to ask our questions in this simple, direct way, which in retrospect seems formulaic, but didn't feel that way at the time.)

"I went by myself," I responded.

"Why did you go by yourself?" he asked.

"I wanted to test myself, to see if I could travel alone and enjoy it," I said.

"Why is it important to you to test if you can travel alone and enjoy it?" he asked.

It was a good question. I thought for a second.

"Because when you've been in a relationship for a while, as I have, you tend to forget what you're like individually," I said. "You become one half of a unit. I wanted to get in touch with that part of myself that's just me, without my partner's influence."

I noticed that this was a much better, and deeper, explanation of the Portugal trip than any of my previous accounts. It certainly provided a clearer view into my psyche than a list of museums and wine bars would have. I felt like I was journaling aloud, and like I had learned something new about myself. "You enter a conversation and you leave a new person," Georgie told us. With good conversation, she says, "life has no upper limit."

At one point, Georgie told us to challenge the "limiting beliefs" we might bring to conversations—those niggling brain fleas that insist we're too boring or fundamentally unlovable. This is probably my biggest obstacle to having better conversations, as evidenced by something that happened on the final morning of the workshop.

That day, I woke up feeling more down on myself than usual. The bartender's comments had stuck with me. *Do I really look like some sort of urchin? Would people treat me better if I got a boob job?* Trying to distract myself on the Tube, I pulled out my phone and read an article about a writer who was mauled by a bear while performing research in Siberia. The animal had cracked open the woman's skull and ripped off her jaw. The writer, who survived, and whose mental health is either extremely poor or unusually robust, called the experience "the bear's kiss"—an intimate entanglement between two mammals, each hungry for something.

The article then mentioned a series of grueling reconstructive surgeries. Suddenly, curiosity ensnared me in its own "kiss." I had to find out the answer to a crucial question: Even though this writer was mauled by a bear, given all the operations she'd had, was she now . . . hotter than me?

I was soon totally consumed by this line of inquiry. I wasn't sure if I was looking for a yes or a no. "No" would bring the sick relief that I'm hotter than at least one person. "Yes" would be great news for the woman, but would also mean I'd have to live with the knowledge that I'm uglier than a bear-mauling victim. (On top of the knowledge that, for some depraved reason, I have an impulse to research such things.)

I google-image searched with the intensity of a homicide detective. I found photos, but then I felt like I had to find more photos, from different angles, and preferably some from before and after the mauling. The automated Tube voice called out "Ladbroke Grove" and "Edgware Road" as I frenziedly punched search terms into my phone, draining my international 5G plan. Even as I did it, I hated myself for being competitive instead of compassionate—*Why do I care? She almost died!*

I had come to one reason why I, and so many others, really struggle with agreeableness: the human animal's total and utter preoccupation with its own self. You have limiting beliefs about yourself, so you fixate on how bad you really are, so you miss opportunities to show interest and empathy toward other people. I thought back to all the times a friend had told me a story, and I listened only for a gap in which to insert my own, similar story. But also about how hard it is to comfort someone suffering through an ordeal you haven't personally endured. I thought about the day I told a professor that I had been evicted from my housing over the weekend, and he robotically responded, "So sorry." And about the friend who begs to hang out but then opens Instagram the second I start talking. Real, human drama is unfolding all around us, but all we want to know is whether we're hotter than a bear-mauling victim.

I knew I had to rewrite this limiting story—one that was standing between me and not only good conversation but true empathy. Mentally, I tried to expand my story to include the off chance that the bartender from that first night was just a creep; I didn't look *that* bad from the flight. And the possibility that this was his bizarre way of hitting on me. And the fact that the bear-mauling victim *herself* cared more about her connection to nature than about the state of her face. And the old chestnut that beauty comes from within—including from your level of agreeableness.

Back at the workshop, Georgie, who is objectively a hottie, told a story about how years ago she thought she was mainly only attractive on the inside, rather than physically. She looked for data to confirm this story: She thought her boyfriends only liked her mind, and that people who smiled at her were weird.

I talked about how I had done something similar on the Tube, trying to figure out if the bear-mauling victim was now hotter than me.

Georgie seemed confused. "Yeeees," she said carefully. "It's similar."

"So what was the verdict?" one of my classmates asked. "Who's hotter?"

"Oh," I said. "It depends on the angle!"

———

Over the coming weeks, I would sometimes struggle to remember these techniques. In a world designed for shallow small talk, discussing emotions, needs, and shared values can feel awkward. While still in London, I FaceTimed Rich and tried to do one of Georgie's exercises with him, but he found it strange and hung up. Then I went out to dinner with a colleague, but we talked about our work and her kids the whole time. I tried to tell her about Georgie's workshop, but the more I explained, the more skeptical she looked.

"Is this a cult?" she asked finally.

But, back in DC, I did feel more in tune with others. One night I met up with another colleague, and, with Georgie's crisp voice in my mind, I was able to root for her without feeling competitive. I delighted in her success and marveled at her work ethic. I didn't explicitly ask what her feelings were, but I could sense them.

Another time, a friend was complaining about work, but I was struggling to follow her story because her job—and her gripes—were so specific. Finally, I interjected with "It sounds like you value autonomy!" That prompted a relieved "Yes!" and a deeper conversational tangent.

Maybe I was having these successes because, thanks to the months I'd spent trying to better myself, I was already different. I wanted different things, and I was pursuing my goals in new ways. Each new personality trait was shifting the others, the way a few brushstrokes can change a painting.

The Boundaries That Unite Us

One day earlier that year, a friend texted to say that she needed me to commit to texting her more regularly. The implication was that I'm a bad friend, which I thought was a valid point.

The thing is, I don't like check-in texts. To me, they have the unsettling air of a boss "checking in" to be sure "everything's okay." I prefer a push mechanism: If I'm feeling bad or need advice, I'll call you, and you should do the same.

I immediately texted one of my other friends to ask if it bothered her that I didn't text her more.

"No," she said. And that's all she wrote.

Clearly, friendship is an inexact science, but I nevertheless wanted my results to improve. I didn't like that so many of my friendships had fallen apart during the pandemic—one ended with a friend yelling at me over dinner; another with a friend yelling at me over lunch. One friendship froze in a flurry of Instagram stories, and another died on a long chain of unread texts. Of course I did have *some* friends, like Anastasia, but it was concerning that she was one of the few who had stood by me for years.

Though some elements of friendship seem tied to extroversion—like the "going out and meeting people" part—others are more connected to agreeableness, like anticipating what your friends need and giving it to them. Agreeable people don't necessarily befriend more people, but their friendships are thicker, more sustaining. As part of my search for agreeableness, I wanted to find friendships, and also to deepen them.

A few months after that text from my friend, I traveled to California to help moderate the *Atlantic*'s "In Pursuit of Happiness" event. In a hotel conference room in Half Moon Bay, I took the stage alongside Miriam Kirmayer, a Canadian clinical psychologist and friendship expert. We were there to discuss the proper care and maintenance of friendships, and to my surprise, the topic was so popular that the crowd spilled out of the room and into the hallway.

During the panel, I deviated from my prewritten prep document and into questions I had about my own friendships, and my role in their scarcity and patchiness. Kirmayer answered them so astutely that afterward I called her for a longer interview.

I asked Kirmayer about all the elements of friendship that it takes an agreeable person to master—like the times when friends let you down, or make you angry, in ways that only people you know well can. For instance, how do you deal with friends who regularly say things that piss you off?

For this, Kirmayer recommended a strategy of assertive communication. When friends bring up a topic you agreed you wouldn't discuss, you could say something like "We said we wouldn't talk about that, and it's important that boundary is respected." You might have to restate the boundary several times, and also reiterate the reason for the boundary: because the topic is hurtful, because it always leads to a fight.

For me, this is where friendships start to unravel. I get pushback from someone, and I assume they're not friend material. Friendship implies ease and fun, while negotiation and diplomacy are the domains of more obligatory relationships, like family and work. If someone's hard to deal with, I've always thought, why deal with them? This is another area in which it's easier to be disagreeable: I've had dozens of friendships silently dissolve, and exactly zero for which I've white-knuckled through a "boundaries" conversation. But Kirmayer explained that boundaries are a way to *preserve* friendships. The reason for the boundary, often, is that it will help you stay close.

In fact, sometimes when it feels like a friend is forcing an apology out of you, it's really an opportunity to relitigate boundaries. With my friend the texter, I should have validated how she felt: "I understand why you get frustrated when I don't text you." But I could also have guarded my side of the fence, since overapologizing can also damage relationships. I could have said something like "But I'm just not a big texter. How else can we stay in touch?" (Regrettably, I did not do this.)

I told Kirmayer that often, the longer I know someone, the more they annoy me—and the more disagreeable I become. Quirks that seemed minor or manageable during the first few brunches start to grate over time. Even Emerson, that great defender of community, wrote that "as soon as the stranger begins to intrude his partialities, his definitions, his defects, into the conversation, it is all over." But I felt like, after a friendship had unspooled in a certain way for years, I couldn't tell a friend to, say, be a better listener or stop giving back-handed compliments.

Kirmayer said this feeling might be a sign that a person needs to diversify their social life. Different friends can serve different needs—you can have a hiking buddy and a venting-about-work buddy. Getting too critical of a friend might mean you're putting too much pressure on them to be everything to you.

Around the time I spoke to Kirmayer, I had signed up for a service whose express purpose was to help me make friends—*best* friends. I joined Bumble BFF, the dating app for friendships. Just like with regular dating apps, the app allows you to swipe "right" on people with whom you might be compatible—but platonically rather than sexually. The app had prompted me to select some interests (choices include astrology, Judaism, and "wine time"), and to answer questions about what I think makes great friendships (I said "vulnerability, kindness, and humor"). I had then messaged a swarm of women and arranged coffee dates of varying levels of awkwardness.

I asked Kirmayer whether I was pursuing the right strategy: Should

I be "dating" lots of different women, or picking just a few with whom to try to develop more meaningful friendships? It's a bit of a balance, she said, but I should be careful not to spread my friendship stamina too thin. "Because we know that frequency and time are important predictors of getting a friendship off the ground, we need to be willing to put in the time," she said.

This comment brought to mind the work of another panelist at that same conference, an author and speaker named Kat Vellos, who had recently published a book about friend-making, *We Should Get Together*. Vellos advocates for something she calls "hydroponic friendship," which involves spending intense periods of time with other people in an effort to "fast-track" a friendship. She even recommends a platonic sleepover, in which a friend comes and stays at your house for the weekend, even if they live in the same town. The goal is to create lots of memories through lots of face time.

This particular idea was too intense for me. I'm in my late thirties, and a lot of my friends have kids. I'm not going to ask them to come spend the night with me; I have enough trouble getting them to spend an evening with me.

But one day I did try out this friendship fast-track, in a way. Some of my new Bumble friends invited me to a Pitbull concert at a faraway stadium in Virginia, beyond the reach of public transit. I agreed to go because I thought it might help us bond. (I also happen to like Pitbull, being, as I am, a fan of Miami and Latin hip-hop.)

So on the appointed night, I loaded the three other career women into my car and put on my inoffensive "Pop Drive" playlist. It rained heavily and we ran late. I kept making wrong turns—I'm a terrible driver, which is something I usually only tell people after we've been friends for a while.

When we finally arrived, we bought Bud Light Lime-a-Ritas and immediately had to go to the bathroom. We traipsed through the mud and the youths and found our seats just as a very moist Pitbull pumped his fist and assured us that it didn't matter if we were Black, white, pink, purple, or Italian, we were going to have a good time tonight. He played all the hits, rapping tirelessly as his celebrity collaborators— Christina Aguilera, Kesha—shimmied on the B-roll projected behind him. Between songs, he gave us pep talks about how only in America could you make it all the way from Miami to Bristow, Virginia.

The night reminded me of the various conferences and reporting trips I'd gone on over the years, in which a bunch of us journalists got thrown together in unusual circumstances for a week or two and emerged as comrades. I'm still friends with some women I traveled to Brazil with ten years ago. All those hours spent interviewing people in favelas and eating chicken necks on farms formed a crucible of accelerated intimacy. Vellos's hydroponic strategy re-creates the friend-making magic of the reporting trip, or the freshman dorm, or the neighborhood playground. If you're not really friends until you've lived through something together, why not live through something together?

After the concert, the Bumble ladies and I spent four hours in the car waiting to get out of the sodden parking lot, inadvertently having the long hangout that Vellos suggested. As the parking attendants stood at the gates, waving ineffectually, we talked divorces and work struggles and bad dates in one sinuous sisterly outpouring.

Even though the concert was muddy and full of drunk children, and even though the night didn't result in everlasting friendship, I'm glad I went. I rarely spend four hours with anyone, and indulging in such a long stretch with this carload of women made me feel like a teenager, talking about whatever, unburdening ourselves, lobbing wacky takes as we grew delirious with exhaustion. It was a two a.m. conversation at two a.m.

Because I had always thought it wasn't possible to make new friends as an adult, I had clung to friendships that made me feel unfulfilled or unheard, figuring that if a friendship wasn't working, I should try harder, because I didn't have any other options. I would leave dinners and happy hours—supposedly "the number-one best thing for my well-being," according to the mental-health listicles—feeling like a frazzled actress after a subpar matinee performance. I reasoned this must just be what friendship is like, that you're supposed to feel slightly worse after being around your friends. And did I really want to start over, to be misunderstood by someone new?

Bumble helped me break free of this mindset of friendship scarcity. I might not find my BFF on Bumble, but I could at least find BFF candidates. If our strained little coffee dates didn't add up to anything, there were always plenty more women to meet, to strike our conversational flints together and see if they spark.

To be sure, I would have preferred to spend this time anywhere other than a godforsaken Virginia parking lot. But in the wise words of Pitbull, "I'm taking all the negatives in my life, and turning them into a positive."

Jesus Was Mocked

On a blazing-hot September day, I reported for my first shift volunteering to serve lunch at a homeless drop-in center near my house in Virginia. Inside, the building was dark and drab, adorned by a few odd selections from the Bible: "Jesus was mocked," read one decorative sign. The center's clients hung out at round tables in the small front room, chatting and waiting for their laundry.

I was issued a nametag, a purple apron, and firm instructions to refuse "seconds" until everyone had been served. "If we give out seconds too early, we run out too early," an older volunteer warned me. "You don't want to run out too early."

The list of agreeableness-boosting personality "challenges" in Nathan Hudson's study includes lots of iterations on volunteering—in addition to literally working for free, he recommends giving to charity and performing small acts of kindness for strangers. Volunteering could be one reason agreeable people are so contented: Various studies have estimated that the happiness lift of regular volunteering feels equivalent to earning anywhere from $1,100 to $80,000 more a year. If that higher figure is to be believed, I made the spiritual equivalent of $4,000 an hour during the twenty-some hours I spent squirting mustard on hot dogs and fetching water bottles for my unhoused neighbors.

My five shifts lasted about four hours each, but the true "rush" began at noon, at which time I was to take orders from our clients and serve up sandwiches, condiments, fruit, chips, drinks, and utensils as quickly as possible. The first day, as I watched the long line of hungry people form, my training from past food-service jobs kicked in and I whirled behind the counter like it was Kids Eat Free night at the deli. When someone asked for a drink, I poured so vigorously that the pitcher's lid came off, spilling lemonade everywhere.

Some people volunteer because they think it will make them feel good, but much of the time, what I saw volunteering made me feel awful. I saw how close people live to the margin and how few luxuries they have. I felt, truly and viscerally, how dumb my problems are, how they shrivel in comparison to real troubles. A common misconception is that poor people, allowed their free choice of foods, will select junk, but in fact nothing on the lunch line was more popular than fresh vegetables. One day, a man asked me for a salad made out of all the sandwich toppings, then sat down and eagerly ate rings of raw white onions. We volunteers were encouraged to eat something ourselves while we worked—it was lunchtime, after all—but I always felt too guilty.

Volunteering also revealed how, often, being agreeable requires being disagreeable—curtly telling people to put their masks on, or to not reach under the partition. Most people were nice and easy, but one man, muttering that he was hungry, grabbed two of everything and then smothered his food with ranch dressing. He wolfed it all down, then got back in line.

This, unfortunately, was against the rules: Not everyone had been served. When the director told him he couldn't have seconds yet, the man started screaming, saying no one was listening to him. Which, in a way, was true. None of us could really know the depths of his hunger and frustration. (As George Orwell noted, "A man receiving charity practically always hates his benefactor.") That day my covolunteer said the devil must be trying to scare me so that I don't come back.

Sometimes it did feel like the devil was coaxing me to quit, pressing on my dual hatreds of monotony and inefficiency. Worse than the busy times were the long stretches when there was nothing to do, and I stood there reading articles on my phone, or looking around longingly for a surface to wipe down. A "fog of dreary senselessness," as Annie Dillard called it, pervaded my afternoons.

This fog was indisputably thickened by my inability to do a thing without declaring myself president of that thing. On just my second day there, my inner McKinsey consultant came out, detecting redundancies yet unable to comment on them on account of my newness. I grumbled, internally, that people should be able to take their own silverware; they usually did so anyway after failing to get our attention. The place's many rules probably have some sort of practical logic to them, but to me they seemed to result, awfully frequently, in my having to tell a starving person that they couldn't have another hot dog.

There were bright spots, too, of course. One man, for instance, walked up to the counter and asked me to dump five spoonfuls of sugar into his coffee.

"Are you sure about that?" I asked. It was a small cup; I didn't want to ruin it.

He nodded. "I want to die sweet," he said.

I smiled. Don't we all?

During every single shift, someone would say something unhinged, but someone else would say something nice. One day a client slid his tray toward the end of the line, where I was handing out desserts. With a shy smile, he said after today he wouldn't need lunch anymore—he had found a job. When one older woman approached the counter, I thought it was to yell at us for being too slow to help her. Instead, she thanked us, saying we were obeying Christ's commandment to provide for "the least of these brothers and sisters of mine." To volunteer is to engage in community service with your fellow man, I found, and your fellow man can be both exasperating and endearing. They can both extinguish your hope and rekindle it at once.

Through volunteering, I learned that I have, deep within me, a motivation to help. I didn't initially feel called to serve, but in another example of how behavior can drive personality, volunteering taught me that I enjoy serving. After spending a day moving sentences around a screen, it felt good to do something tangible, to scoop up potato salad or to hand someone a sandwich. Even more so than devoting myself to the airy world of ideas, I like to fill a hole in society. I like to be needed. As the poet Marge Piercy put it, "The pitcher cries out for water to carry, and a person for work that is real."

"People Are Generally Good"

On Christmas Eve—a time meant for agreeableness but often streaked with just the opposite—I took another personality test, which showed that my agreeableness score had gone up, to "very high." This was in part because I had been intentionally nicer to people around me—my level of the "altruism" facet, once "average," was now considered "high." On top of volunteering, I was paying people compliments, donating books, calling friends just to talk.

At one point I had organized a conversation about abortion with a group of pro-choice and pro-life women, and though it didn't change any minds, it seemed to fade slightly the stark outlines in which we held each other. I apologized to one of the many friends I'd fallen out with during the pandemic. I had dropped everything to help another friend whose family member had become homeless, researching supportive housing and taking her panicked calls.

My higher score wasn't quite the victory that it seemed, though. Scanning down the page of results, under the neuroticism trait, my score on the "anger" facet remained "very high." One day over dinner I asked Rich if I seemed more agreeable lately.

"Eh," he said. "Maybe." He slid his phone across the table, pointing to a text message I had sent him a few days prior:

"clean the fucking house"—no punctuation.

So I'm perhaps not quite ready to teach Sunday school. But there'd been improvement. "You still spike between anger and kindness," Rich said. "But the spikes seem smaller and shorter. And you're less self-centered now."

The most surprising development I saw was the growth in my level of the "trust" facet of agreeableness. My belief that people are "generally good" and "not out to harm me" had risen from "very low" to "about average." If I had to deduce a reason why, it was that all these programs—the anger management, Georgie's workshop, the MBSR—pulled me together with people I otherwise never would have met. Spending quality time with people who are dissimilar to you tends to increase agreeableness, and maybe the real power of those endless Zooms was that they summoned strangers of all stripes into my living room, where my job was not to interview them but to relate to them.

In every type of class—even anger management, to which people had been dragged like surly teens—the participants thanked one another for sharing their experiences, saying they now felt less alone, and that the camaraderie had been uplifting. After years of pandemic loneliness, we were revealing our deepest, quietest battles, and learning with relief that others were fighting them, too. Even if the instructors were useless or flakey, it was the participants who mattered.

Typically my trust for others is tempered by my journalistic skepticism, by my duty to say little, and by the requirement that I later fact-check every word. But in these programs, I wasn't investigating people's confessions. I was bearing witness. I wasn't observing my fellow participants at a remove; I was among them. Much like you can't love a book by reading its reviews, you can't truly trust someone to whom you haven't revealed anything. *You earn intimacy by showing intimacy to somebody.* During my months of agreeableness, I answered humanity's knock, and, subconsciously, learned it came in peace.

7

Get 'er Done:

Conscientiousness

I f you are conscientious, you might have skipped straight to this chapter, racing past the angsty moonbeam stuff in favor of productivity hacks for your already hustle-tastic life. Conscientiousness means getting shit done, never skipping leg day, jumping face-first into your inbox and not emerging until the thing reaches zero, or the heat death of the universe, whichever comes first. Personality tests tend to measure the trait by asking about organization skills, efficiency, and a tendency to stick with one's goals.

It's possible to be too conscientious, of course. Very high levels of the trait can cross the line into perfectionism and rigidity. You can become so regimented that you forget how to enjoy life. But generally, conscientiousness is highly sought after. Because of its association with motivation and persistence, conscientiousness is the trait that best predicts professional success, and it's the one employers prize most. Conscientious people tend to be physically healthier, too, because these titans of impulse control like to exercise and eat right. "Succinctly, conscientiousness is a personality trait that promotes better health, wealth, relationship, and school success," writes the psychologist Brent Roberts. This is precisely why so many people want to become more conscientious.

Conscientious types tend to be morning people and spend more time working. They don't tend to procrastinate. But ironically, as I approached conscientiousness, the final of the five personality traits, I put off writing about it.

The reason is that I am very conscientious, and I have been for most of my adult life. My most recent personality test reported that I'm more conscientious than 93 percent of the population. I hate being late, losing things, or being seen as a slacker. I have multiple overlapping to-do lists, and a calendar I look at daily. I can't remember the last time I missed a deadline. When I need to make a decision, even in my personal life, I talk to experts and write an overview of my findings that I share with other key decision-makers, usually Rich. (Ask me about the "hurricane risk" subdocument in our shared "Florida move" Google Drive folder.) Conscientiousness soothes my neuroticism; I may still be ambushed by misfortune, but at least I've prepared for the worst.

I mostly appreciate my conscientiousness through the absence of minor injuries and inconveniences I'd face if I was *less* conscientious. My friends may have their grumbles about me, but flaking at the last minute isn't one of them. I suspect my bosses' willingness to let me work remotely hinges on my pattern of hitting deadlines like a metronome. And I like how my doctor, after tsking about my thyroid, my ovaries, and other parts of my body, always pauses happily while listening to my strong, steady heart.

"You must exercise a lot," she says with a smile.

"Yes, sure do," I say smugly.

Still, I felt weird about expounding on one of my few strengths. Who wants to hear someone brag about how hard she works? And obviously, when undertaking this project, I didn't want to change my level of conscientiousness, either.

I am this way, though, because I used to not be this way. I learned to be conscientious through trial, error, and a few frighteningly close calls, mostly in my twenties. And this is where I, and the other newly conscientious people I interviewed, can do our favorite thing: be instructive.

I'm far from the only person who has ever evolved from disarray in adolescence to Swiss-watch precision in adulthood. A woman named Julia York has a similar story.

Throughout high school and college, Julia told me, she did the bare minimum. She'd finish just enough of the assigned reading to wing the class discussion, or pump out the entire twelve-page paper the night before it was due. Though her grades were decent, she procrastinated and relied on the pressure of the last minute. At one of her first internships, her boss told her that she didn't take enough initiative.

About three years after college, Julia quit her office job to become a freelance writer. For five months, she told everyone she was becoming a freelance writer. The only problem was that she didn't write much at all. Julia wasn't sure she was qualified to write, so she didn't sit down to try. Overwhelmed, she spent her afternoons watching *Game of Thrones* instead. "It was really jarring to feel like there's something that I am really interested in, but I'm not doing anything about it," she told me.

Julia thought she was just dispositionally lazy. That is, after all, how a lot of us lambaste ourselves after we blow it in some way. But the less freighted way to look at her predicament is as a temporary failure of conscientiousness, not as a permanent character flaw. And luckily for Julia, conscientiousness can grow.

Eventually, Julia ran out of money. She took a job as a receptionist at a high-end hair salon, where she washed towels, ran errands, and cleaned old food out of the fridge. She felt like she had retreated backward five steps while some of her peers were starting grad school. Day after day, running menial errands, she grew afraid that she was going to miss out on her potential, that she would let her life slip by.

Julia read some self-help books, one of which included an anecdote about a CEO who wrote a book by writing for fifteen minutes every day. Julia was surprised; she had always thought that achieving something meant letting it take over your entire life. But the story showed how most people can accomplish at least some version of their goals, not through Herculean pushes but by putting in consistent effort. Maybe she could, too.

A few years ago, Julia decided to try self-employment again—this time as a web designer. But now, she vowed to approach it as a business. She broke her daily calendar down into tranches of time—anywhere from fifteen minutes to an hour—and labeled each time period with a task, a technique also known as "timeboxing." She wrote down the time she was supposed to be at the gym. She made spreadsheets of deliverables for her various clients.

In the office of her home in Spokane, Washington, Julia hung a huge mirror on the wall. With a dry-erase marker, she wrote on it all of her goals for the year, the date her taxes were due, mantras to keep herself motivated, and anything else important. Then she would sit at her desk and look into the mirror, reflected in her own ambitions. "This makes me sound like the Unabomber," she said. But, you know, it worked. There was something about being *with* her goals, looking *at them* in front of her, that made them more tangible.

Julia maneuvered her web-design business toward social-media marketing and content creation, and not long afterward, her first major client found her. Soon, she was making as much as she had at her hair-salon job. Though it wasn't much, "I felt like I had crossed that divide between trying to make it work and it actually working," she told me. Since then, she's quadrupled her monthly income.

Unlike some of the other traits, the psychologist Nathan Hudson has found that merely going through the motions of conscientiousness—making the weekly schedule, putting in the hours of study time—increases conscientiousness, whether you've decided to be more conscientious or not. (Meanwhile, to become less neurotic, a person has to *want* to be less neurotic.) "Just doing conscientious behaviors, whether you realize you're doing them or not, will make you more conscientious," Hudson told me. That was the case for Julia. Simply by using some strategies associated with conscientiousness, like scheduling and writing things down, Julia adopted those behaviors and reversed her self-employment fortunes.

When we spoke, Julia was in her early thirties and still successfully self-employed. These days, she can't fathom not taking initiative. Every day, she uses a paper calendar, a digital calendar, and a checklist app called Todoist. When she writes, she sets an online stopwatch and puts her phone away. She's attained conscientiousness, even though at first it seemed beyond her grasp.

The Challenge of Conscientiousness

To increase conscientiousness, the suggestions from Hudson's "You Have to Follow Through" study include the usual anal-retentive genuflections: preparing for things in advance, laying your clothes out the night before, proofreading, making lists, doing chores, setting reminders, not letting the dishes "soak." Your mother would be very pleased to hear you're doing this. You also, probably, would struggle to do most of this unless you're already pretty conscientious.

That's the thing about conscientiousness: It's hard to do it if you don't already do it. Just like Julia could proclaim herself a freelance writer but not actually do any freelance writing, you can wish that you were better organized or more productive and still not have the faintest idea how to get there. Many of us might be sold on the *idea* of personality change, but conscientiousness exemplifies how difficult it can be in practice: The very behaviors that turn you conscientious require a certain level of conscientiousness to perform. Low conscientiousness can look like a series of bad habits—procrastinating, running late, and overindulging—and as the habit guru James Clear has observed, "the task of breaking a bad habit is like uprooting a powerful oak within us."

Take timeliness, an element of conscientiousness that foils many of us, in part because estimating time is itself a complicated skill. The truth is that *most* people are bad at knowing exactly how long things will take. Most of us don't time our activities, so we have little memory (or the wrong memory) of how long we spent doing them. When the boss asks whether we can get that report done in a week or a month, we don't really know. Instead, we guess, and we tend to guess toward the shorter deadline. Who doesn't like to be optimistic? In the end, that optimism looks like low conscientiousness when we run late.

Oddly, we are more likely to underestimate the duration of a project when it's both a longer and more *familiar* task, according to Michael Roy, a psychologist at Elizabethtown College. As you become more experienced with a task, your brain tends to group its components into bigger "chunks," and then it (wrongly) assumes that three chunks can be dispatched more quickly than ten. Even if you've written the same type of report dozens of times before, you'll forget that it usually takes at least a week just to organize your notes.

Roy says the secret to combatting this underestimation problem is to time yourself as you do things. Again, this seems like a great idea. But it also seems like something only a conscientious person would remember to do.

Even famous promoters of conscientiousness rarely knew how to walk the walk. Benjamin Franklin, who wrote effusively about conscientious virtues like "order," "cleanliness," and "moderation," struggled in practice to maintain this level of self-discipline. In his *Autobiography*, he laid out what he humbly called a "plan for attaining moral perfection," including a schedule for the "twenty-four hours of a natural day": He planned to rise at five a.m., wash, breakfast, and address "Powerfull

Goodness." From eight a.m. to five p.m., he would work. From six p.m. to nine p.m., he would examine the day, and perhaps engage in "music or diversion" before going to bed. It would be the perfect, conscientious day.

However, much like people who flop into bed at 1 a.m. with a sink still full of dirty dishes, Franklin found that "my scheme of Order gave me the most trouble." His careful schedule fell apart when he had unexpected appointments. He also, for the life of him, couldn't keep track of his documents and belongings. (One historian noted of Franklin that "strangers who came to see him were amazed to behold papers of the greatest importance scattered in the most careless way over the table and floor.") "I found myself incorrigible with respect to Order," Franklin wrote ruefully. Do as Ben says, apparently, not as he does.

In fact, as I perused *Daily Rituals*, Mason Currey's book about the habits of creative types, I soon noticed that these weren't routines that fostered conscientious productivity so much as strange rites performed in the throes of procrastination, between shots of alcohol and doses of amphetamines. The novelist Thomas Wolfe got in the writing spirit by fondling his genitals; Patricia Highsmith kept a bottle of vodka by her bed. Currey's subjects would rend their garments about how little work they were getting done and then proceed to do no work whatsoever. Many of them lunged for conscientiousness and landed instead in a speed-addled panic, chain-smoking under the threat of deadlines. The eighteenth-century English writer Samuel Johnson believed that "idleness is a disease which must be combated," but admitted that "I myself have never persisted in any plan for two days together."

Conscientiousness can, indeed, make us feel most "incorrigible." But luckily, there are ways you can overcome this human liability toward languor.

Imagining the Best (and Worst) Case

A sign that you want to increase in conscientiousness might be that you're googling "how to stop procrastinating"—possibly even while putting off some work. To some people who are low in conscientiousness, the future rewards of "good" decisions don't matter as much as the present rewards of "bad" ones. Spending thirty minutes on social media feels good now but will probably have negative consequences later. Spending thirty minutes finishing a work presentation might feel boring now, but will be beneficial later. Guess which option a person low in conscientiousness would choose.

But a technique called episodic future thinking can help correct this cognitive error. The researchers Cristina Atance and Daniela O'Neill describe episodic future thinking as our ability to project ourselves into the future, essentially "pre-experiencing" something, much like we might recall a prior vacation or argument. But instead of remembering the past, the practice entails vividly imagining a future scenario, down to the explicit details—like what you'll be wearing for the work presentation, who will be in the room, and from which deli you'll order a sandwich afterward. This act turns our attention to those far-off rewards, and to what we could be doing now to make them more likely. (Clicking "new slide" on that PowerPoint, alas.)

In studies, episodic future thinking has been shown to promote a variety of conscientiousness-related behaviors, like abstaining from alcohol, nicotine, and overeating. The more frequently and specifically you imagine these futures, the better this works.

This all reminded me of my conversations with Julia, and how different forms of episodic future thinking seemed to spur her along. For one thing, she's always planning. Among the first thoughts she has when she wakes up is *I have to do* this, *so that in two years, I'm at* this *point.*

But initially, I was confused because she—and many others I interviewed—also seemed to be driven to conscientiousness by fear. They weren't imagining positive futures; they were dreading negative ones. "I actually feel like I'm more motivated by fear of not reaching a positive outcome," Julia told me. She'd do anything to avoid going back to another version of the hair salon, to a boring job with no autonomy.

I took this to Donald Edmondson, a professor of behavioral medicine at Columbia University. He clarified that episodic future thinking doesn't mean just daydreaming about the future. It's imagining likely different outcomes—positive *or* negative—that might be influenced by your choices today.

As long as the negativity doesn't become so overwhelming as to be paralyzing, imagining a dark future can be motivating. It can make us think, *What are the behaviors that I have to engage in to offset risk for this future scenario?* Edmondson told me.

In fact, Edmondson added, "the episodes that I use personally are almost always the negative ones." When we spoke, a blood test had recently revealed to Edmondson that he was prediabetic. He knew that put him at a higher risk of developing diabetes, and possibly cardiovascular disease and stroke. He could picture himself in the future, twenty or thirty pounds heavier, struggling to climb up a hill near his house. He visualized his chest tightening, running out of breath, his partner worrying. *Is he having a heart attack?*

Then he asked himself, "What are the changes I would have to make to keep this from happening?" This kind of thinking, though negative, makes the conscientious behaviors of eating right and exercising look more appealing.

On a personal level, I knew exactly what Edmondson was describing. Before I found my way to conscientiousness, I would procrastinate, eat abysmally, and amble along without any real goals. When I started to turn it all around, episodic future thinking—the negative kind—was partly responsible.

Though I made good grades, as a teen my conscientiousness often lapsed. It was like I could *only* make good grades; I couldn't do anything else. In the mornings in high school, I would sleep in so late that, just as my mom was pulling out of the garage, I would slide into the car barefoot, my backpack in one hand and my Steve Madden loafers in the other. On my sprint through the kitchen, I'd shove a raw Pop-Tart in my mouth. One time I was actually late to school, and the teacher let the class vote on whether I should get a detention. They overwhelmingly voted yes.

It wasn't just the lateness. Well into college, I had a bad habit of not opening mail or dealing with paperwork. I didn't have a filing cabinet or anywhere else to store important papers, so I would act as though forms, letters, and the entire US postal system didn't apply to me. As a teen, I would stack documents in a corner of my room and never look at them, which is how I almost threw away the envelope that informed me of my full-tuition college scholarship. A few days before the deadline to respond, I found it stuffed between a bunch of other unsorted mail in a pile on the floor. That letter was worth $100,000.

But now, on Hudson's test, I scored "very high" on conscientiousness. What had changed?

Partly, I grew up and admitted that a fifteen-minute drive will never take eight minutes, no matter how "good" traffic seems. I learned to make checklists and to open my mail. But what really made me more punctual and organized was the possibility of having—or rather, not having—a career in journalism.

This industry is so competitive and cutthroat that conscientiousness is the baseline, the thing you need to have when your editor says your draft is merely "a good start." And any government official is more likely to talk to a reporter who was on time than one who was late, no matter what their first drafts look like.

A few times in journalism grad school in LA, I missed interviews with experts because I failed to realistically assess traffic. I once left my expensive camera on a bus, and I was late to the first meeting of the class taught by my own graduate advisor. Eventually I recognized that these small slipups might cost me a chance at journalism, a career for which I had moved across the country and dedicated two years of my life.

I imagined having put in all this work only to fail, just because I forgot that La Cienega gets hairy after four p.m. I had my own version of Julia's nightmare scenario: I envisioned myself returning to the job I'd had before journalism school, working at a failing nonprofit where my main responsibility was assembling IKEA furniture. Once, my task for the entire day was to set up my boss's new iPhone.

It was unthinkable. Whenever I recalled that place, I cringed. And then I started to be on time.

Finding a Conscientiousness Role Model

At the start of his first semester of college, Zach Hambrick was dropped off by his mother, Genie, and stepdad, Bob. The couple lived in another state, and as they were driving away, Genie grew teary-eyed. She was going to miss her son.

"Don't worry," Bob said. "There's a good chance we'll be coming back to pick him up soon." He meant that young Zach would probably fail out of college. At the time, Zach thought so, too.

Zach grew up in the southwest tip of Virginia, in a small town called Marion. School never grabbed his attention; instead, as a teen he started drinking heavily and playing golf religiously. He graduated high school with a C average and ranked 70th out of a class of 140. His SAT scores were terrible, too, so when it came to college, he didn't have many options.

He applied to two small schools. When he drove up to visit one of them, Marietta College in Ohio, he spent the weekend drinking blended whiskey with some frat brothers. "It turned into a bit of a spectacle," Zach told me.

Concerned he had a drinking problem, Marietta's administrators informed Zach he'd be on probation if he enrolled, he says. That was enough of a threat to make Zach choose the other school, Methodist College (which is now Methodist University), in Fayetteville, North Carolina.

Zach enrolled, but he didn't have high career aspirations. In his remote corner of Appalachia, he didn't know many people with interesting jobs. He decided to stick with what he loved and chose a major in golf management. He bumbled through the first few months without any study skills; he had never really written a paper before.

But then Zach met two people who would help him take his level of conscientiousness from zero to damn near one hundred. In his first year at Methodist, Zach met Ron, a student in his thirties who was finally getting a chance at a higher education. Zach and Ron recognized each other as kindred spirits: two smart, golf-loving guys who were totally unprepared for college. They started studying together, reading dense books by philosophers like Martin Buber. It felt meaningful to swim through such heavy material together. "It was mutually inspiring, in a way," Zach says.

The other person was the director of the golf-management program, Jerry Hogge, with whom Zach loved to talk about the future of the golf industry. Unlike many people, Jerry took Zach seriously. He would encourage Zach's ideas, and he told Zach that he had academic potential. "If you've never been told that, to hear that can be transformative," Zach says. "And I think it was in my case."

Before long, Zach got a filing cabinet and a study-skills book called *Where There's a Will There's an A*. He began following its (quite simple) precepts, like that you should find a quiet place to study and highlight when you read. He finished his first semester with a 2.7 grade point average—much better than he had expected.

Through his friendships with Ron and Jerry, Zach had naturally discovered something that seems to help many people become more conscientious: getting support and advice from others. Many newly minted go-getters rely on role models, guides, or mentors to show them the way. A concept called the "mutually reinforcing orientation" suggests that conscientiousness develops when people start to admire role models who exhibit persistence and self-control. It's not the specter of bad grades that encourages a wayward teenager to study into the night; it's the promise of being like someone they respect.

In fact, relying on the example of others sometimes works better than trying to get motivated on your own. For one recent study, researchers at the University of Pennsylvania rounded up a group of people who said they wanted to exercise more. The researchers told some of the participants to go out and learn an exercise-motivation strategy from someone they knew. But for another group of participants, the researchers themselves provided the exercise-motivation strategy (for example, "for every hour that you exercise, allow yourself fifteen minutes on social media"). Over the course of a week, the participants who learned the strategy from their friends ended up exercising for about thirty more minutes than the group that was given the strategy by the researchers. Learning from their peers might have helped the participants feel more autonomous, increased their commitment to their goals, and created some positive peer pressure. There's something about learning from others, and alongside others, that inspires conscientiousness.

These conscientious role models can be theoretical: You might just ask yourself what a healthy or productive person would do in a given situation. But often, it's someone you know well—and maybe kind of envy. Laura Loker, a writer and illustrator based outside DC, told me she began her transformation from messy to tidy when she moved in with roommates who were very neat. "We collectively raised each other up a little bit," she says.

Similarly, Ron and Jerry gave Zach a license to learn. He felt empowered to be in an environment where "there were people who knew some shit," Zach told me.

After a couple of years, golf management started to bore Zach a little. He took an introduction to psychology class, and right away it engrossed him. He had always been interested in exceptional feats and in measurement, and now he saw these were elements of the study of human behavior.

Zach switched majors to psychology, where he met even more professors who nurtured his curiosity. He decided he wanted to go to grad school for psychology, so he dedicated himself to his schoolwork even further. He spent a week preparing for every test and never turned anything in late. He began studying hard for the GRE, making flash cards and taking dozens of practice tests. Motivating him was a mortal fear that if he failed, he'd have to return to his hometown and become an assistant manager at Wendy's. (There's that episodic future thinking again.)

This kind of deliberate practice is one of the hallmarks of grit, or the relentless pursuit of goals that's highly correlated with conscientiousness, according to the psychologist and *Grit* author Angela Duckworth. Deliberate practice means practicing in order to get better, tracking improvement and drilling repeatedly to reach a stretch goal— the kind of work Zach was putting in at college. But it also means getting feedback from others on how you're doing. "Almost all performers benefit from having a coach," Duckworth told me. "Writers need editors, athletes need coaches, children need parents, and students need teachers." Zach needed Ron and Jerry. It's easier to venture into the unfamiliar world of conscientiousness when there's someone traveling alongside you.

Zach's deliberate practice paid off. When his GRE results arrived in his college mailbox, he opened the envelope and thought, *This is going to change things.* He had done well enough to get into Georgia Tech, a top graduate program. He finished college with a 3.9 grade point average.

Today, Zach is a tenured psychology professor who studies the scientific origins of skills and expertise. Essentially, he studies how people learn to succeed. One of his research-backed tips for people who want to improve on various skills—be it sports or music—is to work with a coach, or a mentor. Find someone who can give you pointers and support along the way. After all, it worked for him.

My conversations with Zach and Julia helped me understand how people can become more conscientious during young adulthood, a pliable time when many of us fail at orderliness and persistence. But plenty of older adults find conscientiousness difficult, too. In fact, aspects of this trait can feel even more elusive when you otherwise have your life together. To learn how to attain conscientiousness later in life, I visited a woman named Dana K. White.

The Process of Elimination

Dana had to guide me by phone to her house; Google hadn't yet mapped out her faraway pocket of North Texas. "Go back the way you came and look for a gray house with a big circle drive," she said.

A golden-haired mom of three and a self-proclaimed former "slob," Dana greeted me in the driveway wearing jeans and a hot-pink shirt. Then she led me inside her house, where everything looked neat and Christmasy: the tree trimmed, the stockings hung, the dining table, unlike most other dining tables in America, cleaned off and ready for eating.

It hadn't always been like this.

For much of her life, Dana could never figure out why she was so intelligent in most ways but couldn't seem to keep her house tidy. Part of conscientiousness is being neat and organized, but this seems to be where even high-achieving, ambitious people struggle. Leading a big and interesting life leaves little time for trifolding your T-shirts.

In high school, Dana's locker was so packed that everything tumbled out whenever she opened it. Her bedroom floor was a knee-deep bog of belongings with a path winding through it. "I was a random putter-downer," Dana told me. Receipts and beauty products would leave her hands and settle onto shelves and floors and in closets, and she would barely notice.

In adulthood, the surfaces of her house were so cluttered that if she was expecting company, it would take her weeks to clean up. Her kids avoided inviting friends over, since they knew it would require a marathon cleaning spree that made their mother cranky. Her husband was willing to help with chores, but because he worked outside the home, Dana felt like the house was mostly her responsibility. She didn't like how messy it was, and she was tired of always losing things. But she wasn't sure how to change, either.

As she sat in church one morning, fretting over the state of her home, Dana decided to try to get organized and to blog about her efforts. She would call the project *A Slob Comes Clean*. "I tried and tried to think of a nicer word than 'slob,'" she wrote. "But I decided that if I was going to do this, I wasn't going to sugar-coat anything."

Dana began with a simple goal: She would do the dishes every day. The dish-doing helped her understand one source of her problems, which was her tendency to see everything as a project. Her approach to other things in life was "just throw myself into something and make it perfect, and then sleep for a week," she told me. But cleaning doesn't work like that; it's an ongoing, iterative process.

Dana found she was going too long between cleanings, then tackling each accumulated mess as a giant, all-day affair. If the sink was filled with dishes, she would wait until it filled a little more. Her family would be drinking out of measuring cups before she ran the dishwasher. Having an empty sink made it easier for her to cook—and to see progress.

The second thing Dana realized was that she simply had too much stuff. A creative former theater teacher, she would collect bric-a-brac—like clothes from garage sales and a cast-iron bathtub—that sat unused. For a while, she thought she could find a system to organize everything. But it turned out she needed to get rid of things, not organize them. Containers, she came to understand, are not meant to help you acquire more stuff; they're a limit on how much stuff you can acquire. The remedy was blunt and simple: She started throwing stuff away. Now, she told me, "I view my entire house as a container. . . . If there's room for it, then I can keep it. If not, I may love it, but I can't keep it."

After about six months of dedicated decluttering, Dana's house was transformed. An entire half bath, previously obstructed by storage, had gradually reemerged. She could host a spur-of-the-moment Friendsgiving without the previsitor panic. All along, she kept posting on her blog, and in the years since, she has expanded *A Slob Comes Clean* into books, videos, and podcasts. She advises people not to buy new storage containers until they've decluttered so much that their stuff easily fits into their existing space. She assures them that you can make progress decluttering even if you only have a few minutes.

During my visit, Dana brought me into a side room so I could see a demonstration of her decluttering process. The room was being used for storage, but her husband hoped eventually to convert it into a study. Dana's focus that day was on tidying a shelf against a wall. First, she looked for obvious trash—old receipts, a broken picture frame—and tossed it into a large gray Kohl's bag. Then she relocated the items that remained—like a Julie Andrews CD—to the places she thought she would look for them first. If it occurs to her that she *wouldn't* go looking for something, it should be tossed: She placed an old mirror studded with hooks into a "donate" box.

Within a few minutes, she had removed enough stuff to reveal a container for storing cords, and the cerulean blue of the shelf underneath. Even she seemed surprised by what a difference a little less junk makes. "If I just look at this right now, it's still super messy," she said. "But if I compare it to what it looked like five minutes ago, I'm like, 'Okay, that was worth my time.'"

————————

Dana had stumbled onto the open secret of home organizing: Most "cleaning" and "organizing" is actually decluttering. Surfaces look neater when there is less stuff on them, and it's easier to clean when you're not wading through old Tupperware and tinsel.

This seems especially true for those who are becoming more organized (i.e., conscientious) after a lifetime of messiness. "In high school, I honestly just had too much stuff for the space that I was trying to keep it in," says Laura Loker, the writer who became neater when she moved in with neat roommates. When she finally got organized, the trick was in accepting that "you have to leave a lot more empty space than you think you need. If it's like Tetris putting everything away, it's not gonna work." Andrew Weintraub, a health-insurance executive who transformed from "Pigpen" to a neat freak, said that one of his main tips is to "throw away, throw away, throw away. Don't worry about what you might need. . . . Use the trash mercilessly."

It's not new, this idea that owning too much can be a perverse kind of hardship. In *The Longing for Less*, Kyle Chayka traces the American roots of minimalism to a twentieth-century philosopher named Richard Gregg, who espoused what he called "voluntary simplicity," or prizing "psychic goods" like friendship and love over physical possessions. "Possessing so much stuff as a consequence of wealth causes nervous strain because we're forced to make so many different decisions every day," Chayka writes, explaining Gregg's philosophy. Except the stuff problem has only grown worse since then: Gregg was concerned about the rise of telephones and motorcars. Think of the nervous strain brought on by a decade of one-day delivery.

Even professional organizers will tell you that minimalism is the secret weapon of the organized. "The biggest impediment to having people put things away is lack of space," says Nicole Anzia, owner of a home-organizing business in DC called Neatnik.

Nicole told me that many of her clients are busy working moms who are too overwhelmed by all the decisions they're making at their jobs and within their families to spend time adjudicating their belongings, too. Washington is full of lawyers and journalists whose desks groan with old papers and notebooks. White-collar professionals in this town can typically afford to buy whatever they need—often, more than they need.

The pandemic added to the object overload. People spent their anxious hours on Amazon, clicking "buy" without thinking about where all those board games and kitchen utensils were going to live. When you have too much, you don't know what you have, so you buy duplicates, which only adds to the mess. Or you spend time looking for things, which stresses people out. Unable to cope, people will throw things in storage. Or they call Nicole.

The first step of Nicole's process is typically purging. To stay organized, Nicole told me, you have to "continually be getting rid of stuff." She recommends going through all your possessions a couple times a year and tossing what you don't use, or throwing away one thing for every new thing you buy.

Do people feel guilty about the seeming wastefulness of this stuff-culling? Oh yes, and that's one of the biggest obstacles. But think of it this way: "Either you're gonna throw it away, or somebody's gonna throw it away," Nicole told me. She paused. "Like when you die, somebody is going to come into your house and throw everything away." So you might as well get it over with.

Doing More by Doing Less

Decluttering is the most glorious conscientiousness advice because it doesn't require you to buy new equipment, or fancy storage units, or a bigger house. It just requires you to throw things away. It's productivity through paring down, not scaling up—and this ethos translates to other elements of conscientiousness, too.

Minimalism, in all its forms, has trickled through the ultra-conscientious world of self-improvement lately. Even some productivity maestros have been forced to admit that no bullet journal or pomodoro timer will allow you to accomplish everything you want, as quickly as you want. You're going to have to pick and choose. In his book *Four Thousand Weeks*, the life-hack columnist Oliver Burkeman describes sitting on a park bench one winter morning, "feeling even more anxious than usual about the volume of undone tasks, and suddenly realizing that *none of this was ever going to work*." Instead, he advocates embracing "finitude," including by limiting your priorities, settling on a relationship and career, and celebrating the "joy of missing out." "Since hard choices are unavoidable, what matters is learning to make them consciously," he writes, "deciding what to focus on and what to neglect, rather than letting them get made by default—or deceiving yourself that, with enough hard work and the right time management tricks, you might not have to make them at all."

This is similar to the philosophy espoused by Greg McKeown in his book *Essentialism*, which implores its readers to worry about accomplishing the *right* things, rather than *more* things. "Only once you give yourself permission to stop trying to do it all, to stop saying yes to everyone," McKeown writes, "can you make your highest contribution towards the things that really matter." McKeown argues you should evaluate decisions in life through something called the 90 percent rule: If something doesn't score at least a 90 out of 100 on your most important decision-making criterion, reject it. (McKeown acknowledges this can be tricky when the person assigning you things is not yourself but a boss of some kind. In those cases, it's worth using the passive-aggressively professional "Which of these other projects should I de-prioritize to pay attention to this new project?")

Essentialism is where I, an extremely conscientious person, have taken things perhaps to the extreme. I wear roughly the same thing every day—usually workout clothes so I can exercise in the middle of the day without changing. I don't carry a purse. I rarely buy home decor, except to cover up weird holes in the walls. I will never plan a wedding. I don't shop for Christmas gifts. I simply don't do anything that I don't value and that will take up precious space, time, and money.

I learned to live this way by being a millennial who graduated into a recession and who has had, more than once, to box up her entire life and move apartments in a weekend. "My generation has never had a healthy relationship with material stability. There are always too few resources at hand or too much competition for what's left," writes the minimalism author Kyle Chayka, also a millennial. Chayka describes living in a series of sublets in his twenties, treating each room like a hotel he might have to leave in a hurry. Maybe the only thing millennials have on other generations is our ability to live minimally in order to survive.

Not everything can be all about efficiency, of course. Every creature has comforts, and I personally spend a fortune on yoga classes, books, and movies. You shouldn't make your life boring or inconvenient for the sake of conscientiousness. But the stories of the newly conscientious people I interviewed suggest that you will accomplish more if your goals are more specific. It will be easier to clean if you have fewer belongings. You'll be more punctual if you are less over-scheduled. After a life spent hacking through a thicket of tasks and tchotchkes, minimalism can feel like reaching a sunlit clearing—a sense of achievement, but with space to breathe.

Decluttering made it easier for Dana to enjoy her house, to know what she has and to remember where it is. Zach's academic performance took off when he narrowed his focus to psychology. Most people enjoy college, where they pick just one major that piques their curiosity, more than high school, which is a forced march through everything from the Krebs cycle to the Hundred Years' War. One woman I spoke to, Sarah Richards, became punctual in her late thirties after a lifetime of lateness. For her, one trick was to stop trying to cram too many tasks into each hour. "Packing is a good example," she said. "I really could do it in thirty minutes. But my God, if I give myself a real two hours to go through my toiletries, to pick my shoes, and to actually think, *What kind of activities am I going to do?* Then I feel so much better, and it just pays off the entire trip."

In this way, simplicity is also the simplest conscientiousness tool. Someone who wants to be more conscientious could start by tossing the clothes and books they no longer want. They could clear their calendar of meetings and engagements that don't provide value. They could bring store-bought cookies to the party, have a smaller bachelorette, and sign their kid up for one less extracurricular activity. Rather than trying to make their life absorb an ever-expanding universe of obligations, they could make it so that their stuff, their interests, and their activities reflect a life that truly lights them up.

You only need to pare down a little before you start noticing the difference. "I think it's really empowering once you start and see a little bit of improvement," says Laura Loker. "To recognize, 'This is actually just something I can learn. It's not like a personality trait that I have to live with forever.'"

Drunk on Efficiency

One day, I finally confessed to my psychiatrist that alcohol might be one reason I was waking up so frequently in the middle of the night.

To be sure, I had insomnia even on nights I didn't drink. But lately, I had noticed that even a glass of wine with dinner interfered with my sleep. Though I technically only drank the seven drinks a week that the medical establishment allots to women, I felt like I needed every single one of those seven.

"What would it feel like to have three drinks a week instead of seven?" my psychiatrist asked.

What would it feel like to shut the fuck up? I thought.

"Hmm, that's a good idea," I said, then promptly forgot about it.

I've always reasoned that I deserved a drink for making it through a stressful day—and every day as a journalist is stressful, so I deserved a drink every day. I also reasoned, as I was working through the extroversion chapter, that I deserved a salve for my intense social anxiety. Whenever I was around new people, I would play a kind of drinking game with myself: Drink whenever you're uncomfortable. The only winner was me, and the only loser was me the next morning.

At one June barbecue at my local pool, I sat down at a picnic table with a group of neighbors I didn't know—something I would never have done before I began this personality-change experiment. The encounter started well enough. We introduced ourselves; my unusual name prompted the usual discussion of ethnic origins. We performed the bizarre midpandemic ritual in which everyone said which brand of vaccine they'd gotten.

The emcee of the barbecue announced that I had won a raffle, and I walked up to retrieve my prize: a terra-cotta plant pot stuffed with some candy and a mini bottle of Jack Daniel's, all wrapped up in clear cellophane.

I sat back down at the picnic table and tried to reenter the conversation. I asked my neighbors about their jobs. I asked them where they'd spent the pandemic lockdown. I asked them how long they had lived in the neighborhood. Then they started talking about their kids and dogs, and I didn't have either.

I asked the only questions I could think of: *What are your kids' names? How did they do with Zoom school? Have you guys done the bike trail to the lake yet?*

Then I was out. I realized with rising panic that I didn't have a single thing to say. I wanted to ask a deep question like "What's the saddest thing that's ever happened to you?" but I thought that might be frowned upon at the Friday Luau Wind-Down.

I hadn't intended to drink that day, but, almost instinctively, I began frantically unwrapping my door prize. I wrestled with the cellophane, then tore through some sort of corrugated ribbon that tied it all together. It sounded like someone boring an ice hole through a frozen lake.

"Do you, uh, want some sauvignon blanc?" asked one of the dads.

"Oh, this is fine," I lied.

"Hey, she *is* Russian," said another dad.

Sure, yeah, Russians and Jack Daniel's, a classic combo. I felt the hot sting of shame, the ignominy of their stares. But then I finally broke through the layers of gift wrap. I opened the tiny Jack and chugged. Just two sips in, I could feel my brain working normally again, out of code red and back into small talk. "Have you guys seen the pawpaws that grow by the creek?" Phew. Some people speak foreign languages better when they're a little sauced, but I speak better, period.

As I was riding my conscientiousness high-horse, I noticed that drinking is one area of this trait where I have room to improve. Conscientious people tend to be healthier, and that includes having a healthier relationship to alcohol. Though "immoderation" is technically part of the trait of neuroticism, numerous studies have found that conscientious people tend to drink less. One review found that low conscientiousness and low agreeableness were in fact the "most robust" predictors of problem drinking. Many people who are low in conscientiousness can't stop doing once-rewarding behaviors after they stop being enjoyable. This often described my relationship to drinking: desperate, without joy.

But, again, people who want to become more conscientious often have no idea how. I've always wondered how on earth some people manage to go their entire lives without drinking, or to stop once they've started. What do they look forward to in the evenings? How do they make it through weddings?

To try to understand, I called up Annie Grace, the author of a book and website called *This Naked Mind*, which aims to help people stop or reduce drinking. In awkward social moments, she said, she sometimes pretends like she's watching the discomfort play out on TV. She doesn't do anything about it. She just observes it. She thinks to herself, *I wonder how long people will let this go.* "I get really curious, like, 'If I don't break this pause, who's gonna break it?'" she told me. I suppose no one has ever been kicked out of a Friday Luau Wind-Down for allowing a stiff silence to extend for too long.

Somewhere around the midway point of my personality project, I began to experiment with my psychiatrist's suggestion of three weekly drinks. I still had a beer or two when out with friends—typically just one or two nights a week. But I found a brand of nonalcoholic beer I liked and swapped it for my one nightly Corona. When I was anxious at home and felt the urge to imbibe, I would tell myself I could have a drink if I could list one way it would improve the situation. Usually, I couldn't.

One night, Rich and I sat down to watch a movie that was highly recommended to both of us by people exactly like us. Our hopes were high. I'm not even going to name the movie here; it was so universally beloved. My favorite thing in the world is to get slightly buzzed while watching a great movie, so I poured a glass of wine and prepared to be transported.

Rich was riveted. He alternately teared up, nodded along, and laughed like he was going to choke. I, however, got the sinking feeling that this was a movie for whimsical people who find CGI karate chops entertaining. What I usually do when I have to watch a movie I hate with someone who likes it is drink more. That way I can resign myself to wasting two hours of my life, and afterward I can form a tipsy half smile and lie that yeah, it was pretty good!

When one of the characters sprouted hot-dog fingers for no reason, I poured myself another chardonnay. But after two sips, I realized I didn't want to be drunker. I just didn't want to be watching this movie. I poured out the wine and went upstairs to read.

The trick, for me, was in seeing alcohol as yet another unnecessary burden I was shouldering for other people—one that I could eliminate like a box of old ornaments. Drinking less was my own form of essentialism: Why do something when you don't have to do it? I'm not as fun when I'm not drinking, but people don't deserve Fun Me all the time. I don't have to say I liked a movie when I didn't. And if no one can think of any more conversation, maybe we should all just go home.

As I appraised the results of my personality experiment, I noticed this was one of the changes that made me feel happiest and most calm. I didn't give up drinking entirely, and I still have inundating weeks (and festive weeks) in which I overindulge. But I do generally have fewer than seven drinks a week. Sometimes it's three, sometimes four. Sometimes it's five, because some wrinkle of uncertainty drove me to the kitchen for an emergency pinot. Maybe it's because I'm already very conscientious, but viewing drinking as a form of excess has helped. In my mind, I've cleansed my life of the extra booze, and everything else seems more in order.

8

Enduring vs. Ending:
On Knowing When to Quit

I can hear the rumbles of protestation already. If, in the service of conscientiousness, the goal is to streamline your life, then how are you supposed to fit in all these personality-change activities? Let's say you want to change on two or three traits—that could mean trying to squeeze a dozen new habits into a life that is already bursting. And if a new activity feels boring, how can you tell whether it's because you're sliding back into reclusion, or if you should just try something else? How do you know when to keep trying to change? Or if you've changed enough?

It's this last question that ran through my brain one day during my first series of improv classes, when our teacher announced we'd be doing a public "showcase" at the end of our lessons—a free performance for friends and family and whoever happened to jog past Pavilion #1 in Rock Creek Park. Immediately, my palms went icy and slick. *That's it!* I thought. *I'm different enough! I should just quit improv now!*

I put the showcase out of my mind for a few weeks. Whenever it crept across my consciousness, I coped through wishful thinking: *Maybe another pandemic will start between now and the showcase and they'll call the whole thing off.* This worked until the night before, when

I kept snapping awake from intense, improv-themed nightmares. I spent the day grimly watching old Upright Citizens Brigade shows on YouTube, trying to figure out how improv should look when it's done correctly. Rich came downstairs and saw me clutching a throw pillow like a life preserver. "I'm nervous on your behalf," he said.

On the evening of the showcase, Rich agreed to drive me to the park. We sped through the hushed streets of suburbia and onto the thundering Beltway, joining the throngs of other Washingtonians heading somewhere to prove themselves. This being before I stopped trying to solve all my problems with alcohol, on the way there I quaffed from a thermos full of merlot.

I was grateful that two of my friends, Marissa and Anastasia, had agreed to come and offer moral support, or at least assist in creating the appearance of a crowd. When we arrived, I left them and Rich in the pavilion's seating area and peeled off with my fellow improvisational actors. Everyone looked hollow-eyed, yet ready, like we were about to invade Normandy. We played some improv games to warm up, then watched from the side as a more experienced group opened for us.

Unfortunately, the other group was very good. They had a deep bench of skilled performers, so each person popped in for just a few seconds, long enough to get a laugh and leave the scene feeling fresh. At one point, I, a person who does not find improv funny, belly-laughed at a scene in which two crime-solvers accidentally scared each other in the woods. (You had to be there.) They all looked remarkably composed and nonsweaty.

Then it was our turn. We formed a line in front of the "audience," if you can call it that, which sat at picnic tables before us. My wine buzz had worn off at that point, laying bare the keen reality that I was about to bomb at something I didn't like, in front of people I didn't know. I flashed back to my early stabs at interacting with adults as a kid, after we had immigrated but before I had learned English. I felt anew the torrid frustration of trying hard yet falling short.

You just have to get through this, I thought, *and then it will be over. You never have to do it again. In fact, since you're only doing it once, you might as well make it count.* This pep talk, remarkably, worked. Alongside extreme stage fright, my brain courses with an immigrant kid's overwhelming desire to do whatever people want in exchange for their approval. I began improvising like they were giving out good SAT scores at the end.

We settled into a common type of scene in which someone is extremely unqualified for their job, for which I played a secretary who kept falling asleep at inopportune moments. My fellow improvisers would request to be put through to various big shots, or to have paperwork faxed, and I would dramatically break into a stage-snore. I probed deep inside myself for the *kind* of person who would be good at this. I heard laughs and judged them to be only 60 percent out of pity. Then our instructor called "scene" and it was over. The unfunny police never showed up to yank me offstage.

Rich had never seen me perform in anything before, and he seemed surprised that I could. Afterward, he said, "Now that I've seen you do it, I don't really know why I thought it's something you wouldn't do."

I didn't know either. I vaguely remembered past boyfriends telling me that I'm not funny, or that I'm so insecure it shows. But why had I been living by their words? Why had I been trying to prove them right? All these years I had been straining to measure up to other people's notions of my personality, when I could have chosen whatever personality made me happiest.

After the showcase, Rich, Anastasia, and I had dinner at a Mexican restaurant where, in college, all the kids would go dancing on Fridays. I said it like this—"everyone would go dancing here on Fridays"—but in reality, I was always too shy to go dancing. Everyone *else* went dancing, and I stayed in my dorm room. Just then, I wished I could go back in time and tell myself there was no reason I shouldn't do it.

Driving home that night, the unlit suburban sky felt friendlier than usual, a cocoon rather than a cavern. I brimmed with enchiladas and relief. Surviving improv made me feel like I could survive anything—as bratty as that must sound to all my ancestors who survived the Siege of Leningrad.

ACTing in Line with Your Values

The improv showcase was an important test of my personality project precisely because it was so outrageously uncomfortable. And at many points, personality change is going to feel like squeezing into a pair of too-small tights or learning some agglutinative new language. You are going to hang out with a group of potential new friends and feel timid and jittery. You are going to be so bored during meditation that you compose an entire work email. You might—as I did—spill someone's Coke on them during a Meetup and learn that this, for better or worse, doesn't get you banned from future Meetups.

But that discomfort doesn't mean you should rethink changing your personality after all. Instead, anxiety can be a sign that you're slipping the surly bonds of habit and truly becoming different. Virtually every voice in the world of self-transformation warns against quitting something just because it doesn't feel right at first. "Don't measure the success of an exposure practice by whether you feel uncomfortable," write Martin Antony and Richard Swinson in *When Perfect Isn't Good Enough*, their guide for overcoming perfectionism. "If you chose an appropriately difficult situation, you *should* feel anxious."

People understandably try to avoid difficult feelings like discomfort, sadness, or anxiety. But those feelings can be a sign that something matters to you, and is therefore worth pursuing. In fact, a type of psychotherapy called Acceptance and Commitment Therapy, or ACT, suggests that what we cherish most is often precisely what prompts deep feelings of anguish and uncertainty. ACT encourages you to identify what it is you care about—your values—and behave in a way that accords with those values, even if doing so frightens you at times. I find it easiest to remember ACT through this acronym: accept your negative feelings (A), commit to your values (C), and take action (T) toward the kind of life you want to live. It can be a helpful sequence to remember when you're trying on new personality traits. In the case of improv, that might mean accepting that I feel stage fright, recognizing that one of my values is to be more outgoing, and doing the showcase anyway.

ACT was originated by Steven Hayes, a psychology professor at the University of Nevada, Reno. Early in his career, Hayes used ACT-adjacent skills to overcome the panic attacks that at times impaired his ability to teach. Rather than fight the panic, he accepted it. A 2006 *Time* magazine profile describes Hayes learning "to be playful with his thoughts, to hold them lightly: You feel panicky? Or depressed? Or incompetent? 'Thank your mind for that thought,' he likes to say." Over the years, Hayes developed this gonzo panic-recovery into the ACT program, which has held up in many clinical studies.

I picked up Hayes's book about ACT, *A Liberated Mind*, to try to learn how to perform ACT on myself. (Hayes says it can be done with or without a therapist.) In the book, Hayes explains that trying to avoid situations that incite fear, like public speaking or socializing, might paradoxically increase the intensity of that fear. Instead, you should try to "defuse" from your thoughts, Hayes writes, or notice that you're thinking them without buying into their content. A form of defusion might be to say to yourself, "I'm having the thought that I'm too anxious to socialize." This doesn't mean you decide you really *are* too anxious and stay in for the night. Think of it like a word of advice from someone you don't totally trust: You can choose to believe your thoughts only to the extent that they serve you.

Then you can decide instead to act in accordance with what you value. Hayes defines values as "enduring, ongoing guides to living," and as distinct from goals, which are finite and achievable. A value might be "be a good parent," for example, while a goal might be "make it to every dance recital this year." You might miss a dance recital but still be a good parent in other ways, and attending the dance recitals doesn't mean you can give up on good parenting the rest of the time. Hayes advises people to do something every day that fits with their values.

"Values" might sound vague—and vaguely religious—but they are the focus of several ascendant mental-health strategies. Many experts recommend discovering your values so that you can behave in a way that honors them. A type of therapy called "behavioral activation" encourages depressed people to perform activities that align with their values—like exercising or caring for their kids—without waiting to feel less depressed first. Even episodic future thinking—in which you build conscientiousness by vividly imagining your future self—involves first probing your values so that your actions can move you closer to them. Committing to your values can help you remain dedicated to changing your personality, even when doing so feels deeply unpleasant.

After I read his book, I asked Hayes to expand on his work in an interview. He's seventy-four, with a perfectly bald head and a youthful vigor. As we talked, I learned that his brother had died suddenly two months prior. Hayes was thinking about the basketball game he'd be attending later, and about how he'd be sitting next to his brother's empty season-ticket seat. "I feel sad talking about that," he said, then paused. "That's what love looks like."

The anecdote illustrates one of the main points of his philosophy, which is that "you hurt where you care." If something is painful or sad, it's often because you value it: Hayes says the most common reaction to acknowledging our values is tears. Because we all have things in our lives that we value, bad feelings are going to be a part of life. You can't avoid them, but you can accept them while doing whatever matters to you anyway.

To identify your own values, Hayes recommends examining your life through four lenses: sweet, sad, heroes, and stories. For "sweet," think about moments in your life filled with deep vitality, connection, or purpose. Why were those moments so meaningful for you? The answer might point to an important value. Under "sad," what are the most painful moments in your life, the ones that ripped your heart open? Why do you think you cared so much about them? For a "hero," think about someone who embodies an attribute you'd like to have. What would it take for you to possess that same trait? And finally, think about how you would write the story of your life. How would you want to be remembered? Those "epitaph" qualities are often the ones we wish we exhibited more in day-to-day life.

When Hayes was describing this framework, I immediately thought of a "hero" in my own life who embodies a value I hold dear. My friend Kathy has a remarkable ability to make friends wherever she goes, and I've always admired it. (According to the Big Five, she'd probably rank high on extroversion and agreeableness.) I love how she makes *other people* feel smart and funny, and I'm jealous of how naturally she scoops up even people she shares little in common with. Kathy moved to St. Louis during the pandemic, and within weeks she was mingling with new friends at dinner parties.

After I learned about Hayes's exercise, in new-friendship situations I started occasionally asking myself, "What would Kathy do?"—yes, like the WWJD bracelets from church camp. One time I even straightforwardly asked her for friendship tips—it turns out one is the rather simple strategy of reaching out to people you only kind-of know and asking them to hang out. It's not that I act exactly like Kathy now. But when I'm deciding between seeing a friend or staying in to watch Netflix, I know what Kathy would do. And I try to do it.

Ideally, values should guide your daily behavior, leading you toward the right thing to do regardless of what's happening in your brain or what happened in the past. Following your values can help provide the energy to perform the often-difficult activities of personality change, since presumably you value the trait you're working toward. Values cast a spotlight on whatever's important, and invite you to step in.

Drop the Rope

The story of a young Canadian law student named Robert offered me a closer look at how Acceptance and Commitment Therapy can work in real life. Growing up, Robert was shy and reserved, in part because he had trouble pronouncing certain words. The shyness compounded on itself, hardening into neuroticism and introversion as he entered his teens. He had friendships, but they were shallow and mercurial. He spent a lot of time reading, watching TV, and playing video games—all activities he could do alone.

Today, he told me, he'd still consider himself an introvert, but he now feels more comfortable behaving like an extrovert, and he's also grown more agreeable, conscientious, and emotionally stable than he once was. He ascribes all of this to the techniques in ACT, which he learned about without a therapist, through reading on his own.

Robert's transformation began when he discovered ACT while re-searching a project for a psychology class in college. He came across a metaphor that resonated: Imagine you're in a game of tug-of-war, and the other guy is pulling the rope as hard as he can. He's stronger than you, so he's always yanking you toward the center. You know you can't win; the best you can do is to resist, to dig your feet into the ground, but it's exhausting. To Robert, his negative thoughts were the other, stronger guy, the one overpowering him. He decided to just drop the rope—to exist alongside the negative thoughts but to stop resisting them. Avoiding discomfort wasn't making him any less uncomfortable; it just mired him in weary inertia.

This meant that he resolved to move forward *despite* his anxiety, instead of *without* anxiety. He began asking questions in class, even if he didn't feel confident. Sometimes when he went out, he would say to himself, "Yeah, I feel anxious." Then he would go anyway. In his first year of law school, Robert ran for student government, and during the debate and campaign process, he focused on "admitting that I was going to be nervous and not trying to avoid being nervous," he says.

One way to push through feelings of discomfort is to ask yourself, if you feel uncomfortable, "what happens then?" I learned this technique from Annie Grace, the sobriety coach behind *This Naked Mind*. If you're in a social situation and say something embarrassing, ask yourself, what happens then? *The person might judge you.* And what happens then? *You might feel embarrassed.* And what happens then? "Just keep pulling the thread until you realize that the thing that happens at the end of that thread is you feel something," Grace says. That feeling might be boredom or humiliation, but, she added, "the thing that I was so afraid of, the thing that I was white-knuckling to make not happen was a feeling. And actually the anxiety I'm feeling about feeling a feeling is worse than the actual feeling." When we allow ourselves to feel discomfort, we often find it doesn't burn as badly as we feared.

By allowing himself to feel discomfort, Robert flourished in law school. He snagged a summer internship with one of the best law firms in his area. He's made close friends and picked up rock climbing, which he sees as a metaphor for overcoming obstacles. When we talked, Robert had a social calendar that would make even a hardened extrovert crawl into bed for some "me time."

Still, there were some things that were too much, even for him.

"In your case, you went to improv?" he asked me. "I would never do that."

"Why?" I asked.

"I'd be incredibly uncomfortable," he said. Then he added, "There's a limit. There's a limit."

———————

The improv showcase did stretch the limits of my discomfort, but in the fall of 2022 I would push them even further. That's when I decided to host my own Meetup group, rather than attend someone else's. This activity combined all my personal bêtes noires: leading something, dealing with large groups of people, trying to sound smart on the fly, and finding parking. Call it extroversion, agreeableness, and emotional stability, all rolled into one vigorous workout.

I organized the group around foreign movies, an esoteric passion of mine that I rarely get to share with others. My entire adult life, I've loved to come home from work, pour a glass of wine, and sink into some unpronounceable drama from Uzbekistan. Then I like to mull it over for a few days, wondering what I would do if I was on the steppe with those characters, covering up a murder committed by my falconer half brother. The only thing better, I thought, would be if I could get people from the Internet to come talk about the Uzbekistan movie with me.

The idea behind the Meetup was that we would watch foreign movies separately, then come together to discuss them. (For COVID and physical safety reasons, I didn't want to invite a bunch of strangers to my house for movie night.) I signed up for an organizer account on Meetup, created the group, and spent the afternoon hitting "refresh" on my browser, watching the "members" tally tick up as our lonely, artsy hearts found one another.

Figuring I would give myself a home-field advantage, for the first Meetup I chose the documentary *Navalny*, about the Russian dissident. For the venue, I selected a restaurant whose Yelp score suggested it was not very popular, and therefore would be more likely to tolerate a large, obnoxious gaggle of movie nerds.

I wasn't nervous driving there, but I soon became so as I sat down at my table, whose reservation had quickly shifted from eight to six and now five. I'm not a natural-born leader, and I've never led a club, a group at work, or anything else, really. I reminded myself of my therapist's advice to "let other people be uncomfortable"—not to try to fill every silence, or to fix every situation that gets unwieldy. But that's easier to do when you haven't invited a bunch of people to come be uncomfortable with you.

People were slow to show up, and for a while I sat alone behind a tri-fold piece of paper that read "Foreign Movie Meetup," like a weird ambassador. When the waitress came by, I ordered several people's worth of food so she wouldn't be irritated by the ever-changing head count.

Even though people gradually trickled in, it did not turn into a smooth evening. I ran out of discussion questions quickly. One person hated the movie. Then two people seemed like they were arguing. Was that okay? I forgot everyone's name and reverted to stage-moderator-style pointing. Then I forgot what I was saying midsentence. Was I supposed to keep people on the topic of the movie, or could I allow them to veer into tangents? I was relieved to see 8:30, the official end of the event.

Luckily, the next thing on my calendar was the professional women's book club that I had signed up for earlier. This, by contrast, *was* a smooth evening. The book-club organizer began by asking everyone their name. Then she asked an icebreaker question—everyone's favorite drink—followed by a list of prepared discussion questions that we ran through in order. The book was about a fraught immigrant family, which got us all talking about our own fraught families, immigrant and otherwise. Afterward, there was some time to chat and catch up.

I mentally took notes on the proper leading of meetings. Clubs work better when the organizer is a little strict, I noticed. People want to know what the rules are; once they do, they're generally happy to follow them. Man is born free, but everywhere he looks for agenda items.

I set about planning my next Meetup more diligently. I printed out some discussion questions from the website of a college film class, and, oddly, from the film club of a Presbyterian church. Symbolism, imagery, mise-en-scène—nothing would escape my learned scrutiny. "How does the film reflect the tensions and optimism of the newly formed European Union?" I made a notecard for that.

The next film we discussed was a 1993 French movie called *Three Colors: Blue*, and it went *un petit peu* better, I'd say. Over the course of our meetings, I found myself awed by everyone's intelligence. I, a child of *Full House* and *Growing Pains*, didn't always pick up on these movies' artistic flourishes, but others in the club did. "Did you notice how the greenhouses were a metaphor for the women in his life?" a participant asked at another meeting. No, no I had not.

As someone who once briefly, but not proudly, dated a man who did not know that Finland was a country, I felt blessed to live in a city where I could order up a panel of strangers who were basically film experts. I looked with pride on the fact that I'd created a forum for my fellow eccentrics. The club had succeeded at its goal of helping me understand movies more deeply, and of seeing how film, perhaps the most classic solo activity, could create a community after all.

Too Much Growth

All of this does not mean, however, that personality change necessitates pursuing every activity you try until you're a cast member on *Saturday Night Live* or ski-jumping in the Olympics. Even when trying on a new trait, you're allowed to just not like things.

In our interview about ACT, Hayes said that "you can change your choices." You can realize you're in pursuit of something you don't truly value: Very few people stay at their first job forever or marry their first-ever date. Deciding to do something different isn't the same as giving up. Even Angela Duckworth, of *Grit* fame, writes, "you can quit." She suggests waiting until a natural stopping point, like the end of the season or semester—or, say, after the improv showcase.

I asked Carol Dweck, the psychologist who developed the "growth mindset," how people should think about the things they're bad at. After all, if you have a growth mindset, aren't all your shortcomings just strengths waiting to gestate? She said it's worth considering whether your failure represents a set of skills you simply haven't learned yet. Is "leading a Meetup" something you think you *could* get better at?

But also, you should ask yourself, do you *want* to get better at it? Time, after all, is finite, and you're not going to master everything. "It's not incumbent upon us to pursue everything we fail at just so we can improve," she said.

This reasoning helped me when I, inevitably, found myself performing personality-change activities I didn't really enjoy. It allowed me to pursue my *value* of extroversion or emotional stability or agreeableness, but to do it in a way that felt more fun and less like a term paper.

After half a dozen meetings, I had to admit that although I could tolerate the discomfort of leading the movie Meetup group, it was not, alas, an expression of my heartfelt values. To answer Dweck's question, I wasn't very good at it, and I didn't really want to get better.

I had organized the group because I wanted to create a community of foreign-movie lovers—to foster extroversion and agreeableness—but instead, it was feeling an awful lot like work. While I think I would have liked being a mere participant, directing the discussions wasn't very enjoyable. Thinking of questions, four-finger-pointing at different panelists—it's the same thing I do when I'm moderating conferences, which I like doing for my job, but not in my free time. It wasn't even furthering a value I had: My value was to "be more extroverted," not "moderate more things." At one meeting, one participant talked over everyone else, to the point where I noticed the other group members getting annoyed. I didn't know what to do about that, and I didn't want to figure it out.

One day at happy hour, I mentioned to one of Rich's friends, Reid, that I ran a foreign-film Meetup. I had somehow forgotten that Reid has seen every movie ever made, twice—once for the plot and once for the cinematography. He's Mr. Foreign Movie Meetup—plus, he lived very close to the restaurant where we met.

Would he like to take over as organizer? He would indeed. With a few clicks in Meetup's backend, I transferred ownership to him.

I decided to find other ways to bond with friends over shared interests. And in the end, I did so in an unexpected way: Months later, I would return to cohost the Meetup with Reid. That is, we both came with questions. We both shared the blame (or the glory) for the movie choice. We both came loaded up with our best facts about Abbas Kiarostami. Together, we led an interesting discussion on a documentary about two brothers who take care of carnivorous birds in New Delhi.

Afterward, Reid told me that having a second person really helped—on his own, he sometimes ran out of questions, leading to an interminable silence. I may be introverted, but I'm at least a professional at coming up with questions. I, meanwhile, appreciated having a coleader who knew so much about cinema, which eased the pressure of weaving a highbrow conversation. That night the Meetup felt real, enshrined. It was officially A Thing. We marveled at how much easier it had been with two people. Things usually are.

The "Real" You

One fall day I faced the neuroscientist Jim Fallon on Zoom, trying to figure out if he still was, or if he ever was, a psychopath. It would make sense if so, given that he had written a book in which he admitted that he's a "borderline psychopath."

But now, he demurred. "I'm not really a psychopath, okay?" he protested to me at one point. On the screen, Jim looked less like a psychopath and more like a gray-bearded grandpa. "I'm normal!" he said. "A lot of the stuff about me being a psychopath was done by journalists who wanted to have a storyline. Because if you're *almost* a psychopath, it's not a story."

I nodded and smiled vigorously at this claim, trying to reassure him that I'm not like *those* journalists. Because I guess I, too, am a bit of a psychopath.

"But . . . your book is called *The Psychopath Inside*," I said carefully, "so I think that maybe led people to think that . . ."

"I do have psychopathy inside," he quickly added, "I do have those traits inside."

The existential debate over Jim's psychopathy began many years ago, when he was in his lab at the University of California, Irvine, finishing up an academic article based on some PET scans he'd acquired of serial killers. The scans revealed low levels of activity in areas of the brain that are associated with empathy and morality—a pattern typical of someone with psychopathy.

After working on that article, Jim sat down to analyze a different set of brain scans he had taken of his own family, which were to serve as a control group in an Alzheimer's study. Then he noticed something odd. These were supposed to be "normal" brains, but the last scan in that pile—his family's pile—looked just like the scans of the psychopaths from the other study. This suggested that "the poor individual it belonged to was a psychopath," Jim would later write. Worried he had mixed up scans from the two studies, he asked a lab technician to break the blind on the psychopath scan and tell him whose brain it belonged to. It was his.

This is how Jim learned that he, shall we say, shares much in common with psychopaths. Not that there weren't warning signs: In his book, Jim writes that he "never truly felt fully emotionally connected" to his wife, and he partied hard, even after his kids were born. He occasionally blew off professional meetings in order to go to bars and flirt with women. He would put other people in danger, like the time he brought his brother to a Kenyan cave known to be a reservoir of the Marburg virus, just because he'd always wanted to visit. Deaths and injuries that anguished other people left him dry-eyed. "I live in an empathetic flatland," he writes. A confirmed psychopath? Maybe not. But he admits to "mild narcissism" and "regular bouts of selfishness."

After Jim learned all this, he decided to become a better person—to hand the psychopath inside an eviction notice. He says his desire to change was prompted by a narcissistic urge to overcome psychopathy, one of the more difficult personality patterns to escape. He told me he wanted to "beat psychopathy." "I know of no case of a teenager or adult who has ever reversed categorical, full-blown psychopathy," he wrote. His competitive streak spurred him to try to become the first.

He began by asking himself, "What would a good guy do?" Then he started performing the routine of a good guy—the dishes, the obligatory family functions, the menschiness. If scientists were to have measured his personality, they might have said Jim was becoming more agreeable. For Jim, being good was exhausting—so much so that he began sleeping longer every night.

But it seemed to be working. After a few months, his wife said, "What's come over you? You're, like, really, really nice."

Jim told her not to take it seriously. He was just playing a game, he said.

"I don't care if you mean it or not," Jim's wife said. "Keep doing it."

Jim's nice-guy act was well underway by the time he and I talked. But here, too, we found Schrödinger's psychopath: Jim couldn't seem to resolve whether, by acting less psychopathically, he was actually becoming less psychopathic. He didn't seem like a psychopath to me—more like an agreeable-enough guy with occasional selfish impulses. But Jim told me that if he doesn't actively try to remember to be a good person, he'll slip back into his old ways. He seemed to dismiss the idea that he was truly different, calling his current behavior "this lie of being a nice guy."

His loved ones don't seem to mind that he's lying, though. All that matters to them is that he became kinder and more thoughtful. Personality is, in part, a performance for other people, and other people are enjoying the new Jim show. "It doesn't have to be this big, sincere thing," he says. "It's just a practical thing of treating people better."

But is it? His story brings up another important question about personality change: Is it real, or is it all an act? Does a person's changed behavior mean they've truly changed? Or if it requires continual effort, does it mean they haven't, really? And does it matter?

Employing Free Traits

Sometimes, when I would tell people I was working on a book about personality change, and that I was nearing the end of it, they'd say something like "So, are you different now?" I heard the implication behind the question: Is this stuff for real? If they try something similar, will they become "different," too?

The answer to that question is, frustratingly, yes and no. It depends on who you ask—and how you think about yourself, your identity, and the nature of the human experience. This is the psychological version of the Ship of Theseus paradox—the thought experiment by ancient Greek philosophers as to whether a ship whose components had been entirely replaced was still the same ship. Greek philosophers being what they were, this paradox was never conclusively resolved, and neither, I'm afraid, is the question of whether behaving and thinking differently means really, permanently, being different. Based on my personality test scores, my attitudes and behaviors did change. But it's up to each person to decide whether that qualifies as a "new personality" or not.

Some experts argue that you can be different even if your personality doesn't change. To them, this question—"Are you different?"—is moot. It may be the same old you inside, they say, but if you can behave differently over significant stretches of time, then it's *as though* you changed. As Jim Fallon found, to those around you, the effect might be the same.

The psychologist Brian Little has a theory that people can employ what he calls "free traits"—occasionally acting out of character in pursuit of an important personal project. Free traits are patterns of behavior you *choose*, rather than inherit or develop over time. This is why a normally very agreeable parent can become a menace if, say, their child's safety is at risk. Or why hard-core introverts can make effortless small talk during important job interviews. It's not that you're behaving hypocritically; it's that you can have multiple authenticities, this theory holds. You can adjust your thoughts and behaviors to suit the situation.

Little says that engaging in free-trait behavior—acting outside your nature—for too long can be depleting. Introverts who are constantly required to behave like extroverts can feel burned out or exhausted, he argues. Retreating to a "restorative niche" can counteract this exhaustion: Picture the introvert disappearing from the raucous party to pet the cat in the bedroom for a while.

Some people switch into their free traits frequently, but you'd never know it because they also spend ample time within restorative niches. This concept reminded me of a week in California during which I moderated two conferences and, between them, attended a fancy dinner at a venture capitalist's house. Toward the end of it all, my mouth hurt from talking. After the last panel of the last conference, I Ubered back to my hotel room, and, overdosed on extroversion, slept for four hours in the middle of the day. Afterward, I felt restored.

In fact, Little and some others say the key to a healthy personality may not be in swinging permanently to the other side of the personality scale but in balancing between extremes, or in adjusting your personality from one situation to another. "The thing that makes a personality trait maladaptive is not being high or low on something, it's more like rigidity across situations," Kathryn Paige Harden, the behavioral geneticist, told me.

A good personality, in this view, is one that can rise to the occasion. It's someone who can deliver the maid-of-honor speech and arrive at her appointments on time, even if she isn't a "natural" extrovert or conscientious type. A person like this, who is willing to flex her personality to meet the demands of the moment, is called a "high self-monitor," according to psychologists. A "low self-monitor," meanwhile, is someone who remains true to themselves, no matter what situation they're in. (The lingo is a bit confusing, but you can think of a high self-monitor as constantly scanning themselves—monitoring—to be sure they're saying and doing whatever's expected of them.) A high self-monitor who is introverted, when faced with a big work presentation, might practice it relentlessly for weeks, trying to overcome her natural shyness. An introverted low self-monitor might, in the same situation, decline to give the presentation at all. Being a high self-monitor allows you to shapeshift when necessary, without rearranging your entire personality.

I found this to be an uplifting take on personality change: that it can be temporary, but still valid. Free traits allow you the flexibility to act out of character while knowing there's something inside you that's constant and steady. Hopefully, this internal, unchanging quality is something positive—your inner thoughtful introvert—but it might also be something you mostly try *not* to act on. Like, in Jim's case, the psychopath inside.

"So, it's okay to be a little bitchy in your heart, as long as you can turn it off?" I asked Harden at one point.

"People who say they're never bitchy in their heart," she said, "are lying."

The Prescription

In 1948, a psychologist named Bertram Forer handed each of his students a supposedly unique analysis of his or her personality. In reality, each analysis was identical, containing generic statements like "You have a tendency to be critical of yourself" and "You pride yourself as an independent thinker." Each student, though, thought the description defined them specifically and accurately. Who doesn't want to be an independent thinker?

Forer's experiment demonstrates why it can be hard to gauge the extent of your own personality change: People see what they want to see, including inside themselves. I'm guessing many people think they're deep, brooding introverts who can, when called upon, transform into ebullient extroverts for an evening. "The problem with self-narratives is that we are the ones writing the story, which means our myths are open to all manner of distortions of what we think we should be like," writes Bruce Hood in *The Self Illusion*.

Even Nathan Hudson, probably the leading scholar of volitional personality change, acknowledges that some personality changes might be in people's heads. In one of his studies, he writes, "Participants may have *believed* their personality traits had changed (despite no change actually occurring) because they observed their own continual success in completing the challenges." (However, as someone whose head is sometimes her greatest enemy, I personally would welcome changes that were only in my head.)

But just as people can experience no real personality change and think they've changed a lot, the converse can be true, too. That is, you might have changed significantly but feel as though you haven't. Personality has an identity component, Hudson told me. It represents who you *think you are*, and that can make it hard to admit when you've outgrown something. You might start to feel calmer, but you still see yourself fundamentally as an anxious person. Your personality test might show that you're now extremely conscientious, but you might hesitate to relinquish your "nutty professor" excuse. This accounts for the scores of people who can effortlessly work a room full of business prospects before sighing and insisting that, really, they're an introvert. It can be hard to give up a long-held piece of yourself.

We might gradually buff away at the rough spots of our personalities—drinking less, getting out more, being nicer—without realizing we're doing it. Or, we might subconsciously explore beyond the barriers we've previously erected for ourselves: In the time that it took me to write this book, one of my interviewees changed careers, from a lawyer to a therapist. "Identity has the power to shape and thus also to constrict," writes the cultural critic Sheila Liming. "That is why so much of human life is devoted to a kind of poking at its edges. We seek to discover who we are by locating the boundaries of what we are willing to be."

The conclusion I came to is that "Are you really different?" is not a universally answerable question. If being an introvert (or closed to experiences or disagreeable, and so forth) is so important to your identity that you don't *want* to change, you are probably not going to change. And when you do try to act against your nature, you'll probably write off the results as short-lived, marginal, or otherwise fake.

But for me, the prospect of a new identity isn't something to avoid. I'm happy to discard my personality labels, even if I can only manage it for a day or two. Maybe I'm an introvert who needs extroversion. I'm a naturally anxious person who can find hard-won moments of Zen. I like people and want the best for them, but I'm always going to keep one sharp, critical eye trained on the world.

I started out envisioning personality change as a tune-up: I would replace the spark plugs and top up the fluids, and in the end I would be driving the best possible version of myself. Then, I thought, I wouldn't have to bother with it again for many months.

But over time, I started to see personality change as more of a process—an ongoing series of choices and commitments that would allow me to live according to my values, to echo the ACT literature. I decided it was more important to choose, each moment, what action to take next, rather than to berate myself for not yet "being different." The only way to *be* different, after all, is to *do* something different.

Hudson has found that for several of the personality traits, people who lack the trait tend to want to grow in that trait. Introverts want to become more extroverted; neurotics want to relax. Some traits function like a balm for their opposite. Similarly, toward the end I saw my personality change as more of a prescription than a cure. It was a daily regimen, not a final state of being. Many people take medication not to treat acute illness but to maintain a state of health. I take the drug Synthroid every day because it keeps my thyroid ticking; I don't stop because my thyroid feels fine. Likewise, I do some of Hudson's personality-change activities—like befriending new people and controlling my anger—even when nothing is wrong. I do them because it's now in my nature.

Understanding this ongoing quality of personality change allowed me to see that there's always a way out; I'm never trapped being a way I don't want to be. The psychologist David McClelland wrote that "personality change appears to be very difficult for those who think it is very difficult . . . and much easier for those who think it can be done." I think it can be done, so I find it doable.

9

Find Your Beach:

How to Keep Changing

The early months of 2023 brought us to Florida again, as we redoubled our efforts to find a new home. This was about as stressful as real estate normally is, except with some idiosyncratic Florida twists. The Zillow description of one house in our price range, for example, read, "Home has flooded multiple times!"

One might ask, understandably, why I was so obsessed with moving. In my life as a working adult, I've only ever lived in and around DC. I've only ever hated it, especially the winter, which is technically only three months of the year but feels, to me, like nine. As day after day of pale light and freezing rain stretches on, I feel like I'm swimming through aspic, choking on its frigid stiffness. A few weeks in, I start to believe that I'll never be warm or happy again.

One January day a few years ago, I thought I'd cheer myself up by getting brunch with a friend at a local diner. Midway through my pancakes, I started crying uncontrollably for no reason—something made more awkward by the fact that "Mambo No. 5" was playing flamboyantly in the background.

A little bit of Monica in my life . . .

"I just can't," I stammered through sobs, "do anything."

A little bit of Erica by my side . . .

My urge to move had to do with seasonal affective disorder, sure. But likely also in play was some writerly inclination to blame underperformance on environmental factors, like a suboptimal view or a chair whose armrests are a smidgen too high. The essayist Sloane Crosley says that writers "become increasingly particular about our conditions until part of us can't help but think of all the work we'd get done if only we were buried alive." As dumb as it may seem, I told myself that the secret to good writing was to never be cold again.

Though initially Rich didn't want to move, eventually my need to not weep away the winter persuaded him, and he (agreeably) agreed to keep looking. Since the last time we had searched for houses in Florida, though, the Federal Reserve had raised interest rates to the highest point in recent memory. This meant that in addition to finding something that would not flood, blow down, collapse into a sinkhole, or get shot up by lunatics, we also needed a house that would cost hundreds of thousands of dollars less than we had originally planned. Instead of welcoming me, I felt like Florida was kicking me away. One mortgage lender, properly suspicious that a writer could afford to live indoors, kept asking me how I knew I would ever write another book. She was apparently unaware that this is the one question you can never ask a writer, along with "Have you written anything I would have heard of?"

A funny thing about this trip: It marked almost exactly a year since my own great dorsal collapse. The previous winter, we'd also traveled to Florida, where I'd suffered the awful prephoto haircut and subsequent petty indignities. It wasn't the worst day of my life, but it was the one during which I realized my personality could turn just about any day into "the worst day." Past Olga tried to solve things with alcohol, yelling, and anxious paralysis. She isolated, slid onto the couch, and refused to go further. Even though the stakes were higher now, I wondered if this time my personality would allow me to remain upright.

Could I maintain all the positive changes I had made, or would I revert to the old me?

This is a hard question to answer scientifically. Nathan Hudson told me psychologists don't yet know how long intentional personality change can last; the studies have only tracked people for a few months after they changed. We all want longer-term studies, but for that you'd have to bang down the doors of the science-funding bureaucrats.

Hudson speculates that personality change is a little bit like weight loss: Many people who lose weight gain it back, while others don't. If someone regained the weight, though, you'd never question whether they lost it in the first place. You'd acknowledge that, not unlike neuroticism or disagreeableness, pounds are difficult to keep off. Similarly, some people abandon their former personality traits for good. Others, though, find themselves retreading well-worn furrows, and are mystified when they wind up in the same old places.

A Ninety-Day Vacation That's Still Going

In 2021, I connected with a young man named Tim Curran, who lives in Omaha, Nebraska—"the pearl of the Midwest," he says, "as nobody calls it but me." He said he had a story of personality change, but neither of us realized at the time just how radical his would be.

Tim is modest and self-deprecating, but he has a big, booming radio voice. In early 2020 he was working a promising, if stressful, job as a sports radio producer. When the pandemic started, and the sports world shut down, Tim's job gave him what he euphemistically calls a "mandatory ninety-day vacation." The furlough came as a blow to Tim, an ambitious twenty-four-year-old who had poured his entire being into work. Even before the pandemic, he'd avoid seeing friends so he could put in longer hours, working nights and weekends. But suddenly, his work, the core of his identity, had evaporated. "I had to look

myself in the mirror and say, 'Okay, what are you going to do now?'"
he told me.

Tim took a critical look at his life. He had to face the fact that over
the years, he had become obese—last he had checked he carried 274
pounds on his six-foot frame. In a photo of him taken in his early twenties, he looked, by his own description, like an out-of-shape forty-year-
old: balding, with a double chin.

He often felt sluggish and physically ill, and the most obvious cul-
prit was alcohol. On his worst days, he would stop by CVS on the way
home, pick up a case of beer, and have fifteen or sixteen cans over the
course of an evening. He had told himself it wasn't a problem because
he could hold down a steady job.

But if it wasn't a problem, he wondered, why did he feel so awful
all the time? Tim resolved to change his personality so that he could
become healthier, and, he hoped, happier. "You've got one shot at this,"
he told himself. "There's time now for a mini reset."

Tim decided to use his furlough to cut way down on drinking, just
to see what happened. Almost immediately, he coursed with new energy, which he channeled into going for a run every day. Soon, gyms
in Nebraska reopened, and he added in strength training three times a
week, cutting the running down to two.

In one year, Tim lost more than one hundred pounds. With the
weight loss—and perhaps also the closure of hair salons—came the decision to accept his baldness and start shaving his head. (Tim politely
called this embracing an "F-U" attitude.)

These changes all reflect greater conscientiousness: Drinking less,
eating healthier, and working out are all things diligent, conscientious
people do. But then Tim started to reevaluate other areas of his life.
For instance, maybe he wasn't actually as introverted as he'd always
imagined himself to be. He would often sulk and grow avoidant if a
friend was slow to respond to a text or to make plans. Sometimes, he
just didn't feel good in his body, so he would stay home. But maybe he

was being too harsh, he thought. He resolved to become more extroverted, FaceTiming his family more, making conversation with strangers, and, once it was safe in terms of COVID, initiating get-togethers with friends.

Tim is, of course, an extreme example of pandemic self-improvement. Not everyone had the time, money, or wherewithal to revamp themselves so dramatically during a public-health emergency. But perhaps what's more remarkable is that he's kept up all these new traits. I first interviewed Tim in April of 2021, and when I talked to him again nearly two years later, he was maintaining his new personality—one that was much more conscientious, extroverted, and emotionally stable.

He still drinks far less than he used to. He works out five days a week. When someone invites him to something, even if it's something he's not sure he'll like, he just says yes. "I don't like EDM, but I'll just go," he says. He sometimes tricks himself into doing things by telling himself, *I am the kind of person who likes it.*

At one point, Tim emceed a big corporate town hall before an audience of a thousand people. He wore a bright red, spangly jacket and made lots of jokes. "That was something I could not have done even five years ago," he told me.

Long-term personality change is more likely to be successful if it's in the service of a "personal project," or a meaningful quest in your life. This can be raising your kids, or helping stop climate change, or, in my case, being a good journalist and partner. What keeps Tim going is that with each thing he's doing, whether it's eating healthily or interacting socially, "it feels like I'm building toward something bigger," he says.

He struggled to pin down exactly what this bigger thing is, though. When pressed, he described it as a carrying on of tradition, of upholding some ineffable sense of duty. He's from a midwestern home where virtue hangs in the air. Tim's grandfather worked hard and raised a family. Tim's father worked hard and raised a family. Tim wasn't going to break from that heritage just to sit alone and drink. He noticed that the people around him spent the pandemic either buckling down or unraveling. He knew in which category he wanted to fall.

The Cult of Real Estate

I wanted to believe I had transformed myself as much as Tim had. And there were some signs that I really was living by my new personality. People around me said I had changed already: Anastasia said my "willingness to do things has gone up," and that I'd become more assertive. This would fall under the umbrella of extroversion—the side of my personality to which she's regularly exposed.

My friend Kathy noticed that I'd become more accepting of the fact that "you are a good and worthy hang and people will want to be friends with you." Kathy and I have a little tradition called "Can I call you and freak out for a sec?" which is exactly what it sounds like. But lately, she noticed that I hadn't been calling and freaking out much, not even for a sec. A reduction in neuroticism, perhaps? "You seem to have a healthier relationship to work in general," she pointed out.

Most importantly, Rich told me he thought I was more easygoing, that my mood was more stable (or less neurotic), and that I communicated better (became more agreeable). I, myself, noticed that I was socializing more, sleeping better, drinking less, and blowing up at Rich moderately—but significantly—less frequently.

When we arrived in Florida, I immediately messaged some local female journalists to hang out. Within a few weeks, I was Rollerblading with one of them. I took a tai chi class and signed up for an unlimited pass at a local yoga studio. I went on several Bumble BFF dates, only one of which was so bad as to be memorable.

But there was also evidence of what economists call regression toward the mean, and what I call my inner striver-immigrant stirring to life, wringing her kerchief, and begging me to think harder about self-preservation. There were times when I felt neuroticism dragging me back into its murky depths.

To help us find a house, I called a Realtor who came highly recommended. When she answered the phone, I was pleased to hear that she had a sophisticated accent, and this was 80 percent of the reason we went with her.

She would turn out to not quite be the worldly cosmopolitan that I imagined. "I carry my gun even in Home Deee-poh," she mentioned melodiously one day.

I'm a reluctant participant in real estate, since real estate, I'm convinced, is a cult. First comes the sleep deprivation: If a "good one" pops up, you rouse yourself at any hour to see it first, lest someone swoop in with a cash offer and steal it out from under you. Actually committing to a house in Florida means calculating some combination of its flooding risk, school district, renovation cost, and resale value. All this trigonometry must be performed while standing in the driveway of the home itself, in twenty minutes or less. Any attempt to resist this pressure, for instance by suggesting we live in an apartment, is met with the cult's solemn incantation: "Renting is just throwing your money away."

No sooner had we set foot on the state's sandy topsoil than we were spending at least six hours a week driving around with Realtor, looking at houses, squinting and trying to imagine ourselves in them. Among other things, we saw: A house in which I opened the electrical panel to reveal rotting wooden boards, and between them, the sky outside. A house that looked amazing in pictures but smelled inside like four animals urinating at once. A flip in a great area, and that looked perfect, except for the backyard swimming pool that had physically popped out of the ground and filled up with rainwater and was now a breeding ground for tadpoles. "These build-ahs really try to rape you," Realtor said, shaking her head.

Discouraged, I called my dad, who said I should simply buy a big, brand-new house in the middle of nowhere—an option we did not want, and perhaps more importantly, could not afford. I talked to my mentor, who said I was insane to move so far away from the media epicenter. "Are there even any other Jews there?" he scoffed. My neuroticism level was ticking up like a taxi meter with every mile.

Just as we had resigned ourselves to living in the middle of the ocean on a sea-steading platform, one day Rich walked into the kitchen holding up a Redfin alert on his phone. A new house had come up in an area that was neither our first choice nor our second, but one we found acceptable. It was shockingly cheap. We texted Realtor and drove over, trying to keep expectations low.

As we pulled up, we saw another prospective buyer burst out the front door. "Had to cut my gym visit short to get a look at this one!" he said. When you put your house on the market, it would be wise to hire your friends to walk in and out of it saying this exact line.

In the front yard, Realtor pulled us aside and whispered to us conspiratorially. "This is a multiple offer situation," she said. "Which means you won't have time to decide. You have a few minutes to take a look, and then you have to tell me today if you want to make an offer."

Since I am working on being more positive, I will say the house had a very nice pool. It also had kitchen tile whose white grout was stained brown from years of spilled barbecue sauce, a carpet the color of a stagnant puddle, beige countertops that must have been the bargain of 2002, and a strange black grime that coated both bathtubs. The woman who lived there seemed to love crafts—she had a highly organized craft room—and it's therefore unfortunate that occasionally picking up a Clorox wipe is not considered "a craft."

Realtor assured me this could all be resolved by throwing $50,000 at some contractors she knows. The place was so dark inside that as Rich and Realtor stood in the cramped kitchen, contemplating everything, they resembled two jaundiced milliners in a Renaissance painting.

Rich, who likes everything, said he liked it. Realtor, who was sick of shepherding us around the Sunshine State, said she liked it. I did not like it, but in the moment I struggled to verbalize why. Fifteen minutes after we had entered, it was the next shopper's turn.

Realtor ushered us outside. "So do you want to make an offer?" she said. "This one is going to go fast."

I'm still struggling to explain to myself what happened next. They both looked at me expectantly. I wanted them to be happy. I wanted everyone to be happy. I could make everyone so happy if I just said yes.

"Um, yes," I said.

"Great!" Realtor yelped. She hopped in her colossal SUV and drove home to write it up.

The following afternoon, Realtor called me.

"I have some good news," she said.

"Um, okay," I said hesitantly.

"Your offer was accepted," she said. "But why do I get the sense that you're a bit nervous about it?"

She must have gotten that sense because I was actively hyperventilating. Not in the good, "we have a home" way but in the "I think I'm dying" way. Because it meant I would have to spend all my money on something I didn't want. Immediately.

I peppered her with questions, asking how much time we had to back out and whether the house was really worth the price it was going for.

"I'm not good at making decisions under this much pressure!" I moaned.

"I feel like you have something going on psy-cho-logically," she said.

She told me to write out the check for the "binder," or the couple thousand dollars that home sellers require in order to hold an offer.

Because buying a home is negotiating with a gun to your head, this needed to be done right away.

I went downstairs and told Rich our offer had been accepted. Then I started sobbing. My chest stiffened and I couldn't breathe. I went running just to have something to do with my legs. As I ran, I tried all the techniques from my neuroticism-reduction practice: to reassure myself that it was just my anxiety talking, that the house was a good deal, to notice what was happening in my body, to breathe through it. I told myself I would have anxiety about any house we picked.

Not entirely soothed, I returned to find there was a new problem: Rich and I had forgotten to bring checks to Florida.

I called Realtor again. She had someone over and she was half speaking to me, half to them. I could tell I was the lesser half—the one who couldn't make up her mind about a house. She told me to just wire the money. Miraculously, because of a fluke of banking hours, this option bought us an extra day to decide.

Life in the Guest House

On that day, I drove to the house that was now technically "ours." I parked a few doors down and tried to take a walk around one of the neighborhood's two possible walking routes: alongside a busy road or alongside a different busy road.

While I walked, I tried out a different way of thinking about my anxiety—one that the researchers who think anxiety is de facto bad would probably not recommend. I didn't note that I was panicking or get curious about the effect of the anxiety in my body. Instead, I listened to what the anxiety was saying.

You see, there is a competing theory to the idea that anxiety is never beneficial. Some psychologists think anxiety can be useful, spurring creativity and motivating us to problem-solve. As the psychologist

Tracy Dennis-Tiwary writes in her book *Future Tense*, anxiety can help narrow attention and heighten focus and detail-orientation. Anxiety can be a form of caring, of our minds highlighting what matters. It tells us that achieving our goals will require effort, and it pushes us to think about what efforts, exactly, we should take. Some studies even suggest that reframing anxiety as a benefit can help people feel less incapacitated by their nerves. "Anxiety evolved to help us navigate uncertainty in life," Dennis-Tiwary told me in an interview. "It evolved to help us focus on potential danger in our future. But to also remember that positive outcomes are still possible."

This is a new way of thinking about anxiety, and by extension, about neuroticism. I still wanted to deflate my neuroticism, but sometimes it seemed like the best way to achieve that would be to *listen* to my anxiety rather than to ignore it.

Dennis-Tiwary dismissed the idea that we should lead lives free of anxiety. "Mental health is not the absence of these uncomfortable feelings," she said. "It is the presence of them. It's our ability to struggle." You are still going to sometimes *feel* neurotic. *Becoming* less neurotic depends on what you do with that feeling.

In this, Dennis-Tiwary echoes the sentiments of the thirteenth-century Persian poet Rumi, who writes that to be human is to be a "guest house" into which one should invite all emotions— "a joy, a depression, a meanness." Even a "crowd of sorrows" should be welcomed, he writes, because each guest has been sent "as a guide from beyond." If anxiety is going to pass through, the trick is to learn from it, then let it move on.

As I walked around the neighborhood, I tried to see where my anxiety was guiding me. Why did I feel like every time I approached this house, I wanted to unzip my skin and run in the other direction? I couldn't tell if it was because I had inherited my dad's fear of spending money, or if my neuroticism was flaring up needlessly, or if it was truly not the house for me.

I called to mind some decisions I'd been 100 percent sure of making. The first time my mom met Rich, and she asked me if "everything about him was satisfactory to me."

"Yep!" I said with the goofy grin of a person who is six months into a relationship.

"*Everything* everything?" she said.

"Everything!" I cooed.

I remembered the joy of accepting my job offer at the *Atlantic*, and the next day marching in to resign from my previous job. I didn't cower or cry in those moments. I felt certain, at ease. I did not feel that way now.

I drove back and canceled the contract, and Realtor pretended not to be mad at me. That night I slept the profound sleep of a baby. Or the dead.

But here's what I didn't do that day: I didn't scream at Rich. I didn't get drunk. I didn't catastrophize. Instead, while in Florida I relied on emotional support from my friends, those people I was reminded exist during all my work on extroversion. "I feel like everyone I know is criticizing all my options while offering no solutions," I whined to Anastasia one day. "I just can't take it right now! I'm on the brink!"

"Well, and for our generation it's especially hard to hear that because we *have* no good options," she said. "We're doing the best we can with what we have available. It's not like you set the interest rates." Our personalities gently patted each other, telephonically.

I saw as an improvement the fact that I could now soften my neuroticism without alcohol and meltdowns. It was a sign that, to paraphrase from the meditation class, things would happen that I didn't like—and I could handle them. The anxiety is still there, a scorching magma beneath my surface, and it probably always will be. As Steven Hayes taught me, I hurt because I care, and as Tracy Dennis-Tiwary taught me, I'm anxious because I care. Neuroticism will continue to visit me, even if its presence lightens. But personality change isn't all or nothing: Just like personality traits themselves, it's a spectrum. You have to appreciate floating through its gradients.

During those months in Florida, I accepted that I didn't know when, exactly, we would find a house we could afford, and I accepted that the stress of not knowing was woven into the search. There are few joys in life that don't lie beyond a field of uncertainty: As Virginia Woolf put it, part of "the beauty of the world" is that it "has two edges, one of laughter, one of anguish, cutting the heart asunder." The laughter of security often trails behind the anguish of doubt.

And some of these doubts would soon resolve themselves. I did not know at the time that, just a few months after our return from Florida, one afternoon I'd notice that my period was a little late. Within a few minutes, I was staring down at a little blue plus sign. The "fucking kid" I had foresworn had glimmered into view—one day in my thirties, in fact, when it was convenient for me. Apparently, much as the only poll that matters is the one on Election Day, the only fertility test that matters is the one you take two weeks after having unprotected sex. Trembling, I called down to Rich in the basement, and he ran upstairs to envelop me in a hug. "You're gonna be a great mom," he said.

Getting pregnant immediately reprograms your brain to prioritize anything that might make your baby's life even 1 percent better. I felt charged with an incredible responsibility, like with every step I was carting around the nuclear football. Within months, Rich and I got married. I whittled my caffeine intake from "concerning" to "almost none." I developed strong and unshakable opinions on the relative merits of car seats. I did whatever I could to reduce my stress and anxiety, which in pregnancy is mostly limited to "take walks." I felt like I, and my personality, had to be good enough for two.

During that intervening, uncertain time, I thought back to something Angela Duckworth, the *Grit* author, had mentioned about what to do when you find your motivation flagging. If you feel reluctant to take on some necessary drudgery—like, say, house hunting—you can try to see it as part of some larger, more meaningful objective in your life. (This is similar to the theory about the motivating power of "personal projects.") Duckworth told me she uses this strategy to spur herself to revise her PowerPoint slides, a process she finds tedious until she reminds herself that it's connected to her larger project of teaching people about psychology. "When I revise this PowerPoint slide, I am being a better teacher. When I'm being a better teacher, I'm increasing psychological literacy," she told me. In my case, this could mean recognizing that the slog of the house search is connected to the higher goal of living in a new home, and of entering the next phase of my life.

This thought process proved helpful to me while we were still in Florida, during another annoying task I performed daily. Though our Airbnb there was billed as a "beach house," to actually get to the beach from said house, you had to cross a busy, four-lane highway. Because this was Florida, where central planning goes to die, there was no crosswalk. Instead, pedestrians were expected to frogger across during a break in traffic. Usually, this required waiting for three to seven minutes, running like hell toward the median, standing atop it as cars raced past you at fifty miles an hour, then sprinting to the other side.

I hated this. To me, it was a harrowing moment during what should have been a peaceful morning run. The crossing process seemed to highlight all my weaknesses—indecisiveness, slowness, anxiety. Some days, I'd think about how if I was bolder, I wouldn't wait for such a long break, and I could make it across sooner. Other days, I'd vividly picture bolting into an oncoming pickup, imagine the metal smashing my body and lifting me off my feet. Once, after I had reached the other side of the highway, I noticed with alarm that my left shoe had been untied the whole time.

Often, changing my personality has felt just like this precarious dance through traffic. I would surge forward—a two-and-a-half-hour improv class!—and then have to stop and rest at the median for a while. I was never quite sure if a new activity spelled momentum or danger.

Sometimes I balked, and watched with bewilderment as other people made it across without an issue. Standing on the other side, they would gloat that, say, meditation worked perfectly for them. I envied their easy, uncomplicated jaunt.

But month after month, I dreaded the highway, or the improv showcase, or the stressful situation du jour, then ran into it anyway. This was what personality change looked like, in the end: fits and starts, with the goal being for the starts to outnumber the fits. The path of change isn't constant, and it isn't always poetic. It can have plateaus and holdups, and objects that are closer than they appear.

About a block later, I'd make it to the beach, which, for all of Florida's many, many flaws, is the state's crown jewel. The beach near us was a broad, alabaster expanse that faded softly into the pulsing Atlantic. Occasionally the wind stirred up the pearlescent sand, and people jogged through it unfazed, as if they were hovering through clouds.

In 2010 Corona launched an ad campaign with the tagline "Find your beach." You've probably seen the ads—the golden beer bottle, the sand, the turquoise sky. Each commercial is a call to steal a bit of happiness in the everyday (with the help, presumably, of beer). I get that this directive can rankle: The writer Zadie Smith, who for a while lived across from a giant Corona ad, called it "a faintly threatening mixture of imperative and possessive forms." But I also understand the reasoning behind it. For me and plenty of other people, there's nothing better than the beach, which functions as both a physical location and an aspirational state of mind, a serene ideal at which to hurl yourself. Granted, your "beach" might be the mountains of Colorado or Central Park on a crisp fall day, but my beach is the actual beach.

Once my feet touched the sand, I would pause and stare into the orphic blue water. At the beach, I felt rescued and renewed. I saw proof of life amid the strip malls and Olive Gardens, and I felt a strengthened commitment to house hunting—but also to extroversion, emotional stability, and agreeableness. The world didn't seem so awful, after all.

This was the reason I had crossed the horrible highway. I was dodging traffic so I could get to the beach, and I was tolerating the stress of real estate so I could find a new house. I was changing my personality so I could live better. When I finally made it across, I felt like a different person.

Acknowledgments

This book owes its life to many people who believed in the idea before I did—and who mostly have better personalities than I do.

Thank you to my amazing agent Howard Yoon, who is emotionally stable and, more importantly, brilliant. Thanks for being in my corner.

Stephanie Hitchcock at Simon Element is one of the book world's best nonfiction-writing minds, and I'm so fortunate that she took this on and shaped it with her incredible expertise. She's the reason this book has heart. Thank you also to Erica Siudzinski, for always being so kind, unflappable, and prompt.

The entire team at Simon & Schuster worked so hard to make this book successful. I'm so grateful to the copy editors and other unsung publishing heroes who do so much to help readers fall in love with books, and to help books find readers.

Thank you to Carrie Frye, the hottest mistress at the funeral, and one who knows exactly when a chapter is hurtling toward doom. Thank you for your wisdom, encouragement, guidance, and agreeableness. Michael Gaynor, I'm forever grateful for your fast fact-checks that are somehow both always thorough and never nitpicky. I live in fear of the day you're no longer available for another "small checking assignment?"

Denise Wills and Honor Jones—thank you for assigning the personality-change story, for your best-in-the-biz editing, and for believing in me. I still owe you an invite to that improv show. In fact, thank you to all my bosses at the *Atlantic* for letting me take book leave and for giving me so many opportunities.

I'm very grateful to Nathan Hudson, Brent Roberts, Matthew Johnson, Kathryn Paige Harden, and the many other researchers who took time out of their busy lives to explain their research to me. I can't thank you enough for your careful work, and for your time. (And a very special thanks to Jim Fallon, who passed away not long after we spoke.) I'm also deeply indebted to the folks who shared their own stories of personality change; your vulnerability and candor help readers feel less alone.

Thank you to my parents, who contributed between 30 and 50 percent of the variance of my personality, and who offered to provide childcare when I got pregnant a little earlier in the book process than expected.

Julie Beck edited several chapters of this book when my eyes were too glazed over to take another pass. She's one of the best writers and thinkers at the *Atlantic*, and her sharp eye was indispensable here. Kathy Gilsinan, baddest and smartest bitch around, read the *whole freaking book!* I'm so grateful to you, girl, and I absolutely owe you one even though you will insist that I don't.

Thank you to all the readers of the personality-change article, of my Substack, and of my other work at the *Atlantic*. There is so much good writing out there, and I'm truly grateful to each person who spends time with my work. It's an honor to be read by you.

Rich, my partner in crime and in so much else, how can I squeeze fifteen years of gratitude into one acknowledgment section? Thank you for your first reads, for your support, and for listening. Thank you, frankly, for the use of your car. Just thank you. I love you.

Appendix

A partial list of the activities I performed in order to change my personality, partly adapted from the study "You Have to Follow Through: Attaining Behavioral Change Goals Predicts Volitional Personality Change" by Nathan W. Hudson, Daniel A. Briley, William J. Chopik, and Jaime Derringer.

(These are still taped to my nightstand.)

Agreeableness 😃

- Volunteer
- Give someone a compliment
- Send a friend an encouraging text
- Apologize even when the other person doesn't
- Write down a nice thing someone did for you
- Reflect on good qualities of people you love
- Make a list of times people kept their promises to you
- Spend time thinking about the good qualities of someone you don't like
- Choose to forgive someone
- Reflect on the circumstances that might be contributing to someone's bad behavior

Emotional Stability 🙏

- Write about a positive thing that happened to you that day and how it made you feel
- List things you're grateful for
- Write about your good qualities
- Write three positive thoughts for each negative thought
- Write down evidence against negative thoughts
- When you wake up, say "I choose to be happy today!"
- Meditate
- Do yoga

Notes

Introduction

7   *I took a scientific personality test:* Nathan W. Hudson et al., "You
    Have to Follow Through: Attaining Behavioral Change Goals
    Predicts Volitional Personality Change," *Journal of Personality and
    Social Psychology* 117, no. 4 (October 2019): 839–57, https://doi
    .org/10.1037/pspp0000221.

10 *I embraced the words of:* Jorge Luis Borges, *Selected Non-fictions*
    (New York: Viking, 1999), 3; and Maria Popova, "The Nothingness
    of Personality: Young Borges on the Self," *Marginalian*, April 10,
    2017, https://www.themarginalian.org/2017/04/03/the-nothing
    ness-of-personality-borges/.

12 *But studies suggest most people:* Nathan W. Hudson and Brent W.
    Roberts, "Goals to Change Personality Traits: Concurrent Links
    between Personality Traits, Daily Behavior, and Goals to Change
    Oneself," *Journal of Research in Personality* 53 (December 2014):
    68–83, https://doi.org/10.1016/j.jrp.2014.08.008.

12 *Even in global surveys across:* Erica Baranski et al., "Who in the
    World Is Trying to Change Their Personality Traits? Volitional
    Personality Change among College Students in Six Continents,"
    Journal of Personality and Social Psychology 121, no. 5 (November
    2021): 1,140–56, https://doi.org/10.1037/pspp0000389.

13 *"Agency causes progress":* Martin Seligman, "Agency and Progress:
    Efficacy, Optimism, and Imagination with Martin Seligman," MIT
    Media Lab, June 11, 2021, https://www.media.mit.edu/videos/ml
    -perspectives-2021-06-10/?autoplay=true.

1
The OCEAN Within: What Is Personality?

16 *From early in his career:* Gordon Allport, *The Person in Psychology* (Boston: Beacon Press, 1968), 382.

16 *His famed "talking cure," or psychoanalysis:* Jeffrey A. Lieberman and Ogi Ogas, *Shrinks: The Untold Story of Psychiatry* (New York: Little, Brown Spark, 2016).

16 *Still, Freud agreed to the meeting:* Allport, *The Person in Psychology*, 383–84.

16 *To Allport, it was an encounter:* Ibid., 383.

17 *"And was that little boy you?":* Ibid.

17 *Psychology is a young science:* "Department of Psychology: About," accessed July 2, 2022, https://psychology.fas.harvard.edu/about.

17 *Theophrastus at one point outlined:* "The Characters of Theophrastus," Eudaemonist.com, 2016, https://www.eudaemonist.com/biblion/characters/.

18 *"The religious view of the human race":* Frank Dumont, *A History of Personality Psychology: Theory, Science, and Research from Hellenism to the Twenty-First Century* (Cambridge: Cambridge University Press, 2010), 15.

18 *However, even Jung cautioned:* Joseph Stromberg and Estelle Caswell, "Why the Myers-Briggs Test Is Totally Meaningless," *Vox*, July 15, 2014, https://www.vox.com/2014/7/15/5881947/myers-briggs-personality-test-meaningless.

18 *Jung's rubric captured the attention:* Merve Emre, *The Personality Brokers: The Strange History of Myers-Briggs and the Birth of Personality Testing* (New York: Doubleday, 2018), 123.

18 *"The more you know about what":* Ibid., 134.

19 *But in time, it turned out:* Stromberg and Caswell, "Why the Myers-Briggs Test Is Totally Meaningless."

19 *The organizational psychologist Adam Grant:* Emma Goldberg, "Personality Tests Are the Astrology of the Office," *New York*

Times, September 17, 2019, https://www.nytimes.com/2019
/09/17/style/personality-tests-office.html.

19 *One detractor even said psychologists:* Annie Murphy Paul, *The Cult of Personality Testing: How Personality Tests Are Leading Us to Miseducate Our Children, Mismanage Our Companies, and Misunderstand Ourselves* (New York: Free Press, 2005), 36.

19 *Rigorous and dutiful, he perused:* Gordon Allport and Henry Odbert, "Trait-Names: A Psycho-Lexical Study," *Psychological Review Publications* 47, no. 1 (1936): 24.

19 *Raymond Cattell, a British-American psychologist:* Dumont, *A History of Personality Psychology*, 172.

20 *In the decades that followed:* Lewis R. Goldberg, "The Structure of Phenotypic Personality Traits," *American Psychologist* 48, no. 1 (January 1993): 26–34, https://doi.org/10.1037/0003-066x.48.1.26.

20 *Starting in the 1970s, Freudian psychoanalysis:* Cody Delistraty, "Untangling the Complicated, Controversial Legacy of Sigmund Freud," *Cut*, September 5, 2017, https://www.thecut.com/2017/09/sigmud-freud-making-of-an-illusion-book.html.

21 *If they could, brothers and sisters:* M. Brent Donnellan and Richard E. Lucas, *Great Myths of Personality* (Hoboken, NJ: Wiley Blackwell, 2021), 150.

22 *They like to be the center:* Daniel Nettle, *Personality: What Makes You the Way You Are* (Oxford: Oxford University Press, 2007), 82.

23 *Agreeable people are warm, altruistic:* Margaret Avison and Adrian Furnham, "Personality and Voluntary Childlessness," *Journal of Population Research* 32, no. 1 (November 2015): 45–67, https://doi.org/10.1007/s12546-014-9140-6.

23 *"High neuroticism infuses everything":* Nettle, *Personality*, 243.

23 *People tend to be happier:* Kristina M. DeNeve and Harris Cooper, "The Happy Personality: A Meta-Analysis of 137 Personality Traits and Subjective Well-Being," *Psychological Bulletin* 124, no. 2 (September 1998): 197–229, https://doi.org/10.1037/0033-2909.124.2.197; and Piers Steel, Joseph Schmidt, and Jonas Shultz, "Refining the Relationship between Personality and

Subjective Well-Being," *Psychological Bulletin* 134, no. 1 (2008): 138–61, https://doi.org/10.1037/0033-2909.134.1.138.

25 *James's father, Henry Sr., devoted:* Robert D. Richardson, *William James: In the Maelstrom of American Modernism: A Biography* (Boston: Mariner Books, 2007).

25 *"In most of us, by the age":* William James, *The Principles of Psychology* (New York: Henry Holt, 1918).

26 *People naturally grow less neurotic:* Olivia E. Atherton et al., "Stability and Change in Personality Traits and Major Life Goals from College to Midlife," *Personality and Social Psychology Bulletin* 47, no. 5 (May 2021): 841–58, https://doi.org/10.1177/0146167220949362.

26 *One study that measured the personalities:* Rodica Ioana Damian et al., "Sixteen Going on Sixty-Six: A Longitudinal Study of Personality Stability and Change across 50 Years," *Journal of Personality and Social Psychology* 117, no. 3 (September 2019): 674–95, https://doi.org/10.1037/pspp0000210.

26 *Another, which followed hundreds of Californians:* Ravenna Helson, Constance Jones, and Virginia S. Kwan, "Personality Change over 40 Years of Adulthood: Hierarchical Linear Modeling Analyses of Two Longitudinal Samples," *Journal of Personality and Social Psychology* 83, no. 3 (September 2002): 752–66, https://doi.org/10.1037/0022-3514.83.3.752.

26 *Yet another found that:* Sanjay Srivastava et al., "Development of Personality in Early and Middle Adulthood: Set like Plaster or Persistent Change?" *Journal of Personality and Social Psychology* 84, no. 5 (May 2003): 1,041–53, https://doi.org/10.1037/0022-3514.84.5.1041.

26 *As the Zen philosopher Alan Watts:* Alan Watts, *This Is It: And Other Essays on Zen and Spiritual Experience* (New York: Vintage, 1973), 70.

27 *"Man first of all exists":* Jean-Paul Sartre, "Existentialism Is a Humanism," in *Existentialism from Dostoevsky to Sartre*, ed. Walter Kaufmann (New York: Penguin, 1956), 349.

27 *Or as Nietzsche cryptically instructed:* Friedrich Nietzsche, *Thus Spake Zarathustra*, Project Gutenberg, https://www.gutenberg.org/files/1998/1998-h/1998-h.htm.

27 *Researchers have found that in cultures:* Wiebke Bleidorn et al.,
    "Personality Maturation Around the World: A Cross-Cultural
    Examination of Social-Investment Theory," *Psychological Science*
    24, no. 12 (December 2013): 2,530–40, https://doi.org/10.1177
    /0956797613498396.

27 *"We all have multiple selves":* Brian Lowery, *Selfless: The Social
    Creation of "You"* (New York: Harper, 2023).

27 *This view is sometimes called:* Bruce Hood, *The Self Illusion: How
    the Social Brain Creates Identity* (New York: Oxford University
    Press, 2012), xv.

27 *This mutability of the self may:* Christian Jarrett, *Be Who You
    Want: Unlocking the Science of Personality Change* (New York:
    Simon & Schuster, 2021), 36.

27 *working more tends to increase:* Nathan W. Hudson, Brent W.
    Roberts, and Jennifer Lodi-Smith, "Personality Trait Development
    and Social Investment in Work," *Journal of Research in Personality*
    46, no. 3 (June 2012): 334–44, https://doi.org/10.1016/j.jrp
    .2012.03.002.

27 *One study found that people:* Jenny Wagner et al., "The First
    Partnership Experience and Personality Development," *Social
    Psychological and Personality Science* 6, no. 4 (January 2015):
    455–63, https://doi.org/10.1177/1948550614566092.

28 *In a well-known study published:* Jordi Quoidbach, Daniel T.
    Gilbert, and Timothy D. Wilson, "The End of History Illusion,"
    Science 339, no. 6115 (January 2013): 96–98, https://doi.org/10
    .1126/science.1229294.

28 *"Human beings are works in progress":* Dan Gilbert, "The Psychology
    of Your Future Self," TED2014, March 2014, https://www.ted.com
    /talks/dan_gilbert_the_psychology_of_your_future_self/transcript
    ?language=en.

28 *In the words of Philip Larkin:* Philip Larkin, "This Be the Verse," in
    Collected Poems (New York: Farrar, Straus and Giroux, 2003).

30 *"James was almost obsessed":* John J. Kaag, *Sick Souls, Healthy
    Minds: How William James Can Save Your Life* (Princeton, NJ:
    Princeton University Press, 2021).

30 *In his writing, James at times:* James, *The Principles of Psychology*, 127.

30 *"My first act of free will":* David E. Leary, "New Insights into William James's Personal Crisis in the Early 1870s: Part I. Arthur Schopenhauer and the Origin & Nature of the Crisis," William James Studies, https://williamjamesstudies.org/new-insights-into -william-jamess-personal-crisis-in-the-early-1870s-part-i-arthur -schopenhauer-and-the-origin-nature-of-the-crisis/.

2

Breaking the Flywheel: The "How" of Personality Change

32 *"Anything that's beautiful in Dallas":* Pamela Colloff, "Lip Shtick," *Texas Monthly*, January 20, 2013, https://www.texasmonthly.com /articles/lip-shtick/.

34 *Conscientious people, for instance, are healthier:* Olivia E. Atherton et al., "Personality Correlates of Risky Health Outcomes: Findings from a Large Internet Study," *Journal of Research in Personality* 50 (June 2014): 5660, https://doi.org/10.1016/j .jrp.2014.03.002; and Margaret L. Kern and Howard S. Friedman, "Do Conscientious Individuals Live Longer? A Quantitative Review," *Health Psychology* 27, no. 5 (2008): 505–12, https://doi .org/10.1037/0278-6133.27.5.505.

34 *A massive meta-analysis of 2,500 studies:* Michael P. Wilmot and Deniz S. Ones, "A Century of Research on Conscientiousness at Work," *Proceedings of the National Academy of Sciences* 116, no. 46 (October 2019): 23,004–10, https://doi.org/10.1073/pnas.19 08430116.

34 *And although introversion is not:* Christian Jarrett, "Why Are Extraverts Happier?" *Research Digest*, July 30, 2016, https://digest .bps.org.uk/2014/03/13/why-are-extraverts-happier/.

34 *It's a "joy to be hidden":* Alison Carper, "The Importance of Hide-and-Seek," *New York Times*, June 30, 2015, https://archive.nytimes .com/opinionator.blogs.nytimes.com/2015/06/30/the-importance -of-hide-and-seek/.

34 *Despite the stereotype of the moody:* Kevin C. Stanek and Deniz
    S. Ones, "Meta-Analytic Relations between Personality and
    Cognitive Ability," *Proceedings of the National Academy of
    Sciences* 120, no. 23 (2023): e2212794120, https://doi.org/10.1073
    /pnas.2212794120.

34 *When neurotic children and teens:* Rebecca L. Shiner, "Negative
    Emotionality and Neuroticism from Childhood through
    Adulthood," in *Handbook of Personality Development*, ed. Dan P.
    McAdams, Rebecca L. Shiner, and Jennifer L. Tackett (New York:
    Guilford, 2019), 375.

34 *Neurotic people are more likely:* Daniel Nettle, *Personality: What
    Makes You the Way You Are* (Oxford, UK: Oxford University
    Press, 2007), 32.

34 *People who are high in emotional stability:* Isabelle Hansson et al.,
    "The Role of Personality in Retirement Adjustment: Longitudinal
    Evidence for the Effects on Life Satisfaction," *Journal of Personality*
    88, no. 4 (September 2019): 642–58, https://doi.org/10.1111
    /jopy.12516; and Morton M. Hunt, *The Story of Psychology* (New
    York: Anchor, 2007), 395.

34 *Some research estimates that a small:* Christopher J. Boyce, Alex
    M. Wood, and Nattavudh Powdthavee, "Is Personality Fixed?
    Personality Changes as Much as 'Variable' Economic Factors
    and More Strongly Predicts Changes to Life Satisfaction," *Social
    Indicators Research* 111, no. 1 (February 2012): 287–305, https://
    doi.org/10.1007/s11205-012-0006-z.

35 *It's not just* having *these traits:* Amanda Jo Wright and Joshua
    James Jackson, "Do Changes in Personality Predict Life
    Outcomes?" *Journal of Personality and Social Psychology* 125,
    no. 6 (December 2023): 1,495–518, https://doi.org/10.1037
    /pspp0000472.

35 *When people do successfully shift:* Nathan W. Hudson and R.
    Chris Fraley, "Changing for the Better? Longitudinal Associations
    between Volitional Personality Change and Psychological Well-
    Being," *Personality and Social Psychology Bulletin* 42, no. 5 (March
    2016): 603–15, https://doi.org/10.1177/0146167216637840.

35 *The prisoner, a man in his thirties, was getting:* Raymond J. Corsini and Danny Wedding, *Current Psychotherapies* (Boston: Cengage, 2011), 12.

36 *The psychologist William R. Miller has studied:* William R. Miller and Janet C'de Baca, "Quantum Change: Toward a Psychology of Transformation," in *Can Personality Change?*, ed. Todd Heatherton and Joel Weinberger (Washington, DC: American Psychological Association, 1994), 253–80.

36 *Afterward, they got divorces:* William R. Miller and Janet C'de Baca, *Quantum Change: When Epiphanies and Sudden Insights Transform Ordinary Lives* (New York: Guilford Press, 2001), 49.

36 *While this tiny study is more:* Janet C'de Baca and Paula Wilbourne, "Quantum Change: Ten Years Later," *Journal of Clinical Psychology* 60, no. 5 (March 2004): 531–41, https://doi .org/10.1002/jclp.20006.

37 *For a 2019 study, Nathan Hudson:* Nathan W. Hudson et al., "You Have to Follow Through: Attaining Behavioral Change Goals Predicts Volitional Personality Change," *Journal of Personality and Social Psychology* 117, no. 4 (October 2019): 839–57, https://doi .org/10.1037/pspp0000221.

38 *Hudson's study found that these challenges:* Nathan W. Hudson et al., "Change Goals Robustly Predict Trait Growth: A Mega-Analysis of a Dozen Intensive Longitudinal Studies Examining Volitional Change," *Social Psychological and Personality Science* 11, no. 6 (June 2020): 723–32, https://doi.org/10.1177 /1948550619878423.

38 *But, as we'll also see:* I'm aware there's been some trouble in the world of psychology lately. In recent years, researchers have tried, and often failed, to replicate many psychological studies— in effect meaning that the original studies' findings might be flukes. This may, understandably, make people less likely to trust studies like Hudson's. But personality psychology is on firmer ground than some other branches of the discipline. According to a recent analysis of different psychological subfields, personality psychology studies have the best track record for holding up over

time and under scrutiny by different researchers. See Wu Youyou, Yang Yang, and Brian Uzzi, "A Discipline-Wide Investigation of the Replicability of Psychology Papers over the Past Two Decades," *Proceedings of the National Academy of Sciences* 120, no. 6 (January 2023): e2208863120, https://doi.org/10.1073/pnas.2208863120.

38 *Along with some colleagues, Mirjam Stieger:* Mirjam Stieger et al., "Changing Personality Traits with the Help of a Digital Personality Change Intervention," *Proceedings of the National Academy of Sciences* 118, no. 8 (August 2021): e2017548118, https://doi.org/10.1073/pnas.2017548118.

38 *If personality is, as F. Scott Fitzgerald:* F. Scott Fitzgerald, *The Great Gatsby* (New York: Scribner, 1925), 2.

39 *When we see that we are:* Raj Raghunathan, *If You're So Smart, Why Aren't You Happy?* (New York: Portfolio, 2016), 225.

39 *"Similarly, it is by doing":* "Aristotle and John Locke: Conversation," *Lapham's Quarterly*, accessed July 8, 2022, https://www.laphamsquarterly.org/conversations/aristotle-%08john-locke.

40 *The participants in the "malleable" condition:* Karina Schumann, Jamil Zaki, and Carol S. Dweck, "Addressing the Empathy Deficit: Beliefs about the Malleability of Empathy Predict Effortful Responses When Empathy Is Challenging," *Journal of Personality and Social Psychology* 107, no. 3 (September 2014): 475–93, https://doi.org/10.1037/a0036738.

40 *Afterward, his patients felt like they:* Richard Wiseman, *The As If Principle: The Radically New Approach to Changing Your Life* (New York: Free Press, 2013), 216.

40 *Kelly's goal was to help:* Nigel Beail and Stacey Parker, "Group Fixed-Role Therapy: A Clinical Application," *International Journal of Personal Construct Psychology* 4, no. 1 (1991): 85–95, https://doi.org/10.1080/08936039108404762.

40 *"No one needs to be the victim":* Stefano Tasselli, Martin Kilduff, and Blaine Landis, "Personality Change: Implications for Organizational Behavior," *Academy of Management Annals* 12, no. 2 (2018): 467–93, https://doi.org/10.5465/annals.2016.0008.

40 *Much more recently, Jessica Schleider:* Jessica Schleider and John Weisz, "A Single-Session Growth Mindset Intervention for Adolescent Anxiety and Depression: 9-Month Outcomes of a Randomized Trial," *Journal of Child Psychology and Psychiatry* 59, no. 2 (September 2017): 160–70, https://doi.org/10.1111/jcpp.12811.

40 *Yet another study found that people:* Hans S. Schroder et al., "Growth Mindset of Anxiety Buffers the Link between Stressful Life Events and Psychological Distress and Coping Strategies," *Personality and Individual Differences* 110 (May 2017): 23–26, https://doi.org/10.1016/j.paid.2017.01.016.

41 *The researchers Adriana Sum Miu and David Yeager:* Adriana Sum Miu and David Scott Yeager, "Preventing Symptoms of Depression by Teaching Adolescents That People Can Change," *Clinical Psychological Science* 3, no. 5 (September 2014): 726–43, https://doi.org/10.1177/2167702614548317.

41 *The best "program" for changing personality:* Hudson et al., "You Have to Follow Through."

3

Dance Like Everyone Is Watching: Extroversion

47 *In lab experiments, extroverts tend to:* Luke Smillie, Margaret Kern, and Mirko Uljarevic, "Extraversion: Description, Development, and Mechanisms," in *Handbook of Personality Development*, ed. Dan P. McAdams, Rebecca L. Shiner, and Jennifer L. Tackett (New York: Guilford, 2019), 326.

47 *People who are extroverted as teenagers:* Catharine R. Gale et al., "Neuroticism and Extraversion in Youth Predict Mental Wellbeing and Life Satisfaction 40 Years Later," *Journal of Research in Personality* 47, no. 6 (December 2013): 687–97, https://doi.org/10.1016/j.jrp.2013.06.005.

47 *Though there's nothing wrong with being:* Zack M. van Allen et al., "Enacted Extraversion as a Well-Being Enhancing Strategy in

Everyday Life: Testing across Three, Week-Long Interventions,"
Collabra: Psychology 7, no. 1 (December 2021): 29931, https://doi
.org/10.1525/collabra.29931.

48 *In one study, introverts even:* William Fleeson and Joshua Wilt,
"The Relevance of Big Five Trait Content in Behavior to Subjective
Authenticity: Do High Levels of Within-Person Behavioral
Variability Undermine or Enable Authenticity Achievement?"
Journal of Personality 78, no. 4 (August 2010): 1,353–82, https://
doi.org/10.1111/j.1467-6494.2010.00653.x.

49 *Early improv was a type:* Doug Gordon, "Author Sam Wasson
Explains How America Invented Improv," Wisconsin Public Radio,
August 8, 2020, https://www.wpr.org/author-sam-wasson
-explains-how-america-invented-improv.

49 *The research on improv's upsides:* Peter Felsman, Colleen M.
Seifert, and Joseph A. Himle, "The Use of Improvisational Theater
Training to Reduce Social Anxiety in Adolescents," *Arts in
Psychotherapy* 63 (April 2019): 111–17, https://doi.org/10.1016/j
.aip.2018.12.001.

51 *The pioneering psychologist Jerome Bruner:* Jerome S. Bruner, *On
Knowing: Essays for the Left Hand* (Cambridge, MA: Belknap
Press of Harvard University Press, 1962), 24.

51 *According to a study that followed:* Shigehiro Oishi and Ulrich
Schimmack, "Residential Mobility, Well-Being, and Mortality,"
Journal of Personality and Social Psychology 98, no. 6 (June 2010):
980–94, https://doi.org/10.1037/a0019389.

52 *George Eliot called a friend:* George Eliot, "The Spanish Gypsy,"
in *The Works of George Eliot,* Cabinet Edition (London and
Edinburgh: William Blackwood and Sons, 1878), 227.

56 *"The needs and wants of others":* Deborah Tannen, *Conversational
Style: Analyzing Talk among Friends* (Oxford, UK: Oxford
University Press, 1984), 4.

57 *People who have lots of weak ties:* Gillian Sandstrom and Ashley
Whillans, "Why You Miss Those Casual Friends So Much,"
Harvard Business Review, April 22, 2020, https://hbr.org/2020/04
/why-you-miss-those-casual-friends-so-much.

58 *While it's true that extroverts enjoy:* Daniel Nettle, *Personality: What Makes You the Way You Are* (Oxford, UK: Oxford University Press, 2007), 81.

65 *Explaining her technique in 1963:* Viola Spolin, *Improvisation for the Theater: A Handbook of Teaching and Directing Techniques* (Evanston, IL: Northwestern University Press, 1999), 4.

67 *But invariably, another man nearby:* Tannen, *Conversational Style*, 77–78.

67 *In general, Tannen notices that the:* Ibid., 121.

67 *Putting a, uh, finer point:* Ibid., 62.

68 *But there's some evidence that I:* Melissa Dahl, *Cringeworthy: A Theory of Awkwardness* (New York: Portfolio/Penguin, 2018), 119.

69 *The students thought about half:* Thomas Gilovich, Victoria Husted Medvec, and Kenneth Savitsky, "The Spotlight Effect in Social Judgment: An Egocentric Bias in Estimates of the Salience of One's Own Actions and Appearance," *Journal of Personality and Social Psychology* 78, no. 2 (March 2000): 211–22, https://doi .org/10.1037/0022-3514.78.2.211.

69 *As the authors of one spotlight-effect:* Thomas Gilovich, Justin Kruger, and Victoria Husted Medvec, "The Spotlight Effect Revisited: Overestimating the Manifest Variability of Our Actions and Appearance," *Journal of Experimental Social Psychology* 38, no. 1 (January 2002): 93–99, https://doi.org/10.1006/jesp.2001 .1490.

70 *Because sharing our thoughts clarifies:* Ralph Waldo Emerson, *The Complete Works of Ralph Waldo Emerson*, Vol. 8: *Letters and Social Aims* (New York: Houghton, Mifflin, 1903), 91.

4

From Overwhelm to Om: Neuroticism

74 *"Anxiety does not necessarily mean":* Alfred Adler and Colin Brett, *Understanding Human Nature: The Psychology of Personality* (London: Oneworld Publications, 1992), 132.

76 *Neuroticism encompasses anxiety, depression:* Shannon Sauer-Zavala and David H. Barlow, *Neuroticism: A New Framework for Emotional Disorders and Their Treatment* (New York: Guilford Press, 2021), 13.

76 *Adverse childhood experiences—stressors like abuse:* Jessica M. Grusnick et al., "The Association between Adverse Childhood Experiences and Personality, Emotions and Affect: Does Number and Type of Experiences Matter?" *Journal of Research in Personality* 85 (April 2020): 103908, https://doi.org/10.1016/j.jrp.2019.103908.

76 *As though it weren't enough:* Roman Kotov et al., "Linking 'Big' Personality Traits to Anxiety, Depressive, and Substance Use Disorders: A Meta-Analysis," *Psychological Bulletin* 136, no. 5 (September 2010): 768–821, https://doi.org/10.1037/a0020327.

76 *including a higher risk of dementia:* Andrew M. Seaman, "Don't Worry: Neuroticism Linked to Alzheimer's Risk in Women," Reuters, October 1, 2014, https://www.reuters.com/article /us-neurotic-alzheimers/dont-worry-neuroticism-linked-to -alzheimers-risk-in-women-idUSKCN0HQ56W20141001.

76 *The trait predicts whether someone will:* Erik E. Noftle and Phillip R. Shaver, "Attachment Dimensions and the Big Five Personality Traits: Associations and Comparative Ability to Predict Relationship Quality," *Journal of Research in Personality* 40, no. 2 (2006): 179–208, https://doi.org/10.1016/j.jrp.2004.11.003.

76 *For whatever reason, we neurotic people:* Rebecca L. Shiner, "Negative Emotionality and Neuroticism from Childhood through Adulthood," in *Handbook of Personality Development*, ed. Dan P. McAdams, Rebecca L. Shiner, and Jennifer L. Tackett (New York: Guilford, 2019), 373.

76 *and our health and quality of life:* Sauer-Zavala and Barlow, *Neuroticism*, 25.

77 *In studies, neuroticism is the trait:* Nathan W. Hudson and Brent W. Roberts, "Goals to Change Personality Traits: Concurrent Links between Personality Traits, Daily Behavior, and Goals to Change Oneself," *Journal of Research in Personality* 53 (December 2014): 68–83, https://doi.org/10.1016/j.jrp.2014.08.008.

77   *"There is no greater risk factor":* Andrea Petersen, *On Edge: A Journey through Anxiety* (New York: Crown, 2017), 77.

77   *Or it might start from:* Ibid., 80.

78   *To paraphrase the poet John Berryman:* John Berryman, "A Point of Age," in *Collected Poems* (Kate Donahue Berryman, 1942).

80   *"I'd seen so many careers":* Dan Harris, *10% Happier: How I Tamed the Voice in My Head, Reduced Stress without Losing My Edge, and Found Self-Help That Actually Works—A True Story* (New York: It Books, 2014), 53.

82   *"The one you feed":* Unwinding Anxiety, Week 3, Module 19, "The Committee in My Head."

82   *Chronic worrying, according to Brewer:* Sauer-Zavala and Barlow, *Neuroticism,* 71.

82   *By doing this, you are supposed:* Judson Brewer, *Unwinding Anxiety* (New York: Avery, 2021), 112.

83   *According to his data, people's anxiety:* Unwinding Anxiety, August 11, 2022, https://www.unwindinganxiety.com/.

84   *No anxiety can hurt:* Petersen, *On Edge,* 167.

84   *Brewer, though, disagrees with this:* Brewer, *Unwinding Anxiety,* 80.

85   *In my readings about Buddhism:* Daisetz Teitaro Suzuki, *Essays in Zen Buddhism* (New York: Grove Press, 1949), quoted in Maria Popova, "D. T. Suzuki on What Freedom Really Means and How Zen Can Help Us Cultivate Our Character," *Marginalian,* March 28, 2021, https://www.themarginalian.org/2015/01/30/d-t-suzuki -essays-in-zen-buddhism/.

85   *"In many ways, anxiety has":* Petersen, *On Edge,* 165.

88   *Indeed, one small study found:* Tony Z. Tang et al., "Personality Change during Depression Treatment," *Archives of General Psychiatry* 66, no. 12 (2009): 1322, https://doi.org/10.1001 /archgenpsychiatry.2009.166.

89   *In studies, neuroticism is associated:* Katherine A. Duggan et al., "Personality and Healthy Sleep: The Importance of Conscientiousness and Neuroticism," *PLoS One* 9, no. 3 (March 2014), https://doi.org/10.1371/journal.pone.0090628.

90 *MBSR is nothing if not established:* Daniel Goleman, "Relaxation: Surprising Benefits Detected," *New York Times,* May 13, 1986, https://www.nytimes.com/1986/05/13/science/relaxation -surprising-benefits-detected.html?searchResultPosition=10.

90 *Meta-analyses stretching back decades have shown:* Paul Grossman et al., "Mindfulness-Based Stress Reduction and Health Benefits," *Journal of Psychosomatic Research* 57, no. 1 (July 2004): 35–43, https://doi.org/10.1016/s0022-3999(03)00573-7.

90 *including by slashing depression and anxiety:* Bassam Khoury et al., "Mindfulness-Based Stress Reduction for Healthy Individuals: A Meta-Analysis," *Journal of Psychosomatic Research* 78, no. 6 (June 2015): 519–28, https://doi.org/10.1016/j.jpsych ores.2015.03.009.

90 *A recently published study even found:* April Fulton, "Daily Meditation May Work as Well as a Popular Drug to Calm Anxiety, Study Finds," NPR, November 12, 2022, https://www .npr.org/sections/health-shots/2022/11/09/1135211525/anxiety -medication-meditation-lexapro.

90 *There are now hundreds:* Jon Kabat-Zinn, *Full Catastrophe Living: Using the Wisdom of Your Body and Mind to Face Stress, Pain, and Illness* (New York: Bantam Books, 2013).

95 *In his book* Full Catastrophe Living: Ibid., 27.

97 *I fixed my mind on:* Thich Nhất Hạnh, *Taming the Tiger Within: Meditations on Transforming Difficult Emotions* (New York: Riverhead Books, 2005), 99.

97 *I knew my only choice:* Jack Kornfield, "The Wisdom of Insecurity," JackKornfield.com, September 15, 2021, https://jackkornfield .com/the-wisdom-of-insecurity/.

98 *Everything changes, including our moods:* Sigmund Freud, *The Complete Letters of Sigmund Freud to Wilhelm Fliess: 1887–1904,* ed. Jeffrey Moussaieff Masson (Cambridge, MA: Belknap Press of Harvard University Press, 1985), 274.

5

Down for Whatever: Openness to Experience

99 *tend to be politically liberal:* Alan S. Gerber et al., "The Big Five Personality Traits in the Political Arena," *Annual Review of Political Science* 14, no. 1 (June 2011): 265–87, https://doi .org/10.1146/annurev-polisci-051010-111659.

99 *"spiritual but not religious":* Vassilis Saroglou, "Religion and the Five Factors of Personality: A Meta-Analytic Review," *Personality and Individual Differences* 32, no. 1 (January 2002): 15–25, https://doi.org/10.1016/s0191-8869(00)00233-6.

99 *and sexually adventurous:* Oscar Lecuona et al., "Does 'Open' Rhyme with 'Special'? Comparing Personality, Sexual Satisfaction, Dominance and Jealousy of Monogamous and Non-Monogamous Practitioners," *Archives of Sexual Behavior* 50, no. 4 (2021): 1,537–49, https://doi.org/10.1007/s10508-020-01865-x.

99 *They have dreams they can:* Michael Schredl and John Rauthmann, "Dream Recall, Nightmares, Dream Sharing, and Personality: A Replication Study," *Dreaming* 32, no. 2 (March 2022): 163–72, https://doi.org/10.1037/drm0000200.

100 *Open people can be "sensation seekers":* Jonathan W. Roberti, "A Review of Behavioral and Biological Correlates of Sensation Seeking," *Journal of Research in Personality* 38, no. 3 (June 2004): 256–79, https://doi.org/10.1016/s0092-6566(03)00067-9.

100 *They spend lots of time:* Julia M. Rohrer and Richard E. Lucas, "Only So Many Hours: Correlations between Personality and Daily Time Use in a Representative German Panel," *Collabra: Psychology* 4, no. 1 (January 2018): 1, https://doi.org/10.1525/collabra.112.

100 *One sign you might be open:* Brian R. Little, *Who Are You, Really?: The Surprising Puzzle of Personality* (New York: Simon & Schuster/TED, 2017), 16.

100 *The trait is usually measured by:* Christopher J. Soto and Oliver P. John, "The Next Big Five Inventory (BFI-2): Developing and Assessing a Hierarchical Model with 15 Facets to Enhance

Bandwidth, Fidelity, and Predictive Power," *Journal of Personality and Social Psychology* 113, no. 1 (2017): 117–43, https://doi .org/10.1037/pspp0000096.

100 *Of all the traits, openness is:* Ted Schwaba, "The Structure, Measurement, and Development of Openness to Experience across Adulthood," in *Handbook of Personality Development,* ed. Dan P. McAdams, Rebecca L. Shiner, and Jennifer L. Tackett (New York: Guilford, 2019).

100 *High openness predicts involvement with:* Daniel Nettle, *Personality: What Makes You the Way You Are* (Oxford, UK: Oxford University Press, 2007), 192.

100 *For especially open people, ideas can:* Ibid., 199.

101 *"He was definitely worried," she writes:* Molly Shannon and Sean Wilsey, *Hello, Molly!: A Memoir* (New York: HarperCollins, 2022).

101 *Despite its relationship with verbal:* Colin G. DeYoung, "Openness/Intellect: A Dimension of Personality Reflecting Cognitive Exploration," in *APA Handbook of Personality and Social Psychology,* ed. Mario Mikulincer et al. (Washington, DC: American Psychological Association, 2015), 369–99.

101 *Open people tend to perform:* Ibid., 385.

102 *One study that compared college students:* Julia Zimmermann and Franz J. Neyer, "Do We Become a Different Person When Hitting the Road? Personality Development of Sojourners," *Journal of Personality and Social Psychology* 105, no. 3 (September 2013): 515–30, https://doi.org/10.1037/a0033019.

102 *Then again, if you can't afford:* David J. Sparkman, Scott Eidelman, and John C. Blanchar, "Multicultural Experiences Reduce Prejudice through Personality Shifts in Openness to Experience," *European Journal of Social Psychology* 46, no. 7 (April 2017): 840–53, https://doi.org/10.1002/ejsp.2189.

103 *These moments "involve absorption in":* Lia Naor and Ofra Mayseless, "How Personal Transformation Occurs Following a Single Peak Experience in Nature: A Phenomenological Account," *Journal of Humanistic Psychology* 60, no. 6 (June 2017): 865–88, https://doi.org/10.1177/0022167817714692.

104 *But a fair number of people:* Alvin Chang, "Your Politics Aren't Just Passed Down from Your Parents. This Cartoon Explains What Actually Happens," *Vox*, November 22, 2016, https://www .vox.com/policy-and-politics/2016/11/22/13714556/parent-child -politics-research-cartoon.

104 *reject their parents' politics as adults:* Emma Goldberg, "'Do Not Vote for My Dad': When Families Disagree on Politics," *New York Times*, August 27, 2020, https://www.nytimes.com/2020/08/27 /us/family-politics-children-democrat-republican.html.

104 *As the personality psychologist Robert McCrae:* Robert R. McCrae, "Social Consequences of Experiential Openness," *Psychological Bulletin* 120, no. 3 (November 1996): 323–37, https://doi .org/10.1037/0033-2909.120.3.323.

108 *Still, psychedelics appear to cause:* Schwaba, "The Structure, Measurement, and Development of Openness to Experience across Adulthood," 506.

108 *"Individuals scoring higher on Openness":* Mark T. Wagner et al., "Therapeutic Effect of Increased Openness: Investigating Mechanism of Action in MDMA-Assisted Psychotherapy," *Journal of Psychopharmacology* 31, no. 8 (August 2017): 967–74, https:// doi.org/10.1177/0269881117711712.

108 *The psilocybin increased openness:* Katherine MacLean, Matthew Johnson, and Roland Griffiths, "Mystical Experiences Occasioned by the Hallucinogen Psilocybin Lead to Increases in the Personality Domain of Openness," *Journal of Psychopharmacology* 25, no. 11 (November 2011): 1,453–61, https://doi.org/10.1177 /0269881111420188.

108 *In one small study, a group:* A. V. Lebedev et al., "LSD-Induced Entropic Brain Activity Predicts Subsequent Personality Change," *Human Brain Mapping* 37, no. 9 (September 2016): 3,203–13, https://doi.org/10.1002/hbm.23234.

108 *Ayahuasca, a ritual drink made:* Nige Netzband et al., "Modulatory Effects of Ayahuasca on Personality Structure in a Traditional Framework," *Psychopharmacology* 237, no. 10 (October 2020): 3,161–71, https://doi.org/10.1007/s00213-020-05601-0.

108 *Psychedelics have also been shown:* Taylor Lyons and Robin Carhart-Harris, "Increased Nature Relatedness and Decreased Authoritarian Political Views after Psilocybin for Treatment-Resistant Depression," *Journal of Psychopharmacology* 32, no. 7 (January 2018): 811–19, https://doi.org/10.1177/0269881117748902.

109 *"Love is the most important thing":* Rachel Nuwer, "How a Dose of MDMA Transformed a White Supremacist," BBC Future, June 20, 2023, https://www.bbc.com/future/article/20230614-how-a-dose -of-mdma-transformed-a-white-supremacist.

109 *In lab rodents, psychedelics appear:* Bill Hathaway, "Psychedelic Spurs Growth of Neural Connections Lost in Depression," *Yale News*, July 9, 2021, https://news.yale.edu/2021/07/05/psychedelic -spurs-growth-neural-connections-lost-depression.

109 *In mice, they reopen so-called critical periods:* Romain Nardou et al., "Psychedelics Reopen the Social Reward Learning Critical Period," *Nature* 618, no. 7966 (June 2023): 790–98, https://doi .org/10.1038/s41586-023-06204-3.

109 *shaking a snow globe:* Nicola Davison, "The Struggle to Turn Psychedelics into Life-Changing Treatments," *Wired UK*, May 12, 2018, https://www.wired.co.uk/article/psychedelics -lsd-depression-anxiety-addiction.

109 *or lubricating cognition:* Michael Pollan, "The New Science of Psychedelics," Trippingly, September 23, 2020, https://www .trippingly.net/lsd-studies/2018/5/5/the-new-science-of-psychedelics.

109 *Curiously, the increased openness spurred:* Brandon Weiss et al., "Examining Psychedelic-Induced Changes in Social Functioning and Connectedness in a Naturalistic Online Sample Using the Five-Factor Model of Personality," *Frontiers in Psychology* 12 (November 2021), https://doi.org/10.3389/fpsyg.2021.749788.

109 *decrease not only neuroticism specifically:* D. Erritzoe et al., "Effects of Psilocybin Therapy on Personality Structure," *Acta Psychiatrica Scandinavica* 138, no. 5 (June 2018): 368–78, https:// doi.org/10.1111/acps.12904.

109 *depression for at least a year:* Natalie Gukasyan et al., "Efficacy and Safety of Psilocybin-Assisted Treatment for Major Depressive

Disorder: Prospective 12-Month Follow-Up," *Journal of Psychopharmacology* 36, no. 2 (February 2022): 151–58, https://doi.org/10.1177/02698811211073759.

113 *At work, whenever someone clapped:* Henrick Karoliszyn, "The Agony and the Ecstasy: Using the 'Party Drug' MDMA to Combat PTSD," NOLA.com, May 13, 2019, https://www.nola.com/gambit/news/the_latest/article_9daca885-f64d-53bf-b586-afd9ddb7a918.html.

115 *The researchers at MAPS, who connected:* Michael C. Mithoefer et al., "3,4-Methylenedioxymethamphetamine (MDMA)-Assisted Psychotherapy for Post-Traumatic Stress Disorder in Military Veterans, Firefighters, and Police Officers: A Randomised, Double-Blind, Dose-Response, Phase 2 Clinical Trial," *Lancet Psychiatry* 5, no. 6 (June 2018): 486–97, https://doi.org/10.1016/s2215-0366(18)30135-4.

115 *And the openness was what:* Wagner et al., "Therapeutic Effect of Increased Openness."

119 *Months after I connected with Lori:* Liz Essley Whyte, "Ecstasy Drug Trials Missed Suicidal Thoughts of Subjects," *Wall Street Journal*, August 5, 2024, https://www.wsj.com/health/healthcare/ecstasy-drug-trials-missed-suicidal-thoughts-of-subjects-888ebfa1.

122 *"Each of us is several":* Fernando Pessoa, *The Book of Disquiet* (London: Penguin Books, 2001), 327.

122 *"Literature," he famously argued:* Ibid., 107.

122 *"Life is what we make of it":* Ibid., 371.

6

Plays Well with Others: Agreeableness

125 *Studies suggest agreeable parents are warmer:* Amaranta D. de Haan, Peter Prinzie, and Maja Deković, "Mothers' and Fathers' Personality and Parenting: The Mediating Role of Sense of Competence," *Developmental Psychology* 45, no. 6 (November 2009): 1,695–707, https://doi.org/10.1037/a0016121.

125 *They view their children more positively:* Peter Prinzie, Amaranta de Haan, and Jay Belsky, "Personality and Parenting," in *Handbook of Parenting*, ed. Marc H. Bornstein (New York: Routledge, 2019), 797–822.

125 *The agreeable are likable:* Dimitri van der Linden et al., "Classroom Ratings of Likeability and Popularity Are Related to the Big Five and the General Factor of Personality," *Journal of Research in Personality* 44, no. 5 (October 2010): 669–72, https://doi.org/10.1016/j.jrp.2010.08.007.

125 *help people in need:* Meara M. Habashi, William G. Graziano, and Ann E. Hoover, "Searching for the Prosocial Personality," *Personality and Social Psychology Bulletin* 42, no. 9 (July 2016): 1,177–92, https://doi.org/10.1177/0146167216652859.

125 *forgive people who wrong them:* Jennifer L. Tackett, Maciel M. Hernandez, and Nancy Eisenberg, "Agreeableness," in *Handbook of Personality Development*, ed. Dan P. McAdams, Rebecca L. Shiner, and Jennifer L. Tackett (New York: Guilford, 2019), 459.

125 *They tend to have better relationships:* Kelci Harris and Simine Vazire, "On Friendship Development and the Big Five Personality Traits," *Social and Personality Psychology Compass* 10, no. 11 (November 2016): 647–67, https://doi.org/10.1111/spc3.12287.

125 *They laugh, nod, and smile:* Marta Doroszuk, Marta Kupis, and Anna Z. Czarna, "Personality and Friendships," in *Encyclopedia of Personality and Individual Differences*, ed. Virgil Zeigler-Hill and Todd K. Shackelford (London: Springer Nature Switzerland, 2019), 1–9, https://doi.org/10.1007/978-3-319-28099-8_712-1.

126 *Women tend to be more agreeable:* Tackett, Hernandez, and Eisenberg, "Agreeableness," 443.

126 *Agreeable people aren't more financially:* Angela L. Duckworth et al., "Who Does Well in Life? Conscientious Adults Excel in Both Objective and Subjective Success," *Frontiers in Psychology* 3 (September 2012), https://doi.org/10.3389/fpsyg.2012.00356.

126 *But the agreeable are rich:* Harris and Vazire, "On Friendship Development and the Big Five Personality Traits," 656.

126 *have a better quality of life:* Michael P. Wilmot and Deniz S. Ones,

"Agreeableness and Its Consequences: A Quantitative Review of Meta-Analytic Findings," *Personality and Social Psychology Review* 26, no. 3 (February 2022): 242–80, https://doi.org/10.1177/10888683211073007.

126 *A study that tracked hundreds:* Christopher J. Boyce and Alex M. Wood, "Personality Prior to Disability Determines Adaptation," *Psychological Science* 22, no. 11 (October 2011): 1,397–402, https://doi.org/10.1177/0956797611421790.

127 *As the personality psychologist Donn Byrne:* Donn Byrne, "Interpersonal Attraction and Attitude Similarity," *Journal of Abnormal and Social Psychology* 62, no. 3 (1961): 713–15, https://doi.org/10.1037/h0044721.

127 *Though "anger" is technically a facet:* Ryan Martin, *Why We Get Mad: How to Use Your Anger for Positive Change* (London: Watkins, 2021), 167.

127 *Agreeable people tend to both get:* Fangying Quan, Rujiao Yang, and Ling-Xiang Xia, "The Longitudinal Relationships Among Agreeableness, Anger Rumination, and Aggression," *Current Psychology* 40, no. 1 (August 2020): 9–20, https://doi.org/10.1007/s12144-020-01030-6.

128 *Agreeableness seems to help people:* Scott Ode, Michael D. Robinson, and Benjamin M. Wilkowski, "Can One's Temper Be Cooled? A Role for Agreeableness in Moderating Neuroticism's Influence on Anger and Aggression," *Journal of Research in Personality* 42, no. 2 (April 2008): 295–311, https://doi.org/10.1016/j.jrp.2007.05.007.

129 *"The strenuous soul must fight":* Peter N. Stearns, *American Cool: Constructing a Twentieth-Century Emotional Style* (New York: New York University Press, 1994), 30.

129 *The twentieth-century mandate to "stay cool":* Ibid., 1.

130 *But, she admits, she's scared, too:* Elissa Schappell, "Crossing the Line in the Sand," in *The Bitch in the House*, ed. Cathi Hanauer (New York: William Morrow, 2002), 202.

130 *One of the main reasons some people:* Martin, *Why We Get Mad*, 69.

131   *"It is well not to see"*: John W. Basore, *Seneca: Moral Essays* (New York: Putnam's Sons, 1928), 281.

131   *His other anger-management techniques included:* Simon Kemp and K. T. Strongman, "Anger Theory and Management: A Historical Analysis," *American Journal of Psychology* 108, no. 3 (1995): 397–417, https://doi.org/10.2307/1422897.

131   *playing the lyre:* Seneca, *On Anger* (Montecristo Publishing LLC, 2020).

131   *"I was never comfortable enough"*: Martin, *Why We Get Mad*, 17.

134   *People high in agreeableness tend:* Daniel Nettle, *Personality: What Makes You the Way You Are* (Oxford, UK: Oxford University Press, 2009), 162.

134   *Empathy—"made of exertion, that dowdier"*: Leslie Jamison, *The Empathy Exams* (Minneapolis: Graywolf Press, 2014), 23.

136   *Conversation is, as Vivian Gornick:* Vivian Gornick, *The Odd Woman and the City: A Memoir* (New York: Farrar, Straus and Giroux, 2015), 99.

136   *Yet in a study by the:* Michael Kardas, Amit Kumar, and Nicholas Epley, "Overly Shallow? Miscalibrated Expectations Create a Barrier to Deeper Conversation," *Journal of Personality and Social Psychology* 122, no. 3 (2022): 367–98, https://doi.org/10.1037/pspa0000281.

140   *As Kate Murphy writes:* Kate Murphy, *You're Not Listening: What You're Missing and Why It Matters* (New York: Celadon Books, 2019), 61–63.

143   *And the fact that the:* Leslie Jamison, "The Bear's Kiss," *New York Review of Books*, November 7, 2022, https://www.nybooks.com/articles/2022/10/20/the-bears-kiss-in-the-eye-of-the-wild/.

145   *Agreeable people don't necessarily befriend:* Harris and Vazire, "On Friendship Development and the Big Five Personality Traits."

147   *Even Emerson, that great defender:* Ralph Waldo Emerson, *Essays: First Series* (Boston: Phillips, Sampson, 1857).

148   *This comment brought to mind:* Kat Vellos, *We Should Get Together* (Kat Vellos, 2019).

150   *But in the wise words:* Judy Faber, "Pitbull Sinks His Teeth into

New Album," CBS News, July 16, 2007, https://www.cbsnews
.com/news/pitbull-sinks-his-teeth-into-new-album/.

151   *Volunteering could be one reason:* Elizabeth Hopper, "Want to Be
Happier? Try Volunteering, Study Says," *Washington Post*, July 28,
2020, https://www.washingtonpost.com/lifestyle/2020/07/29
/volunteer-happy-mental-health/.

151   *to $80,000 more a year:* Francesca Borgonovi, "Doing Well by
Doing Good: The Relationship between Formal Volunteering and
Self-Reported Health and Happiness," *Social Science & Medicine*
66, no. 11 (June 2008): 2,321–34, https://doi.org/10.1016/j.socsci
med.2008.01.011.

152   *As George Orwell noted:* George Orwell, *Down and Out in Paris
and London* (New York: Houghton Mifflin Harcourt, 1933), 184.

152   *A "fog of dreary senselessness":* Annie Dillard, *Teaching a Stone to
Talk* (New York: HarperCollins, 2007), 34.

153   *As the poet Marge Piercy:* Marge Piercy, "To Be of Use," Poetry
Foundation, accessed November 21, 2022, https://www
.poetryfoundation.org/poems/57673/to-be-of-use.

154   *Spending quality time with people:* Christian Jarrett, *Be Who You
Want* (New York: Simon & Schuster, 2021), 146.

7

Get 'er Done: Conscientiousness

157   *Very high levels of the trait:* T. A. Widiger and W. L. Gore,
"Personality Disorders," *Encyclopedia of Mental Health* (2016),
270–77, https://doi.org/10.1016/b978-0-12-397045-9.00092-6.

157   *Because of its association with:* Michael P. Wilmot and Deniz S.
Ones, "A Century of Research on Conscientiousness at Work,"
Proceedings of the National Academy of Sciences 116, no. 46
(September 2019): 23,004–10, https://doi.org/10.1073
/pnas.1908430116.

157   *it's the one employers prize most:* Paul R. Sackett and Philip T.
Walmsley, "Which Personality Attributes Are Most Important

in the Workplace?" *Perspectives on Psychological Science* 9, no. 5 (2014): 538–51, https://doi.org/10.1177/1745691614543972.

157 *"Succinctly, conscientiousness is a personality trait":* Brent W. Roberts and Patrick L. Hill, "The Sourdough Model of Conscientiousness," in *Building Better Students: Preparation for the Workforce,* ed. Jeremy Burrus et al. (New York: Oxford University Press, 2017).

158 *Conscientious types tend to be:* Christoph Randler, Michael Schredl, and Anja S. Göritz, "Chronotype, Sleep Behavior, and the Big Five Personality Factors," *SAGE Open* 7, no. 3 (August 2017), https://doi.org/10.1177/2158244017728321.

158 *spend more time working:* Julia M. Rohrer and Richard E. Lucas, "Only So Many Hours: Correlations between Personality and Daily Time Use in a Representative German Panel," *Collabra: Psychology* 4, no. 1 (January 2018): 1, https://doi.org/10.1525/collabra.112.

160 *Unlike some of the other traits:* Nathan W. Hudson, "Does Successfully Changing Personality Traits via Intervention Require That Participants Be Autonomously Motivated to Change?" *Journal of Research in Personality* 95 (December 2021): 104160, https://doi.org/10.1016/j.jrp.2021.104160.

161 *Low conscientiousness can look like:* James Clear, *Atomic Habits* (New York: Avery, 2018), 22.

162 *In his* Autobiography, *he laid out:* Benjamin Franklin, *Autobiography of Benjamin Franklin* (New York: Henry Holt and Company, 1916).

163 *The eighteenth-century English writer Samuel Johnson:* Mason Currey, *Daily Rituals: How Artists Work* (New York: Knopf, 2013).

164 *The researchers Cristina Atance and:* Cristina M. Atance and Daniela K. O'Neill, "Episodic Future Thinking," *Trends in Cognitive Sciences* 5, no. 12 (2001): 533–39, https://doi.org/10.1016/s1364-6613(00)01804-0.

164 *In studies, episodic future thinking:* Kristin N. Javaras, Molly Williams, and Arielle R. Baskin-Sommers, "Psychological Interventions Potentially Useful for Increasing Conscientiousness,"

Personality Disorders: Theory, Research, and Treatment 10, no. 1 (January 2019): 13–24, https://doi.org/10.1037/per0000267.

169 *A concept called the "mutually reinforcing":* Roberts and Hill, "The Sourdough Model of Conscientiousness," 16.

169 *For one recent study, researchers:* Katie S. Mehr et al., "Copy-Paste Prompts: A New Nudge to Promote Goal Achievement," *Journal of the Association for Consumer Research* 5, no. 3 (May 2020): 329–34, https://doi.org/10.1086/708880.

172 *"I tried and tried to think":* Dana White, "About Me," A Slob Comes Clean, accessed December 14, 2022, https://web.archive .org/web/20110609044251/http:/www.aslobcomesclean.com:80 /about-me/.

174 *Except the stuff problem has only:* Kyle Chayka, *The Longing for Less: Living with Minimalism* (London: Bloomsbury, 2020).

176 *"Since hard choices are unavoidable":* Oliver Burkeman, *Four Thousand Weeks* (New York: Farrar, Straus and Giroux, 2021).

176 *"Only once you give yourself":* Greg McKeown, *Essentialism: The Disciplined Pursuit of Less* (New York: Currency, 2014), 4.

177 *Chayka describes living in a:* Chayka, *The Longing for Less*, 12–13.

180 *Though "immoderation" is technically part:* Christian Hakulinen et al., "Personality and Alcohol Consumption: Pooled Analysis of 72,949 Adults from Eight Cohort Studies," *Drug and Alcohol Dependence* 151 (June 2015): 110–14, https://doi.org/10.1016/j .drugalcdep.2015.03.008.

180 *One review found that low conscientiousness:* P. Priscilla Lui et al., "Linking Big Five Personality Domains and Facets to Alcohol (Mis)Use: A Systematic Review and Meta-Analysis," *Alcohol and Alcoholism* 57, no. 1 (January 2022): 58–73, https://doi.org /10.1093/alcalc/agab030.

180 *Many people who are low:* Daniel Nettle, *Personality: What Makes You the Way You Are* (Oxford, UK: Oxford University Press, 2009), 141.

8

Enduring vs. Ending: On Knowing When to Quit

186 *Instead, anxiety can be a sign:* Paraphrase from John Gillespie Magee Jr.'s poem "High Flight," https://www.poetryfoundation .org/poems/157986/high-flight-627d3cfb1e9b7.

186 *"If you chose an appropriately":* Martin M. Antony and Richard P. Swinson, *When Perfect Isn't Good Enough* (Oakland, CA: New Harbinger Publications, Inc.), 141.

187 *A 2006 Time magazine profile:* John Cloud, "The Third Wave of Therapy," *Time,* February 13, 2006, https://content.time.com /time/subscriber/article/0,33009,1156613,00.html.

187 *I picked up Hayes's book:* Steven C. Hayes, *A Liberated Mind: How to Pivot Toward What Matters* (New York: Avery, 2019).

188 *A type of therapy called:* Jessica F. Magidson et al., "Theory-Driven Intervention for Changing Personality: Expectancy Value Theory, Behavioral Activation, and Conscientiousness," *Developmental Psychology* 50, no. 5 (May 2014): 1,442–50, https:// doi.org/10.1037/a0030583.

194 *Even Angela Duckworth, of* Grit*:* Angela Duckworth, *Grit: The Power of Passion and Perseverance* (New York: Scribner, 2016), 241.

197 *This suggested that "the poor":* James H. Fallon, *The Psychopath Inside: A Neuroscientist's Personal Journey into the Dark Side of the Brain* (New York: Current, 2013).

198 *"I know of no case":* James Fallon, "How I Discovered I Have the Brain of a Psychopath," *Guardian,* June 2, 2014, https://www .theguardian.com/commentisfree/2014/jun/03/how-i-discovered -i-have-the-brain-of-a-psychopath.

200 *The psychologist Brian Little has:* Brian R. Little, *Who Are You, Really?: The Surprising Puzzle of Personality* (New York: Simon & Schuster/TED, 2017).

201 *The lingo is a bit confusing:* Stefano Tasselli, Martin Kilduff, and Blaine Landis, "Personality Change: Implications for

Organizational Behavior," *Academy of Management Annals* 12, no. 2 (2018): 467–93, https://doi.org/10.5465/annals.2016.0008.

202 *"The problem with self-narratives is":* Bruce M. Hood, *The Self Illusion* (New York: Oxford University Press, 2012), 236.

202 *In one of his studies:* Nathan W. Hudson et al., "You Have to Follow Through: Attaining Behavioral Change Goals Predicts Volitional Personality Change," *Journal of Personality and Social Psychology* 117, no. 4 (October 2019): 839–57, https://doi.org/10.1037/pspp0000221.

203 *"Identity has the power to shape":* Sheila Liming, *Hanging Out* (New York: Melville House, 2023), 50.

204 *Hudson has found that for:* Nathan W. Hudson and Brent W. Roberts, "Goals to Change Personality Traits: Concurrent Links between Personality Traits, Daily Behavior, and Goals to Change Oneself," *Journal of Research in Personality* 53 (December 2014): 68–83, https://doi.org/10.1016/j.jrp.2014.08.008.

204 *The psychologist David McClelland wrote:* Tasselli, Kilduff, and Landis, "Personality Change."

9

Find Your Beach: How to Keep Changing

206 *The essayist Sloane Crosley says:* Sloane Crosley, *Look Alive Out There: Essays* (New York: MCD, 2018).

209 *Long-term personality change is more:* Brian R. Little, *Who Are You, Really?: The Surprising Puzzle of Personality* (New York: Simon & Schuster/TED, 2017).

214 *As the psychologist Tracy Dennis-Tiwary:* Tracy Dennis-Tiwary, *Future Tense: Why Anxiety Is Good for You (Even Though It Feels Bad)* (New York: Harper Wave, 2022), 7.

215 *Some studies even suggest that reframing:* Jeremy P. Jamieson, Matthew K. Nock, and Wendy Berry Mendes, "Changing the Conceptualization of Stress in Social Anxiety Disorder," *Clinical*

Psychological Science 1, no. 4 (August 2013): 363–74, https://doi
.org/10.1177/2167702613482119.

215 *Even a "crowd of sorrows"*: Rumi, "The Guest House," All Poetry,
accessed December 14, 2023, https://allpoetry.com/poem
/8534703-The-Guest-House-by-Mewlana-Jalaluddin-Rumi.

217 *There are few joys in life*: Virginia Woolf, *A Room of One's Own*
(London: Hogarth Press, 1931).

219 *I get that this directive*: Zadie Smith, "Find Your Beach," *New
York Review of Books*, June 9, 2022, https://www.nybooks.com
/articles/2014/10/23/find-your-beach/.

Index

About the Author

Olga Khazan is a staff writer for the *Atlantic*. Prior to that, she was the *Atlantic*'s global editor. She has also written for the *New York Times*, the *Los Angeles Times*, the *Washington Post*, *Vox*, and other publications. She is a two-time recipient of the International Reporting Project's Journalism Fellowship and winner of the 2017 National Headliner Award for Magazine Online Writing. For now, she lives with her husband and son in Northern Virginia.